The Charity of Nations

The Charity of Nations

Humanitarian Action in a Calculating World

Ian Smillie and Larry Minear

Kumarian
Press, Inc.

The Charity of Nations: Humanitarian Action in a Calculating World
Published 2004 in the United States of America by Kumarian Press, Inc.
1294 Blue Hills Avenue, Bloomfield, CT 06002 USA

Production and design by Rosanne Pignone, Pro Production
Copyedited by Beth Richards
Proofread by Jody El-Assadi, A Proofer's Touch
Index by Barbara DeGennaro

The text for Charity of Nations: Humanitarian Action in a Calculating World
is set in Janson 10/12.
Printed in the United States of America on acid-free paper by Thomson-Shore, Inc.
Text printed with vegetable oil-based ink.

∞ The paper used in this publication meets the minimum requirements of the
American National Standard for Information Sciences—Permanence of Paper for
printed Library Materials, ANSI Z39.48-1984

Library of Congress Cataloging-in-Publication Data
Smillie, Ian.
The charity of nations : humanitarian action in a calculating world /
    Ian Smillie and Larry Minear.
        p. cm.
    Includes bibliographical references and index.
    ISBN 1-56549-190-4 (pbk. : alk. paper) — ISBN 1-56549-191-2
        (cloth : alk. paper)
1. Humanitarian assistance—Political aspects. 2. Humanitarianism—Political aspects.
    3. International relations. I. Minear, Larry, 1936– II. Title.
HV553.S57 2004
    361.2'6—dc22
                                                            2004010847

13 12 11 10 09 08 07 06 05   10 9 8 7 6 5 4 3 2   First Printing 2004

Contents

Maps and Tables

Maps

Table

Abbreviations

ADB	Asian Development Bank
AEI	American Enterprise Institute
AFRC	Armed Forces Ruling Council (Sierra Leone)
ALNAP	Active Learning Network for Accountability and Performance
ANSO	Afghan NGOs Security Office
APEC	Asia-Pacific Economic Cooperation
ASEAN	Association of East Asian Nations
AREU	Afghanistan Research and Evaluation Unit
AusAID	Australian Agency for International Development
BBC	British Broadcasting Corporation
BHR	Bureau of Humanitarian Response (USAID)
BMZ	Ministry of Development (Germany)
BPRM	Bureau of Population, Refugees, and Migration (US)
CAP	Consolidated Appeals Process (UN)
CECI	Centre Canadien d'étude et de la cooperation internationale
CFET	Combined Fund for East Timor
CIDA	Canadian International Development Agency
CNN	Cable News Network
CNRT	National Council of Timorese Resistance
CPA	Coalition Provisional Authority (Afghanistan)
DAC	Development Assistance Committee (OECD)
DART	Disaster Assistance Relief Team (USAID)
DEC	Disasters Emergency Committee (GB)
DFID	Department for International Development (UK)
DHA	Department of Humanitarian Affairs (UN)
DRC	Democratic Republic of the Congo
EC	European Community

ECOSOC	Economic and Social Council (UN)
ECHO	European Community Humanitarian Office
ECOMOG	Economic Community Military Observer Group
ECOWAS	Economic Community of West African States
ETAN	East Timor Action Network
ETISC	East Timor Ireland Solidarity Campaign
EU	European Union
FAd'H	Forces Armées d'Haiti
FAO	Food and Agriculture Association (UN)
FEWS NET	Famine Early Warning Systems Network
Fretilin	Revolutionary Front for an Independent East Timor
GB	Great Britain
GDP	Gross development product
GM	Genetically-modified food
GNP	Gross national product
GO	Governmental organization
HDRs	Humanitarian Daily Rations
HIV/AIDS	Acquired Immune Deficiency Syndrome
HPG	Humanitarian Policy Group (ODI)
IASC	InterAgency Standing Committee (UN)
ICRC	International Committee of the Red Cross
ICVA	International Council of Voluntary Agencies
IGAD	Intergovernmental Authority on Development (East Africa)
IDPs	Internally Displaced Persons
IFRC	International Federation of Red Cross and Red Crescent Societies
IMF	International Monetary Fund
INTERFET	International Force for East Timor
ISAF	International Security Assistance Force (ISAF)
KBR	Kellogg, Brown & Root
LRD	Linking relief and development
MSF	Médecins sans Frontières
MSTC	Making Sense of Turbulent Contexts (World Vision)
NATO	North Atlantic Treaty Organizations
NGO	Nongovernmental organization
NOW	Nepean Outreach to the World
OAS	Organization of American States
OAU	Organization for African Unity
OCHA	Office for the Coordination of Humanitarian Affairs (UN)
ODA	Official development assistance
ODI	Overseas Development Institute (UK)
OECD	Organisation for Economic Co-operation and Development

OFDA	Office of Foreign Disaster Assistance (USAID)
OIOS	Office of Internal Oversight Services (UN)
OLS	Operation Lifeline Sudan
OPEC	Organization of Petroleum Exporting Countries
OSCE	Organization for Security and Cooperation in Europe
OTI	Office of Transition Initiatives (USAID)
PLO	Palestine Liberation Organization
PRT	Provincial Reconstruction Team (Afghanistan)
PSO	peace support operation
PVO	Private voluntary organization (US)
RAF	Royal Air Force
RUF	Revolutionary United Front (Sierra Leone)
SAHIMS	Southern Africa Humanitarian Information System
SCF	Save the Children Federation/Fund
SDC	Swiss Agency for Development Cooperation
SIDA	Swedish International Development Agency
SPLA	Sudanese People's Liberation Army
TFET	Trust Fund for East Timor (World Bank)
SMART	Standardized Monitoring and Assessment of Relief and Transitions (OFDA)
SRSG	Special Representative of the Secretary-General (UN)
SUV	Sports utility vehicle
UDT	União Democrática Timorense (East Timor)
UK	United Kingdom
UN	United Nations
UNAMA	UN Assistance Mission in Afghanistan
UNAMET	UN Mission in East Timor
UNAMIR	UN Assistance Mission in Rwanda
UNAMSIL	UN Mission in Sierra Leone
UNDAC	UN Disaster Assessment Team
UNDP	UN Development Programme
UNDRO	UN Disaster Relief Organization
UNFPA	UN Fund for Population Activities
UNHCR	UN High Commissioner for Refugees
UNHCHR	UN High Commissioner for Human Rights
UNICEF	United Nations Children's Fund
UNMISET	United Nations Mission of Support in East Timor
UNSC	UN Security Council
UNTAET	UN Transitional Administration for East Timor
UNV	United Nations Volunteers
URD	Urgence Réhabilitation Développement (NGO)
USAID	US Agency for International Development
USGET	United States Support Group for East Timor
WFP	World Food Programme (UN)

To the memory of
Sharon Capeling-Alakija

Introduction

In recent years, the moral necessity of humanitarian action is no longer self-evident and has become a matter of debate. A contributing factor is the unevenness of the response to emergencies, with human need going largely unaddressed in some crises while being inundated with attention and resources in others. The humanitarian "imperative" is difficult to take seriously when its application is so tattered. Another factor that casts a long shadow is the increased commercialism of the humanitarian world. The big business aspects of the aid enterprise make it seem entrepreneurial and opportunistic, thus undermining claims to a higher and nobler status. Equally disturbing, the effectiveness of humanitarian action—whether driven by moral, political, or economic considerations—often seems self-defeating. This much-vaunted imperative has also been discredited by activities that prolong suffering, fuel and extend wars, delay peace agreements, and marginalize local leadership and institutions.

As a result of the very mixed reviews of their work, aid organizations find themselves faced with the challenge of defending—or, in some quarters, reinstating—the humanitarian imperative, now downgraded from a given to a desideratum. "Human rights and humanitarianism are not unassailable moral goods," writes David Rieff. "They are ideologies—as questionable as neoliberalism or communism or Christianity." As a result, the case for their compelling claim on international action and resources has become a matter of public debate. "The virtue of the political," Rieff concludes, "is that the case for making the most tragic of all public decisions becomes controversial and a matter for public debate, rather than some kind of categorical moral imperative whose need to be undertaken is deemed to be self-evident."[1]

Today, aid and human rights organizations spend vast amounts of time and energy making a timely case for humanitarian action, framing need in terms of national security rather than of moral compulsion. In some ways it is as though the Cold War never ended, as though every dollar and every euro spent abroad must be calculated in terms of an immediate self-interest rather than in human terms, or even—as de Tocqueville called it—in terms of self-interest properly understood. Such a "proper" understanding might well heed Dickens's 1843 *Christmas Carol* warning, when the ghost of Christmas Present shows Scrooge two desperate children: "This boy is Ignorance. This girl is Want. Beware them both, and all of their degree, but most of all beware this boy, for on his brow I see that written which is Doom, unless the writing be erased."

Human rights and humanitarianism enjoy a status in international law that political and religious ideologies have never been able to claim. Humanitarian law, human rights law, and refugee law have evolved steadily in scope and precision over the last century and are now endorsed by most of the world's nations; they are not fictions of the overwrought do-gooder's imagination. In fact, as one authority puts it, "the effectiveness and efficiency of humanitarian and human rights activities [are] enhanced by how much they are firmly grounded in international legal principles and how much those principles are upheld."[2]

In embracing or reaffirming the humanitarian imperative, organizations thus encounter several problems. If the imperative is really what it purports to be, agencies must respond to human needs in every situation where people lack the bare essentials for continued existence or where fundamental rights are abused. Few agencies claim such global reach or mount such far-flung programs. A second complication is economic, or more precisely, commercial. Aid agencies have institutional imperatives that influence their decisions about whether, when, and where to engage. Staying at home because a given situation is too perilous for would-be beneficiaries or for agency staff is rarely seriously considered. For institutional reasons, a relief agency cannot afford to be absent from a major crisis. Fundraising, image, and relations with major donors may suffer if an agency is not seen to be present. Yet every agency concedes that in scores of crises it is not on the front lines. How compelling is the humanitarian imperative if aid organizations don't provide succor everywhere—even if there are good institutional reasons for such selectivity?

This book makes a case for the humanitarian imperative as a legitimate claim for action by the myriad organizations that make up the humanitarian enterprise. At the same time, it examines the political and commercial erosion of that imperative and the need for measures to restore its integrity. The "political economy of humanitarianism" describes the processes by which resources to relieve suffering and protect rights are mobilized, allocated, and used. It is not so much about the application of humanitarian principles as it is about how, why, and to what extent these principles characterize the day-to-day work of the humanitarian sector. The political economy perspective employed by this book examines the extent to which humanitarian activities are based on the needs identified by people in distress, as opposed to reflecting what humanitarian agencies think the political traffic will bear and what they think donors will provide in the way of charitable donations and institutional grants. The study also examines the extent to which humanitarian action is supply- rather than demand-driven, and shaped by overt or hidden influences—some of them more legitimate than others.

Our original working title was *Passing the Buck*. Referring to money as "bucks" first came into English usage more than two hundred years ago, when deer skins—buckskins—were used as a unit of exchange. The term is also used in poker to describe a counter that is passed between players. To "pass the buck" has come to mean to "shift the responsibility." Churchill spoke of "passing the buck to some other futile body." Referring to his own desk, President Truman said, "The buck stops here." The humanitarian buck gets passed in two ways. Where humanitarian action is concerned, there is obviously a large transfer of resources intended to meet human needs and to protect the human rights of people affected by natural and human-caused crises. Many players are involved in this transfer of resources. All are happy to accept credit for humanitarian accomplishments but are equally ready to shift the responsibility for failures to other parties: that is, to pass the buck.

We changed the title for several reasons. *The Charity of Nations* seems apropos because humanitarian action is widely viewed as an optional, voluntary undertaking rather than a rights-based activity integral to a civilized, law-abiding, and peaceful world. There is at present no humanitarian regime—that is, no set of standards, enforcement sanctions, and accountabilities—as there is in the refugee, trade, or nuclear nonproliferation spheres. The prevailing animus in the humanitarian sector is to try hard and do the best possible job with limited available resources, not to acquit oneself of certain specific obligations.

This book is about where the buck stops, in terms of how resources are used and where the responsibility for that use lies. It is an attempt to answer fundamental questions about the humanitarian enterprise. What drives governments and aid agencies to respond to urgent human need around the world? Why do they respond with alacrity in some instances and with collective foot-dragging in others? Why do governments pursue policies that cause human disasters, and then with great fanfare intervene to mop up the detritus? Why do some crises get the lion's share of the resources—political and diplomatic, humanitarian and military—while others are essentially forgotten? To whom are governments accountable in meeting their obligations? Can they be held to higher standards? How can the world's humanitarian apparatus hold its own against rampant political and commercial intrusions?

Some readers of an early draft of this book found our approach politically naïve. In their judgment, the work of humanitarian organizations in the highly politicized settings of civil wars—although avowedly neutral in principle—is certain to have political repercussions, even if such agencies don't espouse the cause of one side or another. Moreover, as agencies increasingly tackle the policies that create suffering, their advocacy involves them directly in the political arena. We have seen ample evidence of the interactions between humanitarian organizations and the political sphere. However, while aid agencies do not function in a political vacuum, political actors, whether on the giving or receiving end, play a risky game when they politicize the agencies' work. Micromanagement often denies humanitarian activities not only their designed human benefits but also their positive political contributions.

Chapter 1 outlines the principles, the players, and the changes affecting the humanitarian enterprise today. Chapters 2, 3, and 4 examine crises in Sierra Leone, East Timor, and Afghanistan, covering the full panoply of humanitarian action and inaction in each setting over the past twenty-five years. These three particular chapters are based on field research conducted by the authors between 2001 and 2003, augmented by other material and by personal experience dating back more than three decades. We have focused on Sierra Leone, East Timor, and Afghanistan first because we were looking for protracted emergencies in different parts of the world that could teach different lessons and, second, because they illustrate in microcosm the difficulties of the prevailing charitable model of humanitarianism.

Sierra Leone demonstrates the fine art of "forgetting" serious emergencies when there are no apparent high-profile political issues at stake such as those in Kosovo, Bosnia, or Afghanistan. Sierra Leone also demonstrates the enormous cost of remedial humanitarian and peacekeeping action when an emergency—one that certainly would have cost much less to address earlier in its evolution—can no longer be ignored. East Timor shows how humanitarian assistance actually *can* work when donors are prepared to read from the same song sheet, even if they are twenty-five years late and even if their motivations are largely political. By contrast, Afghanistan demonstrates not just the relentlessly political perversion of the humanitarian ideal. It reveals as well the more generalized inability of the humanitarian system as presently constituted to function coherently—even when the political stakes in getting it right are high and even when practitioners make a conscious effort to do so. Chapter 5 deals with specific issues arising from emergencies in Sudan, Haiti, Bosnia, and Southern Africa.

Building on these examples, the remaining chapters examine the major drivers shaping the humanitarian enterprise: foreign policy imperatives (Chapter 6) and domestic politics in donor countries (Chapter 7). Chapters 8 and 9 look at some of the pathologies that result from these foreign and domestic political influences: scrambles for attention and market share, abandoned principles, forgotten emergencies, widespread mistrust, and an absence of objective criteria for making financial decisions.

The final chapter takes liberties not often found in books about humanitarian activities. In fact an early reader, well versed in donor reluctance to consider fundamental change, said we must have been "inhaling" when we sketched out our conclusions. After further visits to countries in crisis and after participating in a meeting of donors and front-line agencies where there was lengthy debate about whether they were "agreeing," "endorsing," or just "elaborating" a plan for improved humanitarian donorship, we decided that cautious recommendations would probably be well received—and instantly forgotten.

Chapter 10, therefore, takes a more sweeping approach. It makes the case for a new conceptual humanitarian center—an agreed-upon set of basic definitions and policies that are clear enough to avoid the ambiguities and confusion that exist today. It recommends a strengthened multilateral core and a major rededication to multilateralism. It calls for a shift from voluntary donor contributions to an assessed funding formula. It makes the case for a much more powerful UN coordinating and managerial function that is more accountable and answerable to the public instead of to self-serving governments, and it recommends major changes in the way donors deal with the NGOs that today deliver more than 60 percent of all humanitarian assistance. It calls for greater accountability, a new approach to building public understanding and confidence, and more money.

This book draws on the research and writings of the Humanitarianism and War Project since its inception in 1991 (see description on the final page of the book). This study would not have been possible without support from many in the humanitarian community who are deeply concerned about its problems and who are dedicated to improving its effectiveness. We talked to hundreds of practitioners in the course of our study, in more than a dozen donor capitals from Canberra to Stockholm; at UN agency headquarters in New York, Geneva, and Rome; and on the ground in Afghanistan, Sierra Leone, and East Timor. Financial assistance was provided by the governments of Australia, Canada, Sweden, and Switzerland; by the UN Office for the Coordination of Humanitarian Affairs; and by five private organizations (CARE Canada, Oxfam America, Trócaire, World Vision Canada, and Aga Khan Foundation Canada). We are grateful to many colleagues who have commented on parts of the manuscript, especially to Peter Walker, Tom Weiss, Antonio Donini, and Steve Lubkemann, who labored over the full text. The Rockefeller Foundation provided a wonderfully peaceful month at its study and conference center in Bellagio, without which we might never have finished the work. We thank all of them for their assistance and their trust. The authors alone, of course, are responsible for the contents of the book, as well as any errors or omissions.

Ian Smillie
Larry Minear
The Humanitarianism and War Project
Tufts University
May 2004

1

The Humanitarian Enterprise Today

Charity begins at home, and justice begins next door.
—Charles Dickens, *Martin Chuzzlewit*, 1844

The humanitarian idea is elegant in its simplicity: In the context of natural and man-made disasters, every person on the globe has a right to life-saving assistance and to protection of their basic human rights. The concept of helping people in trouble is as old as civilization and not a little complicated by concerns—dating from the Elizabethan poor laws and *Martin Chuzzlewit*—about "charity" and the motives of givers and receivers. Today, the legal obligation to help citizens is first and foremost that of their governments. However, when governments are unable or unwilling to meet their responsibilities, humanitarian organizations, and occasionally foreign governments, step in. What might be termed a global humanitarian enterprise has evolved over the years, providing emergency succor and protecting fundamental rights during wars, natural disasters, famine, and plague. Humanitarian action includes providing relief material and protecting human rights, advocacy, education, and reminding parties in conflict of their obligations under humanitarian law.

But the humanitarian idea, in reality, turns out to be far more complex. The right to humanitarian assistance is only vaguely articulated in international law, itself a hotly contested domain.[1] The implementation of human rights is left to governments, which for political reasons are often reluctant to hold their peers' feet to the fire, no matter how egregious their shortcomings. And while governments are technically obliged to allow outsiders access to those people whom they themselves cannot assist, there is no companion obligation on outsiders to come to the rescue. Unlike membership dues in the United Nations and contributions for peacekeeping, all humanitarian resources are completely voluntary, a matter of the charity of nations and the kindness of strangers.

To complicate matters further still, outside governments often take sides in international conflicts, undercutting their objectivity and throwing human rights considerations to the political wind. Governments under duress have priorities and preoccupations that extend beyond, or sometimes even preempt, the basic human rights of their citizens. And rebel groups in civil war situations—now the most common form of conflict—accept few legal obligations and often are immune to most forms of external pressure. The rights of civilians caught in these conflicts are thus increasingly difficult to enforce.

The humanitarian enterprise, too, has its own contradictions. The plethora of international groups—UN organizations, government aid agencies, private relief and rights groups, the Red Cross movement—is bewildering in its diversity. All embrace humanitarian principles, but beneath the surface are many different understandings of those principles. As with governments, a variety of factors—political and diplomatic, economic and commercial, institutional and organizational—intrude into lifesaving work. The dynamics of charitable contributions by governments are far more complex and calculating than the term "benevolence" might suggest.

Since the fall of the Berlin Wall and the winding down of the Cold War, humanitarianism has become a big business, now involving some $10 billion annually. This figure includes expenditures on humanitarian aid and postconflict peace activities from traditional donor governments (members of the OECD's Development Assistance Committee) and non-DAC donors, as well as public donations to NGOs and the Red Cross movement.[2] Competition in the aid marketplace has increased by leaps and bounds. More private aid agencies, with varying degrees of competence and credibility, now swing into action with each new crisis. The welter of institutions is as baffling to governments in distressed areas as it is to the taxpayers in donor countries who want to help. New actors now mingle with the traditional players and include private corporations such as Bechtel and the British Crown Agents and military contingents such as the Marine Expeditionary Force or the Royal Air Force. In recent conflicts, some governments have employed private security companies—mercenaries—to protect their interests. While deputizing hired guns has proved to be a recipe for confusion and lack of accountability, protecting humanitarian flanks has become a growth industry for security officials and consultants.

Lost in the shuffle of international players, traditional and newly-minted alike, are host governments and civil society organizations in recipient countries, which, for all their weaknesses, offer the best long-term hope for avoiding future emergencies. In fact there is a certain irony about and misplaced emphasis on the *international* aid apparatus when the preponderance of humanitarian action in many crises is carried out by individuals and local institutions. Nevertheless, the wishes and capacities of "beneficiary populations" themselves frequently do not figure in the design of humanitarian initiatives nor do they serve as a point of accountability for the activities mounted.

At the end of his term as president of the United States, Dwight Eisenhower said,

> In the councils of government, we must guard against the acquisition of unwarranted influence, whether sought or unsought, by the military-industrial complex. The potential for the disastrous rise of misplaced power exists and will persist. We must never let the weight of this combination endanger our liberties or democratic processes. We should take nothing for granted. Only an alert and knowledgeable citizenry can compel the proper meshing of the huge industrial and military machinery of defense with our peaceful methods and goals, so that security and liberty may prosper together.[3]

Today, rather than working together, traditional humanitarians and what might better be called "the military-commercial complex" find themselves increasingly jockeying for position in conflicts around the world. Progress made over the past decade to coordinate bona fide humanitarians has been undercut by the presence and functions of this new breed. These actors have their own institutional needs and political patrons, their comparative advantages, as well as their inherent limitations.

The simple humanitarian idea that people in extremis have a right to relief and protection is thus subject to a host of countervailing and intrusive forces. Some are political, reflecting the international and domestic policies of the would-be helpers. Some are economic, reflecting the self-interest of helpers delivering what they have in their cupboards rather than what desperate people need. Some are such a mishmash of politics, economics, commercial calculation, guilt, and solidarity that making sense of them is almost impossible. Against their better judgment, for example, drought-stricken African countries were pressed by the United States to accept genetically-modified food aid in 2002. Concerns about biodiversity and possible future risks to agriculture aside, the countries all ran the risk of having their future farm exports boycotted throughout the European Union. But refusal of the aid, in the short term, ostensibly would have condemned people to death, a policy that is difficult to explain in the world of well-meaning humanitarians.

Much has changed in the world of humanitarian action since the end of the Cold War. The number of emergencies has grown dramatically. During the United Nations' first forty years there were thirteen peacekeeping operations, mostly in the Middle East and aimed primarily at preventing the renewed outbreak of hostilities between states and the consequent humanitarian emergencies. After 1988, however, there was a major change. Regional, ethnic, and intrastate animosities, which had been held in check by great-power Cold War interests, overflowed across Central Asia, the Balkans, and Africa. Longstanding wars and conflicts that had been off-limits for reasons of superpower geopolitics (e.g., Angola, Mozambique, Cambodia) were dumped unceremoniously onto the United Nations's doorstep.

In the seven years between 1988 and 1995, twenty-six new UN peacekeeping operations were authorized, double the number of the previous four decades. Conflicts have become more typically internal to single countries rather than international, generating massive numbers of internally displaced people and civilian victims of war. Humanitarian aid has tripled in a decade, mostly at the expense of longer-term development spending—and yet it is still far from adequate. Emergencies are more protracted, and they are no longer restricted to the developing world. National sovereignty has lost much of its sanctity, and sovereign authorities have more widely accepted humanitarian and human rights obligations. There is more discussion about, if not significantly more resources devoted to, the prevention of conflict. Interactions between humanitarian activities and political-military strategies have increased but an accepted template for the relationship has yet to emerge.

Effective humanitarian action is now seen variously as a complement to political objectives and as a substitute for political action at the preventive and even the remedial stages of protracted emergencies. The traditional and well understood East-West political parameters of humanitarianism have changed entirely, leaving much of the political roadmap uncharted and perilous. After a decade and a half of major post–Cold War confusion, some long for the clarity of the bipolar Communism versus anti-Communism world, which at least served as a kind of global positioning system for humanitarian action. The terrorist attacks of September 11, 2001 and the response to them have introduced a new political and security overlay on international efforts to assist and protect the world's most vulnerable people.

During the 1970s and 1980s, humanitarian aid represented less than 3 percent of all official development assistance. In the years since 1999, it has taken 10 percent of the total, mostly at the expense of dwindling supplies of longer-term development assistance. And as emergency assistance has become a larger piece of a smaller pie, it has attracted heightened visibility, importance, and expectations. At the same time, the humanitarian enterprise has become both more self-critical and more criticized. Part of the attention has shifted from the act of transferring assistance to people in trouble to the quality and the longer-term impact of the resources transferred. History, as it turns out, did not end in 1989, taking humanitarian action with it. Instead, humanitarian engagement has subsequently become both more global and more complex.

As would be expected in times of major upheaval, the roles of humanitarian agencies are evolving apace. Nonstate humanitarian actors have assumed larger and more high-profile roles. Multilateralism is finding new modes of expression, through devolution to regional groupings and "coalitions of the willing," and this is testing older ways of responding to humanitarian crises. There are now more players, and more types of players in the field. Everybody, it seems, wants a piece of the multibillion-dollar action. Ironically, the peace dividend anticipated at the end of the Cold War never materialized, but more conflict has meant more work for humanitarians and more business for those providing food and hardware and for those analyzing the effects of such labors.

We use the term humanitarian enterprise to describe the global network of organizations involved in assistance and protection. Humanitarianism is the act of people helping people. It is a service, a calling, an expression of human solidarity. It involves not only a philosophy but also a set of deliverables. An expression of ethical concern, humanitarianism is also a business driven by market forces and by agencies seeking to maintain and expand market share. This arena has a few saints, a great many dedicated humanitarian professionals, and not a few hustling entrepreneurs, fly-by-nighters, freebooters, and purveyors of snake-oil.

There are five sets of humanitarian actors: United Nations institutions, government aid agencies, international nongovernmental organizations (NGOs), members of the Red Cross and Red Crescent movement, and local NGOs and other civil society institutions based in countries facing emergencies. Many of the actors have been around for decades. Some in the UN group came onto the scene following the creation of the United Nations in 1945. The UN family of organizations developed over a period of years: UNICEF (1946), the Office of the High Commissioner for Refugees (1951), the World Food Programme (1961), and later the UN Development Programme, the Office of the High Commissioner for Human Rights, and the Office of Project Services. Some UN organizations had precursors that preceded the United Nations itself, including the International Labour Organization (1919) and the Food and Agriculture Organization (1943). The World Bank, a specialized agency of the United Nations system, increasingly involves itself in conflict prevention and postconflict activities. UN institutional development mirrors a trend toward greater specialization and division of labor within the humanitarian enterprise. It has also heightened the complexity involved in directing a burgeoning cast of characters.

Evolving in tandem with these organizations, a body of international law provides a conceptual framework for humanitarian action. Key elements include the UN Charter (1946), the Universal Declaration of Human Rights (1948), the Geneva Conventions of 1949 and Additional Protocols of 1977, and a convention relating to the Status of Refugees (1951). In more recent years, the International Convention on the Rights of the Child (1989) and the Guiding Principles for the Treatment of Internally Displaced Persons (1998) have afforded additional protection to children and those uprooted within their own countries, as distinct from refugees who have crossed international borders. The International Criminal Court (2002) added a new mechanism for investigating and prosecuting crimes against humanity, genocide, and war.

Overall, this body of conventions has produced an increasingly comprehensive international legal framework for worldwide humanitarian action, even though it is still a patchwork and, in times of crisis, a weak reed. The mandates and access specified are neither ensured nor enforced, although they do provide a set of norms and expectations according to which the behavior can be measured. Periodic discussions flag the need to update further the existing provisions, only to conclude that, in the present political climate, changes would doubtless constrict rather than expand humanitarian space.

A second cluster of actors is made up of donor governments and their various bilateral aid agencies: the U.S. Agency for International Development (USAID), the Canadian International Development Agency (CIDA), the Swiss Agency for Development Cooperation (SDC), and a dozen others. The traditional "donors' club" represented by the Development Assistance Committee (DAC) of the Organization for Economic Cooperation and Development (OECD) has some 22 members, most with their own bilateral aid programs. In recent years the cast of donors has expanded to include countries such as South Korea, India, Iran, Russia, Turkey, and Lithuania.[4] In the 1970s and 1980s, members of the Organization of Petroleum Exporting Countries (OPEC) also joined the donor club. Many bilateral aid agencies operate their own direct programs in humanitarian crises. But mostly they seek out operational partners in the form of UN agencies, international NGOs, local civil society groups, and host government ministries. With the formation of the European Community Humanitarian Office (ECHO) in 1992, European governments and their aid agencies sought to orchestrate common aid programs in crisis areas, in addition to their continuing bilateral operations.

For the uninitiated, trends in the bilateral sector hold a number of surprises. For example, the United States remains by far the world's largest contributor to relief and development overseas. It also spends the largest amount of any government on assistance for the settlement of refugees within its own borders.[5] But taken together, European contributions to relief assistance exceed those of the United States by a wide margin: in 2001, Europe spent $2.55 billion on emergency aid, compared with $1.97 billion spent by the United States.

Other calculations further dull the luster of the United States as the world's leading humanitarian actor. As a percentage of gross national product (GNP) and on a per capita basis, the United States ranks near the bottom of the DAC league tables. Of 22 DAC member countries, the United States ranks twenty-second in the percentage of its GNP committed to development assistance, including emergency relief. In 2001, the governments of five countries—Denmark, Norway, the Netherlands, Sweden, and Luxembourg—met or exceeded the agreed ODA target of 0.7 percent of ODA, with Denmark achieving a remarkable 1.03 percent. The United States stood at 0.11 percent.[6] On a per capita basis, these five pace-setting countries provided between $37 and $50 on behalf of each of their citizens in 2001. In comparison, the United States government spent $6.90 per capita and Japan spent $1.70. Such data confer humanitarian superpower status on several smaller nations and call into question ritual U.S. appeals to other countries for greater burden sharing.

A third calculus trims American contributions further still. A disproportionately larger share of U.S. emergency aid takes the form of food assistance than is the case for other countries. Few analysts dispute the indispensability of food in certain emergencies. However, market-driven fluctuations in supplies and prices have often made the United States an unreliable supplier of commodities. The United States provided more than half of the world's emergency food aid in 1999 through 2001; the European Union, the world's next largest food aid donor, decreased the level of its food aid shipments during this period, while Japan increased its share. Of all inputs pledged against UN consolidated appeals in 2001, about half was in the form of food, much of it channeled through the UN World Food Programme (WFP). But if it were to be stocked solely in anticipation of likely need, the world's humanitarian cupboard would undoubtedly have a smaller food pantry and larger stocks of other relief items. Many analysts see food aid as Exhibit A in the distorted political economy of foreign assistance. Donors tend to provide what they have in excess rather than what people in crisis require or request.

In fact African governments, pressed to lower trade barriers as part of the process of international globalization, have become increasingly critical of food assistance and its impact on their domestic markets. They argue that the cost to the United States and the European Union of protecting domestic agricultural production results in higher annual subsidies per head of *livestock* than the yearly incomes of the poorest *people* in food-importing countries. The presidents of Mali and Burkina Faso, who say that cotton provides their "ticket into the world market," have noted that subsidies paid to some 2,500 "relatively well-off [American cotton] farmers has the effect of impoverishing some 10 million rural poor people in West and Central Africa" whose livelihoods depend on cotton exports.[7]

A third group of humanitarian actors is composed of international NGOs. Some NGOs have antecedents in the nineteenth century in the form of religious and missionary undertakings. The British Anti-Slavery Society (now Anti-Slavery International), formed in 1787, is "the oldest human rights and humanitarian nongovernmental organization in the world."[8] Save the Children was established in England in 1919, Oxfam during the Second World War. CARE began in 1945 in the wake of World War II, World Vision in 1950. Other NGOs are of more recent provenance. Médecins sans Frontières (MSF) was born in 1971 after a policy dispute within the International Committee of the Red Cross (ICRC) during the Biafra/Nigeria crisis, over the ICRC's insistence on working on both sides of the conflict and muting its public criticism of the Nigerian authorities. There are now MSF sections in some eighteen different donor countries.[9]

Despite the long histories of large numbers of international NGOs, this group of nonstate actors has only recently surfaced on the screens of many policy makers. Government officials are now aware that the world's largest NGOs actually provide more aid than do some donor governments. NGOs are active in more countries than many governments, and they carry more credibility with taxpayers than do government aid agencies. Indeed, some individual NGOs have country programs with larger budgets than the government ministries to which they relate. Many of the major international NGOs have been granted official consultative status at the United Nations and its various specialized organizations, which—to the chagrin of some governments—gives them still greater influence.[10]

NGOs differ in size, sources of income, and geographic and programmatic areas of activity. Because of their independent and particularistic nature, it is difficult to tally the size of their budgets as a sector. In 2001, however, NGOs raised an estimated $1.5 billion in private donations for humanitarian assistance. In addition, they programmed roughly one-third of all bilateral humanitarian assistance and as much as half of the humanitarian funds managed the major UN agencies. In short, it is likely that NGOs manage about 60 percent of all humanitarian funding—hardly "bit players."

NGOs are also taken with increasing seriousness by insurgent movements, in part because of their influence on the international stage. Often NGOs organize themselves into issue-oriented networks—

human rights groups provide a case in point—for purposes of advocacy and solidarity. As a result, two analysts note, "Network actors bring new ideas, norms, and discourses into policy debates, and serve as sources of information and testimony."[11] However, networks of global dimensions have their vulnerabilities as well. One aid official working in the Democratic Republic of the Congo reports being warned by an insurgent guard at a roadblock that he would meet the same fate as had colleagues from his agency a few weeks earlier in the Caucasus, a continent away. He took the warning seriously.

NGO income sources vary in nature and scale. According to one study, "Some NGOs receive an overwhelming share of their income from official agencies. Action Contre la Faim in France received 70 percent of its income from official sources, and more than 85 percent of the funding for the International Catholic Migration Commission is from governments and UN agencies. At the other end of the spectrum are NGOs that raise more than three-quarters of their income from the public. World Vision USA, for instance, received only 23 percent of its income from government in 2001, Oxfam GB 28 percent, and the Lutheran World Federation just 20 percent."[12] Some NGOs take no government funding.

The pros and cons of accepting official funding from governments or the United Nations are a matter of debate among NGOs. Some argue that taking government money gives them a place at the table where policies are shaped. Others worry that doing so may inhibit their advocacy and their ability to criticize governments when they are seen as part of the problem. For their part, governments have differing policies toward NGOs. Some treat them as wholly-owned subsidiaries and, in effect, extensions of government policy. Others go to great lengths to protect the independence of the NGOs they fund.

The fourth group of humanitarian actors, the Red Cross and Red Crescent movements, form something of a distinct set. The ICRC was founded in 1863 and is based in Geneva. National Red Cross and Red Crescent Societies exist in 181 countries around the world. And the Geneva-based International Federation of Red Cross and Red Crescent Societies (IFRC), founded in 1919, knits the societies together. The ICRC, which in 2003 had 79 missions in conflict areas, is mentioned by name and function in international humanitarian law. These functions include the protection and assistance of civilians and ex-combatants in settings of international and internal armed conflict, including visits to prisoners of war and civilian internees. The national Red Cross and Red Crescent societies assist a total of some 233 million persons annually, using some 97 million volunteers and paid staff. The Red Cross movement is a truly global network, spanning donor and recipient countries. By contrast, the major NGOs have far fewer national members—Save the Children has twenty-six, MSF eighteen, Oxfam eleven, and CARE ten—most of them in donor countries.[13]

Like NGOs, the Red Cross movement has evolved in recent decades. Not only has the size and complexity of each of the institutional components grown; so too has the scale of their activities, the size of their budgets, and the extent of their global reach.[14] The movement's principles, which include neutrality, impartiality, and independence, are shared by most other humanitarian organizations, although in varying degrees, as will be seen in later chapters. In 2003, the combined international budgets of the ICRC and IFRC stood at $723 million. Taken together with the budgets of national societies funded from locally generated resources, this confirms the movement's status as one of the world's major humanitarian players.

The fifth set of actors, indigenous NGOs and civil society institutions based in conflict zones, is simultaneously the potentially most important and the least appreciated humanitarian player. These local actors tend to set the stage for higher profile international actors, even though the show is playing in their hometown, and they often express bitterness at being relegated to the role of baggage handlers for the international jet set. Because humanitarian enterprise is predominantly an expatriate show, the lead roles typically go to outsiders, and even the tickets are priced out of local reach. Even international NGOs with strongly expressed commitments to building local institutions are, for the most part, anything but nurturing of local capacities.

The frequently-heard grievances of host governments and local NGOs during emergencies, from Afghanistan to East Timor, have a great deal of merit. During the first Gulf crisis in 1990–1992 when the internationals fled from Iraq and Kuwait, neighboring states in the region represented the forward line of humanitarian response. The people and government of Jordan shouldered the initial burden, as more than a million people fled into their country. When the Kurds converged on the Turkish border, the first assistance came from local families, communities, and the Turkish Red Crescent Society. In Iran, most of the aid was mobilized by national, provincial, and local governmental authorities. In Sierra Leone, local NGOs complained bitterly when foreign agencies twice fled a rebel advance on Freetown, taking the keys to food warehouses with them.

Local humanitarian actors are in some cases the most historically rooted of the five sets of institutions. "Long before international efforts were developed to respond to the needs of people uprooted by war and persecution," writes Elizabeth Ferris of the World Council of Churches, "individuals and private groups provided immediate assistance to those forced from their homes." As early as the mid-nineteenth century, in many countries their activities had laid the organizational foundation for "the capabilities that were channeled into relief activities in the early decades of the twentieth century."[15]

Joining these five sets of traditional humanitarian actors are some relative newcomers. One group, largely unquantified and scarcely noticed until recently, consists of Muslim contributors making donations in the form of *zakat*, an obligatory Islamic religious duty, or *wakf*, a form of charitable endowment. Remittances through informal or parallel systems such the *hawala* have also accounted for significant financial volumes to countries in need, such as Somalia. Other groups, such as for-profit contractors and military personnel, began with bit parts in the early post–Cold War era but have expanded their roles and carved out niches for themselves that affect the overall character of the enterprise.

Since the winding down of the Cold War, international military forces have assumed a wider array of humanitarian roles. As UN peacekeepers or national contingents deployed into Somalia, Bosnia, or Rwanda, international military forces have been involved to varying degrees in three broad tasks: providing security for civilians and humanitarian organizations in violent settings, helping aid agencies do their job, and supplying hands-on emergency aid.

The military's contribution to humanitarian work has been uneven. Oddly, military units have sometimes been *least* committed to providing security and *most* interested in conferring hands-on aid—precisely the reverse of what humanitarian agencies would like.[16] As actors whose primary functions reflect political objectives and direction, the military differs fundamentally from humanitarian institutions. In many cases, human needs activities are part of a campaign to "win hearts and minds." Nevertheless, in some circumstances they have demonstrated that they can make a positive contribution to humanitarian endeavors. For their part, contracting firms and consultants are now getting a larger share of the humanitarian market, although predominantly in high-profile, well-funded emergencies.

The twin trends of for-profit action and the expanded roles of the military converge in another development: the growing use of private security firms by the U.S. military. Private-sector companies now carry out a range of tasks aimed at supporting U.S. forces and the communities with which they interact. In Iraq in 2003, the Pentagon signed several multibillion-dollar contracts with Kellogg, Brown & Root (KBR), a subsidiary of the energy giant Halliburton. One contract was designed to get Iraqi oil fields up and running; another harnessed KBR as "a kind of for-profit Ministry of Public Works," as one journalist put it, for U.S. troops in Iraq. In this case, civilians from the private sector performed work that the military used to do for itself, such as prepare its meals, wash its laundry, build and maintain its bases.[17]

The new breeds of actor are in some ways particularly suited to the post–Cold War scene. Internal armed conflicts make humanitarian access more difficult for the traditional actors, placing a premium on security. The ideology of the marketplace, reflected in greater privatization of social services in developed countries, seems like a natural for the more competitive world of social and economic reconstruction abroad. However, the new international military and commercial contractors have been received with ambivalence by traditional humanitarian actors. Aid agencies find the competition threatening, as indeed it sometimes is. Military and for-profit contractors have a task-oriented mentality that may show results sooner than NGOs, which are more consultative and interactive. "The private sector will always be capable of responding more rapidly and [offers] easier decision-making" than NGOs and UN agencies, even though the latter may be cheaper, says USAID's deputy administrator Frederick Schieck.[18] But not everyone agrees that traditional aid groups are the best bargain in town, including a reporter on a visit to Iraq: "[T]he Iraqi people need help, regardless of whether that comes from people in camouflage uniforms riding in dusty Humvees, or from elegant men in ponytails driving gleaming SUVs. It is fascinating to see how much more morally serious the people in the Humvees seem to be—and how much readier the people in the SUVs are to despise the army than to effectively better the lot of the Iraqis."[19]

Ponytails and SUVs aside, aid agencies have more substantive concerns than such worries about the "more morally serious people in the Humvees." In their view, humanitarian action is an art as well as a discipline, a matter of solidarity and continuity as well as of commercial contracts and military exit strategies. Neither contractors nor troops with aid responsibilities are—first and foremost or exclusively—humanitarian in their mandates. They come and go with a given emergency, unlike humanitarian or development workers who may have been in a country for years before a given crisis and who may well stay on for many more years. Thus while the military and private contractors may make specific and indispensable humanitarian contributions here and there—lift capacity into Goma, protection of civilians in the Pristina stadium, construction of refugee camps in Albania, restoration of law and order in East Timor—the new breed is no substitute for the old.

The chapters ahead delve into whether the humanitarian system is, in fact, even remotely systematic. First in a list of problems are the glaring gaps—for example, between assistance, which many agencies are qualified to provide and for which ample funding is often available, and protection, which is far more demanding, more political, and less well resourced. Another gap is the relative underfunding of prevention in relation to remedial action. The humanitarian enterprise is better at stanching wounds than at anticipating and preventing injury. Yet another gap concerns the prevailing narrow definition of relief and the difficulty of finding resources for reconstruction and development. Funds restricted to emergencies and funding procedures with little built-in flexibility respond badly to the broad panoply of humanitarian need. Such need is usually nonlinear, replete with deep roots and vastly different pathologies. Finally, there is a gap in the system's responsiveness to need wherever it exists. "What constitutes a humanitarian crisis, its magnitude and its nature," reports a study by the Overseas Development Institute, "is at present a matter largely of subjective interpretation."[20] Declarations of emergencies and the allocation of resources to them tend to be political and media driven rather than needs based.

Second, a number of indispensable functions are not managed well by the humanitarian system as it exists today. Assessments of need are patchy. Resource mobilization for individual crises is uneven; the amounts requested for various crises and the percentages received show vast disproportionality in relation to need. "Over the past three years," observes a study of appeals between 2000 and 2002, "the average requests have ranged from $38 per head to $304 per head. Contributions per beneficiary range from $20 to $177."[21] Monitoring and evaluation have also been weak, with little feedback into agency programming and little apparent effect on subsequent funding patterns.

Fourth, the basis for choosing funding partners is often not clear. Does an NGO receive funding to deliver emergency health services because it has a better track record than other NGOs, the UN, and military or commercial competitors, or do personal and political connections play a key role? Is a military contingent asked to build a road because it can do so more quickly, because it can gain access to local sources of intelligence, or because troops need to be kept occupied? Will the award-winning private contractor really install water and sanitation in a refugee camp more quickly and cheaply than the NGO specialist? In many cases the answer is not clear.

As a result, the humanitarian enterprise is characterized by a surprising degree of mistrust and antipathy: between donors and UN agencies; between UN agencies and their implementing partners; between international NGOs and civil society organizations in host countries; and between humanitarian actors and institutions with political, diplomatic, military, and peacekeeping responsibilities. The lack of standard donor definitions, priorities, timeframes, and reporting requirements places the onus for efficiency and effectiveness on delivery agencies. As a result, they are unable to perform to their own satisfaction or to that of most donors.

Even the concept of humanitarianism itself is a matter of debate. The lack of a structural view to probe the root causes of violence often gives humanitarian action a bad name. For example, the expressions of solidarity by European and American politicians with the people of strife-torn West Africa, and high-level hand-wringing in the UN Security Council in mid-2003, conveniently ignored the fact that arms, diamond, and timber sanctions aimed at stopping money flow to combatants were routinely being broken. Cosmetic humanitarianism abounds. A case in point: the 1996 announcement made with great fanfare by then-U.S. Secretary of State Madeline Albright. While refusing to sign the new convention to ban landmines—a humanitarian initiative of extraordinary urgency and high potential impact—the United States would establish its own fund to assist the victims of landmine explosions.

Even humanitarian organizations differ among themselves about how humanitarianism should be defined and approached. In a structural sense, many problems that require humanitarian redress have their roots in inequalities of power, in a lack of representative forms of government, in tribal and ethnic tension, and in patterns of international trade and finance. "In eastern DRC, for instance," says Sarah Collinson, "most aid agencies see themselves as engaged in relief, and thus not directly concerned by structural issues to do with the war economy. Yet the cycle of boom and bust in the coltan trade indicates that economic changes at a global level can be just as much 'disasters' in humanitarian terms as a drought or military offensive."[22]

Some aid agencies are committed, whether directly or through their membership in coalitions, to address problems upstream before they result in new or continued suffering. Many faith-based groups embrace a justice agenda and, while not necessarily choosing sides in a given conflict, do not make the principle of neutrality their first and great commandment. Others take a more circumscribed view. The ICRC, for example, attaches central importance to the concept of neutrality, which limits the attention it devotes to structural causes of suffering. Its viewpoint is reflected in the comment by analyst Max Glaser: "Aid providers are not responsible for the causes of conflict and the suffering it produces, and it is an illusion indeed to expect that humanitarian agencies are capable to address 'root causes' of conflict."[23]

Whatever their interpretation of their own role, humanitarian agencies of all stripes have become more aware in the past decade of the importance of understanding the contexts in which they work. World Vision International has even coined some new acronyms: MSTC, for "making sense of turbulent contexts," and SCPIs, for "situations of chronic political instability." Through a manual and training sessions for field staff, the agency provides analytical tools for understanding the political lay of the land so that humanitarian activities and presence do not exacerbate the underlying problems.[24]

Finally, there is an obvious and growing cynicism among governments in their use of humanitarian activities as a substitute for decisive political and military action. This imposes a high toll on public willingness to endorse global engagement on issues of human survival. For several years the Bosnian crisis was treated as a humanitarian problem rather than as a political and military issue. Until the Rwandan genocide had ended and the need for international peacekeepers had largely passed, that emergency was also treated by most UN Security Council members as a humanitarian problem rather than a political or security issue. Palestine absorbs huge amounts of humanitarian spending, in part because Israel is not fulfilling its obligations under the Geneva Conventions to meet the food and medical requirements of people in its occupied territories. In all three cases, humanitarian action became a fig leaf for political and military inaction. Given the continuing instability in all three regions, there has been no great political acuity in this, nor have humanitarian needs been particularly well served. The humanitarian stage often provides a semblance of action rather than lasting or effective movement on life-and-death issues.

The next four chapters examine how some of these issues have played out in specific emergencies: Sierra Leone, East Timor, Afghanistan, and elsewhere. The subsequent four chapters scrutinize the drivers of humanitarian action: the overt and the hidden persuaders, the policies and politics, the scramble for attention and money, the growing intrusion of security concerns, and the consequences of subordinating the rather simple concept of saving lives to political, managerial, and institutional priorities.

2

Forgetting Sierra Leone

By now we are all familiar with the day when the world changed and unspeakable acts of terror took the lives of more than 5,000 civilians. I am referring, of course, to January 6, 1999, when rebel gunmen killed, maimed and raped their way across Freetown, Sierra Leone's capital.

—David Keen[1]

Nobody cares much about Sierra Leone. Until 2000, it held little strategic, political, or economic interest for any great power. Its decade-long humanitarian crisis was treated accordingly until a major United Nations peacekeeping mission was almost derailed by a rebel army that hacked the limbs off children to make its political point. The international media, more interested in refugee camp sex scandals than starvation, mostly ignored the crisis. Most aid agencies had trouble raising funds for Sierra Leone, and UN appeals—always low, even compared to what was requested in less acute emergencies—rarely met half of their target. In the humanitarian financing sweepstakes, Sierra Leone was not a winner.

This small West African country, one of Britain's first colonies in Africa, was founded by former slaves returning from Canada, Britain, and the United States in the late eighteenth century. Known in colonial times as "the white man's grave," Sierra Leone's inhospitable climate and the malaria-bearing *Anopheles* mosquito conspired to ensure that the colony was a drag on the colonial exchequer for most of its time under British rule. The roots of its terrible civil conflict, which lasted from 1991 until 2002, actually predate independence, which was granted in 1961.

Britain did little to develop the colony. The first motor roads into the interior were not laid down until the 1940s, and some of the largest towns were without secondary schools until after independence. Administrative and democratic institutions inherited by the newly independent

country were little more than a veneer. Much of the economy revolved around the diamond industry, but most of the country's diamonds were alluvial, scattered over large areas of several districts. This created policing problems as well as administrative, political, and economic difficulties, all of which offered wide scope for deliberate mismanagement and corruption.

The first military coup took place in 1966. The civilian government that succeeded the military in 1967 lasted a remarkable twenty-five years, but at a cost. The two presidents during that period, Siaka Stevens and Joseph Momoh, presided over a steep descent into political oppression and economic ruin. Opposition parties were banned, the diamond industry and other assets were stripped, and development moved relentlessly in a negative direction. Because Sierra Leone had no resources of significant value to the great powers and because it had never become a pawn in cold war politics, it was of little interest to donors, and aid money was limited.

Rampant corruption helped make this a self-fulfilling situation. For many years, Taiwan maintained an embassy and an aid program in return for Sierra Leone's support at the United Nations. Israel maintained an embassy and a small aid program, mainly because of Lebanese interests in the diamond industry, and because of Sierra Leone's flirtations with the PLO and Iran. But these were sideshows in an otherwise dozy donor community complemented by the small programs of a handful of international NGOs. In 1990 Sierra Leone received $63.4 million in development assistance. While this may seem like a substantial amount at $14.50 per capita, it was far less than most other African countries. Zimbabwe, still in the good books of donors, received $69 per capita that year; Cameroon received $59 and Ghana $39.

By 1991, Sierra Leone had dropped to last place on the UN Human Development Index. That year, a small band of rebels crossed the border from Liberia and attacked a police post. It was the unlikely start of a war that would eventually displace half of the country's population and take the lives of as many as 75,000 people. The war was ostensibly about democracy, justice, and equity, although the manifesto of the Revolutionary United Front (RUF)—copied largely from the writings of revolutionaries elsewhere, revolutionaries with much better bona fides—would not actually become known for several years.

Led by a former army corporal, Foday Sankoh, the RUF was in its initial stages a cipher, a combination of disaffected youth, political dissidents, and opportunists. The RUF had no ethnic following, and unlike most African conflicts, there were no cold war antecedents. Sankoh had trained in Libya, where he met another would-be leader, Charles Taylor of Liberia. Taylor had begun his own guerrilla war against the government in Monrovia in 1989, and in supporting the RUF, he was striking a blow at both the Economic Community of West African States (ECOWAS) and the government of Sierra Leone. ECOWAS had sent a peacekeeping force (ECOMOG) to Liberia, and for years—using Freetown as a rear supply base—it thwarted Taylor's fight for power. In supporting the RUF, Taylor was therefore aiming at several birds with the same stone: He intended to destabilize both Sierra Leone and ECOMOG. In addition, he saw possibilities in Sierra Leone's diamond fields, less than a hundred miles from the Liberian border.

By 1995 much had changed in Sierra Leone. A military coup had ended the inept and terminally corrupt civilian government, installing the National Provisional Ruling Council (NPRC) in its place. The RUF now controlled the best diamond areas and was exporting gems via Liberia to pay for weapons. And its war, ostensibly against injustice and poverty, was now manifested in brutal attacks on civilians. In addition to its widespread use of sex slaves and child soldiers, the RUF committed the most horrific acts of brutality, chopping the hands and feet off civilians, many of them babies. As a terror tactic, and as a way of limiting civilian presence in its areas of control, the technique was as successful as it was barbarous. Preceded by its reputation, the RUF was often able to conquer areas without firing a shot.

In 1995 the country carried a debt that equalled 177 percent of GNP, a burden exceeded by only seven other countries in the world. Life expectancy was only thirty-nine years and the adult literacy rate was less than 25 percent. Seventy percent of the country's schools had been destroyed in the fighting, and only 80 of the 500 health centers were functioning, most of them in and around the capital, Freetown.

The humanitarian situation was grim. UN estimates in March 1996 placed the number of Sierra Leonean refugees who had crossed into Guinea and Liberia at 330,000. Freetown held an estimated 750,000 displaced people, many living with family and friends. A further million or more displaced people had moved into towns up-country, and 900,000 had registered for food aid. In all, 2.1 million people—half the population of the country—had been forced to abandon their homes and livelihoods. About half of the displaced people were said to be managing reasonably well without assistance, living with friends and family. A further 210,000 lived in camps, where they were dependent on others for some aspects of their survival. Many had adopted what aid agencies like to call "coping strategies," such as traveling by day to farming plots within a five- or ten-mile radius of the towns where they sheltered at night. A third category, of about half a million people, were entirely destitute, camping where they could in towns and cities, or surviving in camps with the help of relief supplies.

A September 1995 UN report said that there was adequate relief food available for the "accessible" populations, although such a statement concealed a number of problems. The most prominent was the inability of relief agencies to get food convoys through to the affected areas. Relief agencies were regularly attacked by the RUF, and often by Sierra Leonean soldiers posing as rebels. Soldiers by day, rebels by night, people called them "sobels." In December 1995, the WFP reported malnutrition reaching "frightening levels." However the overall UN response remained dramatically limited compared with other countries. In Liberia, a country with only 60 percent of the population of Sierra Leone, the 1995 consolidated UN appeal totalled $65 million, and more than 80 percent of the requirements were met. In Sierra Leone, a UN appeal for less than $20 million was only half subscribed. Sierra Leone was what relief agencies call a "forgotten emergency."

This is perhaps not surprising, given an almost conspiratorial effort by donors to pretend that everything in Sierra Leone was under control. An August 1995 UNDP report on aid to Sierra Leone devoted only one paragraph to the war, made no mention of the humanitarian situation, and a section on "constraints to development" contained a one-line reference to the security situation.[2] This is not to suggest that UN agencies were ignoring the humanitarian needs; they were doing what they could with the meager resources available. But there was an almost pathological effort to avoid the suggestion that the Sierra Leone situation was out of control. A British report at the time noted that the UN's Department of Humanitarian Affairs in New York had

> . . . argued for a declaration of a state of "complex emergency" in Sierra Leone. This would unleash a whole set of responses, including the appointment of a UNSRSG [Special Representative of the Secretary·

General], a Humanitarian Coordinator, and new arrangements for UN working in Sierra Leone. However the UN Secretary General's Special Envoy, the UN Resident Coordinator, and the [government] are all united in the opposition to this. They argue that such a declaration would be politically inept, as it would undermine the authority of the Government and signal to the RUF that the international community has lost faith in the present administration. It would create the impression that Sierra Leone is a "failed country" . . . and undermine confidence-building efforts. Aid agencies also fear from experience elsewhere that the declaration of a "complex emergency" in Sierra Leone would give license to all sorts of ill conceived aid inputs and appointments of coordinators with conflicting mandates. . . ."[3]

The report implied that the actual declaration of a complex emergency was needed to ensure an appropriate UN response. This was not the case. UN Under-Secretary General Peter Hansen, speaking about Sierra Leone at the time, made the point that a declaration would not change reality one way or the other for the average Sierra Leonean. A complex emergency *is*; it is not designated. UN agencies can (or at least should be able to) reconfigure themselves to deal with an emergency, regardless of what has been "declared." Nevertheless, the British report recommended that "the U.K. should oppose any calls in New York or Geneva for the declaration of a 'complex emergency.'"

The report posited some short-term scenarios for the country's future. In a calculation that added up to 105 percent, it said that there was a 15 percent chance of the situation either normalizing or improving, and a 30 percent chance that it would remain as it was. There was a 40 percent chance of the situation "getting worse" and a 20 percent chance of "apocalypse." At one point or another during the next five years, all of the scenarios came to pass.

In 1995 the NPRC—clearly losing the military battle to the RUF—brought in a South African mercenary company called Executive Outcomes. Within weeks, using superior communication techniques, better training, and helicopter gunships, Executive Outcomes had pushed the RUF back from Freetown and had cleared the diamond areas. The RUF sued for peace and, pressured by donors and Sierra Leonean civil society, the military permitted elections to take place. The new civilian government, led by a former UN official, Ahmad Tejan Kabbah, negotiated a peace deal that was signed in Abidjan, the capital of Côte d'Ivoire, in November 1996. Among the provisions: Executive Outcomes had to go. John Hirsch, U.S. ambassador to Sierra Leone at the time, later called their departure a "fatal mistake,"[4] but Kabbah was under intense donor pressure to reduce government expenditure. The IMF in particular objected to the $1.8 million cost of maintaining Executive Outcomes each month. In retrospect, however, given the $3 to $4 billion that the donor community would eventually shell out to rescue

Sierra Leone, $1.8 million a month looks reasonable. Compared with the $1.9 million that UN Mission in Sierra Leone (UNAMSIL) would eventually cost the donors *every day*, Executive Outcomes would have been a bargain, especially if they had inflicted a decisive defeat on the RUF.

A six-month twilight period now ensued during which Sierra Leoneans began to hope that the worst was past. Then, in May 1997, another coup took place. Johnny Paul Koroma, a major already in jail for involvement in a previous coup plot emerged as the leader of the Armed Forces Ruling Council (AFRC). The Kabbah government fled with most of the diplomatic corps and aid agencies to the nearby capital of Guinea. ECOWAS extended the military mandate of ECOMOG to Sierra Leone and demanded that the junta step down. The UN Security Council and the Commonwealth concurred. In defiance, however, Johnny Paul—as he was commonly known—made a power-sharing pact with the RUF, and soon rebels were running free in the streets of the capital. The results were devastating. Politicians who had not fled the country for exile in Conakry found themselves victimized by the new regime. Journalists were murdered. Rape, theft, and torture became the predominant ethic of the new government. Banks remained closed, the civil service ceased to function, and commerce ground to a halt.

No government anywhere recognized the AFRC. As a result of the coup and growing insecurity, major aid programs were suspended, and the United Nations placed a petroleum and arms embargo on Sierra Leone. The Kabbah cabinet remained largely intact, operating in conjunction with Sierra Leone's small diplomatic corps and UN agencies from hotel rooms in Conakry. Although most humanitarian NGOs also left the country when the coup took place, a handful returned, and while some donors—the European Community, Netherlands, and the United States—continued to provide them with funding, others did not. Most notable among the latter was Britain's Department for International Development (DFID), which suspended humanitarian assistance as well as development aid on the grounds that its use for humanitarian purposes could not be guaranteed. Combined with the fuel and arms embargo, however, the suspension of aid was seen by some humanitarian agencies as part of a package. "In effect," an ActionAid official said, "aid became a political tool of international diplomacy, contrary to the [NGO] Code of Conduct which says that 'Aid will not be used to further a particular political or religious standpoint.'"[5] Since when, it might be asked in counterpoint, have governments ever paid much attention to NGO codes of conduct?

The situation in Sierra Leone deteriorated rapidly. Fighting continued, food shortages grew, and more people were displaced. Relief supplies that did get through were subjected to hijackings, and the humanitarian situation, grim before the AFRC takeover, became worse. Those few humanitarian agencies that continued to operate in Sierra Leone—notably the ICRC and some European NGOs—came under increasing pressure from the Kabbah government-in-exile to stay out of the country. Even funding from the European Community Humanitarian Office (ECHO) and U.S. was seriously curtailed. Marc Sommers says, "Politics overwhelmed humanitarianism in Conakry."[6] Not only did the political agenda—to get rid of the AFRC—become paramount, relief supplies became part of the equation. The UN resident coordinator, Elizabeth Lwanga, sided with the exiled President Kabbah, and her relationship with agencies operating in Freetown degenerated, as one report puts it, "into mutual antipathy and contempt. Very serious allegations were made about her refusal to 'stand up' for humanitarian principles and agencies."[7]

Some NGOs accused the British government and DFID of the same approach. One critic of those favoring regime change later said of Britain, "their strategy worked: holding back humanitarian aid helped Kabbah get back into Sierra Leone."[8] Had the RUF and the AFRC remained in power, however, the humanitarian situation undoubtedly would have become considerably worse. None of the protagonists had calculated how many lives might have been saved had British aid been freely given, and none had calculated how much the AFRC might have filched—and what this might have added to its life expectancy. But writing with hindsight, Toby Porter describes the period "as one of the most shameful episodes of humanitarian inaction in modern times. Those encouraging the policy [of withholding aid] may well have been in breach of the Geneva Conventions."[9]

Writing about other wars, Alex De Waal begs to differ: "At the end of the day, relief organizations will always make charitable works their priority, which means that human rights concerns will be fudged or jettisoned. In the short term, people may be fed or treated as a result—an outcome not to be despised. But this is at the cost of addressing more fundamental political and human rights concerns."[10]

The trade-offs between providing and withholding aid in the service of political objectives became the subject of charge and countercharge, accompanied by much *Sturm und Drang*. DFID Minister Clare Short was questioned by a British Parliamentary Committee on the subject almost a year later. A member of parliament asked her about criticism from ActionAid. Short said, "ActionAid's allegation is completely false. They are saying we used humanitarian aid for political purposes. The suggestion being the humanitarian aid was needed but in order to bring about a political solution we took a decision not to supply humanitarian aid to needy people to increase the pressure for a political solution. That is a complete and absolute lie."[11] In response, ActionAid's chief executive did not buy her explanation, referring again to "DFID's apparent pursuit of political objectives through the restriction of humanitarian aid to Sierra Leone. We have expressed particular worry that this may reflect an important shift in DFID policy without public acknowledgment by the government."[12]

The principles involved in this debate are as vexed as they are important, and they will arise again in later chapters. In Sierra Leone, however, the debate about humanitarian aid at this time obscured a larger failing on the part of the countries providing it. The AFRC and its RUF partners had not just formed an illegitimate government; they were perpetrating some of the worst human rights violations since the war began. The fact that those wringing their hands in Conakry could find nothing more powerful than humanitarian aid to think about—either as weapon or as succor—demonstrates an all too typical Western approach to African conflicts. It would take two more years before Britain, alone among Western nations, would decide that a military response was required to deal with the security problem in Sierra Leone.

By the time the debate was playing itself out in London, the AFRC had dissolved, pushed out of Freetown along with the RUF after a military onslaught by ECOMOG. Oddly, ECOMOG failed to pursue them, and so they lived to fight another day. Although their leader, Foday Sankoh, had been jailed, the RUF continued to run roughshod over the diamond areas and large parts of the countryside. Hundreds of thousands of refugees continued to live across the borders in Guinea and Liberia, and a million or more people remained displaced. Hunger was widespread, disease was unchecked, and thousands suffered from bullet wounds and mutilation.

A casual observer might be forgiven for thinking that by 1998, after all it had been through, Sierra Leone might have started to receive greater humanitarian attention. At a political level, however, the UN Security Council deferred entirely to the ECOWAS initiative, relying on ECOMOG troops to defend civilians and West African diplomats to maintain the fiction that there was still some sort of peace process amid the ruins of the Abidjan agreement. "African solutions for African problems" became a rallying cry for those permanent members of the Security Council who refused to consider any kind of enhanced UN role in Sierra Leone. The aid effort suffered as well. The UN Consolidated Appeal asked donors to contribute $20.2 million that year to help it deal with all of the refugees, all of the displaced people, and all of the health and food needs of Sierra Leone. By the end of the year, less than half of the funds requested had arrived. The world seemed determined to keep Sierra Leone in its place as a "forgotten emergency."

The AFRC period reflected a "getting worse" scenario. What happened in 1998 and 1999 was apocalyptic. Some time afterwards, British Sierra Leone-watcher David Keen wrote the words used at the beginning of this chapter: "By now we are all familiar with the day when the world changed and unspeakable acts of terror took the lives of more than 5,000 civilians. I am referring, of course, to January 6, 1999, when rebel gunmen killed, maimed and raped their way across Freetown."[13] The two-week RUF invasion of Freetown was as clear a signal as any that the RUF were butchers, that ECOMOG was incapable of dealing with the challenge, and that ECOMOG, as an African solution to an African problem, was not going to work.

In fact ECOMOG had been an experiment, one that Western governments hoped might relieve them of responsibility for dealing with Africa's wars. The United States was particularly reluctant after Somalia to be drawn into another African conflict, and although President Clinton had stood at the Kigali airport in Rwanda well after the genocide there, saying "Never again," he didn't mean it. The UN—controlled by the five permanent members of the Security Council: Britain, Russia, France, China, and the United States—had failed Somalia. It had done little more than run away from Rwanda, and it was about to pull its peacekeepers out of Angola, where there was no peace to be kept. Sierra Leone was thus caught between a political rock and a hard place called "apathy." The days of the lackluster ECOMOG were numbered, but Tejan Kabbah was told that there was no chance whatsoever of a UN peacekeeping force arriving to take their place. Faced with an impossible situation, Kabbah bowed to growing international pressure for another peace arrangement with the RUF. There could never be a military solution, he was told; the solution had to be political.

What then occurred must go down in the annals of international diplomacy as one of the most cynical and disgraceful episodes of all time. Jesse Jackson, "Special Envoy for the President and Secretary of State for the Promotion of Democracy in Africa" had already been to Freetown and Monrovia. In 1998 he had urged President Kabbah to "reach out" to the RUF in order to make peace, and had upset virtually every Sierra Leonean alive—and many South African anti-apartheid activists—by comparing the RUF with South Africa's ANC. Somehow, he assumed, a power-sharing agreement would "promote democracy."

Prominent members of the U.S. Congressional Black Caucus then became involved. Many were close to Liberia's Charles Taylor, recently elected president in a ballot that he promised would result in more war, should he lose. New Jersey Representative Donald Payne, a personal friend of Taylor, wrote to Kabbah, urging negotiations. "Successful negotiations must be without precondition and include the permanent release of Mr. Foday Sankoh," Payne wrote.[14] Under direct personal pressure from Jesse Jackson and U.S. State Department officials, and with a rapidly dwindling military capacity to resist the RUF, Kabbah finally agreed to a cease-fire and released Foday Sankoh, who joined him for negotiations in Lomé, the capital of Togo. There, over a marathon

45-day negotiating session, U.S. officials and others helped draft a peace deal. What resulted, on July 7, 1999, was a blanket amnesty for all RUF fighters. In addition the RUF was given four ministerial posts in Kabbah's government, and vice presidential status was conferred on Foday Sankoh. As icing on the cake, he was also made head of a new commission to oversee the country's diamond resources.

The RUF had demonstrated that butchery paid off. Instead of being punished, they were rewarded, assisted in the process by the most powerful government on earth. At precisely the same moment that NATO was spending billions of dollars to save Kosovars from human rights abuse, much worse atrocities were being generously rewarded in Sierra Leone. Instead of going to prison, Foday Sankoh was made vice president. As a prize for eight years of diamond theft, he was put in charge of the country's entire mineral wealth. Assistant U.S. Secretary of State Susan Rice bragged at the time that "the U.S. role in Sierra Leone . . . has been instrumental. With hands-on efforts by the president's special envoy Jesse Jackson, Ambassador Joe Melrose, and many others, the United States brokered the cease-fire and helped steer Sierra Leone's rebels, the Kabbah government, and regional leaders to the negotiating table."[15]

UN officials as well as representatives of ECOWAS and the British government also had participated actively in the negotiations. But when UN Special Envoy Francis Okello sought permission from New York to initial the deal with the others at the table, someone at the UN headquarters woke up to meaning of the words "absolute and free pardon and reprieve to all." The UN High Commissioner for Human Rights, former Irish President Mary Robinson, raised objections, and Okello was instructed to append a handwritten note saying that the UN did not acknowledge the application of the amnesty to "acts of genocide, crimes against humanity, war crimes and other serious violations of international humanitarian law." There were no such compunctions in Washington at the time, but six months later a U.S. State Department spokesman, Philip Reeker, would say, "The United States did not pressure anybody to sign this agreement. . . . We neither brokered the Lomé peace agreement nor leaned on President Kabbah to open talks with the insurgents. . . . It was not an agreement of ours."[16]

Reeker had good reason for trying to distance the administration retroactively from the Lomé agreement. Apart from its grotesque rewarding of criminality, it was destined to fail. Peter Takirambudde of Human Rights Watch said that the agreement represented "a major retreat by all the parties—the UN, the Clinton Administration, the others. For the rest of Africa, where there are rebels in the bush, the signal is that atrocities can be committed—especially if they are frightening atrocities. The lesson to other rebels is that half measures will not do."[17] The moral of the tale, it seems, was that the more egregious the human rights violations, the more they would be rewarded.

The Lomé Agreement included provision for a new peacekeeping force. When the Security Council passed its resolution creating UNAMSIL in October 1999, its attention may have been diverted away from detail and away from the implications of what they were doing by events ocurring in Kosovo and East Timor. In June 1999 the Security Council had mandated a NATO peacekeeping force in Kosovo, and this was building toward 40,000 troops as the Lomé agreement was being signed. (The NATO war against Yugoslavia was in aid of 750,000 refugees and displaced people who had fled Serbian human rights abuse—approximately one-third the number of displaced and refugee Sierra Leoneans.) East Timor, reeling from postreferendum violence, had in September seen the arrival of the first of more than 10,000 Australian peacekeepers, mandated by the Security Council. (East Timor has a total population of 850,000 people.) Perhaps the Security Council felt, given its willingness during these critical weeks to support peacekeeping operations in Kosovo and East Timor, that it could no longer ignore Sierra Leone. Perhaps the Security Council actually believed that the spurious Lomé Agreement would hold, that the RUF had changed and would be satisfied with half of the pie, that there would be a peace to keep—and that pigs would fly past the UNAMSIL reviewing stand.

It is more likely, however, that the members of the council expected "African solutions" to continue providing a fig leaf for their lack of attention. Certainly they assumed that 12,000 ECOMOG troops would remain in Sierra Leone, and that many would simply be re-hatted under UN colors. Other troops, it was thought, would be drawn from countries in the region. It might thus be possible to create UNAMSIL by writing a few checks and issuing some blue helmets. But Nigeria, which had provided most of the ECOMOG troops—losing an estimated 1,000 men in the effort and spending upwards of a million dollars a day—had had enough. Newly elected President Olusegun Obasanjo announced that Nigeria was pulling its troops out of Sierra Leone. A scramble ensued to find new troop-sending countries. Finally, as the Nigerian forces withdrew, troops from India, Zambia, Kenya, and other countries arrived. But many were poorly equipped, and although UNAMSIL had an assertive mandate under Chapter VII, few understood that they might be placed in harm's way. And those who eventually *were* placed in harm's way were unprepared to defend themselves. In short, the genesis of UNAMSIL was based on several false assumptions: that the RUF intended to live up to the agreement it had signed; that if it did not,

UN troops had a mandate to get tough; and that faced with the need to get tough, they would be willing and able to do so.

Less than a year after the Lomé agreement was signed, on May 2, 2000, reports began to reach Freetown that UNAMSIL troops had been detained, and possibly kidnapped, up-country by RUF forces. When the dust settled a few days later, it turned out that several had been killed and more than 500 captured and relieved of their vehicles and weapons. It was an unprecedented attack on a UN peacekeeping mission, and on the United Nations itself. By May 6, an RUF advance on Freetown was under way and there was understandable panic, not only among civilians and in the government, but within UNAMSIL and among the humanitarian community. All remembered what had happened in January the year before, and for the third time in thirty-six months, the humanitarian community in Sierra Leone prepared for evacuation. One UNAMSIL worker recalls a rumor that the RUF were already in Freetown. "We had information that they were still three or four days away," he recalled. "I drove to UNAMSIL. It was one of the most surreal sights of my life. The place was in chaos—soldiers arguing, shouting, drinking, fistfights, an atmosphere of chaos. I tried to find the Chief Military Observer to tell him that the rebels were not in Freetown, that they still had time—" presumably to prepare a defense.[18]

Britain, not a contributor of troops to UNAMSIL, took swift action. On May 7, a Hercules transport aircraft arrived at Freetown's Lungi airport with an advance force of 250 British paratroopers, ostensibly to secure the airport for the evacuation of British nationals. The following day, more troops arrived and Foreign Minister Robin Cook announced the diversion of the British aircraft carrier *Illustrious* to Sierra Leone, along with a frigate, a helicopter carrier, and three support ships. By May 12, the ships had arrived. Over the next few days, British troops engaged RUF probes, doing something the UN forces had never done: they fired back—with punishing effect on RUF forces that had rarely experienced such an event. The British troops held a much publicized amphibious landing on the beach and actively patrolled the streets of Freetown. British helicopters hovered over the capital and flew sorties up-country, while most of the captured UNAMSIL troops were quickly herded by the RUF across the Liberian border and eventually to freedom.

During a critical one-week period, when many were predicting the full collapse and withdrawal of UNAMSIL and an end to the basic principles of UN peacekeeping, the British moved with incredible speed. Although fighting would continue for another six months, the writing was on the wall for the RUF. If they needed further confirmation, it came four months after the British troops arrived. On August 25, eleven soldiers of the Royal Irish Regiment were captured by a gang of freelance thugs known as the West Side Boys. Held for ransom in a remote jungle hideout, the soldiers did not have long to wait. On September 12 the camp was hit by British paratroopers, flown out specially from Britain for the occasion. They freed all eleven, along with twenty-two other captives, some of them sex slaves. Twenty-five West Side Boys were killed, and the group was never heard from again.

Why did Britain act? Speculation at the time revolved around commercial interests, like those so often defended in Africa by France, but these were somewhere between negligible and nonexistent. It may be that Britain wanted to rehabilitate its ethical foreign policy, tarnished a year earlier in a convoluted arms deal for the government in exile that contravened a UN embargo. The colonial legacy and Commonwealth connection inevitably played a part. Tony Blair's father had once taught at Fourah Bay University and there was rumored to be a sentimental connection. Here was something, UN-watchers said, that Britain could do to help justify its seat on the Security Council in future diplomatic battles. But most of this is fairly thin gruel beside the stated reason, which was to defend a legitimate government from takeover by thugs, and to defend a UN peacekeeping force that was on the verge of collapse at a moment in time when the UN's peacekeeping role—after several failures—was being reinvented. Undoubtedly there was also a calculation, not unlike that made by the U.S. military in Somalia a decade earlier, that a military intervention would succeed. In this case, they were right.

Sierra Leone's CNN moment had at last arrived. With the RUF assault on UNAMSIL, the world's news media flooded into Freetown. Stories about RUF atrocities, diamonds, and the very future of the United Nations became headline news around the world. Outraged by the RUF affront, the Security Council upgraded UNAMSIL from 6,000 to 16,500 and then to 17,500 troops, making it the largest UN peacekeeping mission, not just at that time, but of *all* time. In the coming months, squabbles over the military chain of command were resolved and a new force commander was appointed.

In addition the UN's coordination of humanitarian activities took a turn for the better. Since the time of the AFRC two years earlier, relations between the UN and the rest of the aid community had been strained. Elizabeth Lwanga was gone, and in 1999 Kofi Annan appointed a senior Nigerian diplomat, Oluyemi Adeniji, as his Special Representative. As SRSG, Adeniji became head of UNAMSIL and the ranking UN officer in Sierra Leone. Much of his first year was taken up with worries about the military situation, crisis management, and high-level political negotiations. The coordination of humanitarian affairs was not his long suit, and although he was a seasoned diplomat, his relations with the humanitarian community in Sierra Leone were poor. Soon, however, a deputy SRSG was appointed, one with the skills, knowledge, and patience needed to handle the humanitarian crisis. Alan Doss had been UN Resident Coordinator in Thailand during the Cambodian crisis, had served in several African countries, and had most recently directed the United Nations Development Group, created by Kofi Annan as a key feature of his reform program for the United Nations. In other words, he knew how the UN worked.

In addition to being a senior member of UNAMSIL, Doss was made UNDP Resident Representative, UN Resident Coordinator, UN Humanitarian Coordinator, and the UN Designated Official responsible for the security of UN agencies in Sierra Leone. Carrying a British passport, he inspired confidence in Sierra Leone's most important donor. Being competent, communicative, and apparently owning a clock with twenty-six hours in every day, he was soon able to overcome many of the rivalries and enmities that had built up over the years. He began chairing weekly meetings of the heads of UN agencies. He attended weekly meetings of an NGO forum. He listened, he responded—he *coordinated*.

In September 2000, the RUF began a new military adventure. Its forces attacked refugee camps in Guinea, south of Conakry. While the Guinean army was engaged there, a larger RUF force attacked further east, driving toward the diamond fields of Guinea's forest region. But the Guinean army was able to move quickly and dealt the RUF a crushing defeat. By November, it was clear to the RUF that their leader, Foday Sankoh, jailed in the aftermath of the attack on the UN, would not be released from prison. It was equally clear that expansion of the territory it controlled was out of the question, and that the possibility of an RUF military victory in Sierra Leone had ended with the arrival of better-equipped, properly mandated UN troops. The RUF also knew that if they posed any real threat, British troops would likely find them and kill them. After ten years of murder and mayhem, therefore, they agreed to another cease-fire. This one, however, would hold. A year later, President Kabbah declared the war over. Elections were held in May 2002, and the RUF—deluded in thinking that it might have some electoral popularity—received fewer votes than there were men under its command. Sierra Leone's nightmare was over.

The nightmare was over, but the problems were not. The threat of violence remained as long as young men could not find work and as long as the diamond fields remained unpoliced. Next door, Liberia was once again in flames, and tens of thousands of refugees were crossing into Sierra Leone. Hundreds of thousands of Sierra Leonean refugees had to be repatriated, a million or more displaced people had to be resettled, and the entire education and health infrastructures had to be rebuilt. In previous years, regardless of need and regardless of the amounts requested, the UN consolidated appeals (CAPs) had rarely met more than 50 percent of target. This held true in 2002, when a request for $98.5 million was placed before donors. A little more than half of the request was covered. Three-quarters of the requested food aid arrived, but only a third of the health projects were funded, and even then, the money arrived late. No funding was provided for malaria, Sierra Leone's worst health problem, or for HIV/AIDS. The water and sanitation sector was badly underfunded, and no money was provided through the CAP for shelter, rehabilitation, and employment services for ex-combatants.

There was so little money to help people return to their homes that UNAMSIL began to provide military vehicles, provoking a row with certain NGOs about the use of military assets for humanitarian purposes. MSF-France denounced what it called a rushed effort to "evict people from the camps, claiming that the war is over now and everyone needs to go home." Who, it asked, "is going to be responsible for the people's rights at the end of the day? Who is supposed to be sure that this repatriation and resettlement program takes place in humane and voluntary conditions and that the basic services that all people have a right to are provided for them? Who, at the end of the day, will put the people before the peace process?"[19] They might well have asked two other questions: Would people rather have stayed in crowded, dirty, underfunded camps than go home? And who would pay for what everyone was demanding of the UN?

Much debate occurred during the AFRC period about the need to keep humanitarian efforts separate from political and military objectives. These debates continued and current wisdom in some quarters claims that humanitarian agencies could have provided much more relief to RUF-held areas had the UN not been seen as siding with the government.[20] The truth, however, is that the RUF was always dangerous, unpredictable, and more than a little prone to the theft of relief goods. Over the years it kidnapped many aid workers and made it impossible for any lengthy or meaningful relief effort to take place in its territories. This was not because the neutrality of humanitarian agencies was compromised by their association with the government or the UN; it was because this behavior was the trademark of a loose-knit guerrilla army that had perfected the art of manipulating and terrorizing civilians.

To continue the debate about the use of UNAMSIL vehicles after the RUF was a spent force, even in the fear that the RUF might somehow come back to life and be prejudiced against those who had moved refugees in a UNAMSIL truck, was too much for some NGOs. While MSF, Action Contre la Faim, and a few others steadfastly refused to do so, most NGOs gradually took a more pragmatic view. High church neutrality had been a means to an end during the AFRC period, but was now a hindrance to helping those in need and no longer served a useful purpose.

≈

No weapon of mass distraction is more powerful than a sex scandal, and the one that rocked the Sierra Leonean aid community in 2002 highlights the power of the media and its effects on the aid industry. The scandal also illustrates the problem of trying to make long-term plans in a short-term business, as well as the danger of ignoring what in manufacturing terms is called preventive maintenance. The story begins in September 2001, when two consultants working for Save the Children Fund (SCF)/UK and UN High Commissioner for Refugees (UNHCR) reported widespread sexual abuse of women and children in refugee and internally displaced persons (IDP) camps. The perpetrators were the employees of several humanitarian agencies.[21]

> The team received allegations of abuse and exploitation against 67 individuals based in a range of agencies responsible for the care and protection of refugee and IDP communities. The agencies that are possibly implicated in some way include UN peacekeeping forces, international and local NGOs, and government agencies responsible for humanitarian response.

The report, leaked to the media, literally exploded onto world headlines. The BBC covered it this way:

> The United Nations High Commissioner for Refugees has sent a team of investigators into refugee camps in west Africa following the revelation that large numbers of children have been sexually exploited by aid workers there. The scale of the problem—revealed in an overview of a report by the UNHCR in conjunction with the British-based charity Save the Children—has surprised relief personnel. The unpublished report . . . is based on a study of more than 1,500 people interviewed over six weeks last October and November. An unspecified number of interviewees complained that they or their children had to have sex in order to get food and favours. Over 40 aid agencies—including the UNHCR itself—were implicated, and 67 individuals—mostly local staff—named by the children. Some under-age girls said United Nations peacekeepers in the West African region were involved.

Under the emotive headline, *"Agencies Hid Scandal of Aid Workers Who Bought Child Sex with Food,"* The Guardian reported the story this way:

> The widespread sexual abuse of young girls in refugee camps in West Africa in exchange for food and aid was well known but consistently

covered up by senior aid workers, it was claimed yesterday. The allegations were made in the wake of the leaking of a report for UNHCR and Save the Children UK which revealed that aid workers have been involved in extensive sexual exploitation of refugee children, offering food rations in return for sexual favours. More than 40 agencies have been named in the report, including many well-known charities. The report was originally 80 pages long but 16 pages were released to the public. One aid worker, who did not want to be named, said the full report contained even more damaging allegations, including the names of all the charities involved.[22]

Others were quick to condemn. Jonathan Potter, head of People in Aid, put out a statement saying, "The UNHCR/Save the Children report on sexual exploitation of refugees in West Africa made me recoil. I have not seen the full report and cannot vouch for the truth of the revelations, but the allegations outraged me on behalf of those with whom we are all trying to work."[23] A report by the Humanitarian Accountability Project noted a shift in attention away from service provision toward greater protection, "even though the connections between [this] issue and broader related accountability problems was in many respects overshadowed by the search for a rapid response specifically to the sexual and gender-based violence."[24] Other issues, it said, were side-lined by this "grander accountability scandal."

The report reminded humanitarian agencies everywhere that the protection of refugees and displaced persons is as important as the provision of services. This means that agency staff need skills, guidelines, and adequate supervision. It may also have reminded them of the fact that their work is open to public scrutiny, and that the media can play a huge part in shaping how they are perceived and behave. The report led to significant changes in programming throughout the humanitarian community. A Joint United Nations Code of Conduct was developed as part of an interagency action plan, and this was passed on through the delivery system to the UN's NGO implementing agencies. WFP, for example, began attaching the code of conduct to all letters of understanding with implementing agencies. WFP also initiated training and sensitization sessions for its own staff, and a zero-tolerance policy on sexual abuse by humanitarian workers.[25]

UNHCR came in for particular criticism over the issue, because at the time the agency was said to have had only two protection officers in all of Sierra Leone. In fact the number may have been higher, but there is little dispute about the inadequacy of the agency's protection effort. Although UNHCR did not dismiss the severity of the problem or the need for remedial action, the organization might be excused for having too few protection officers, given its inability to attract an adequate budget for the caseload it was dealing with—and the more general inability of UN agencies to attract adequate funding for anything in Sierra Leone. Reductions in spending on activities that do not provide immediate relief might be forgiven as understandable, even if they increase the risk of other problems. The choice can be likened to reductions in preventive factory maintenance in favor of additional production. With each day that passes, the risk of breakdown increases, but some managers are judged only on meeting production targets. Under this kind of pressure, a manager might understandably calculate that machinery—which he knows needs maintenance—might not, in fact, break down. In this case, however, it did.

Or did it? There is a bigger issue associated with this story—it was in significant ways untrue. Humanitarian agencies were given copies of the SCF/UNHCR report with a brief annex outlining the findings regarding their specific organization. Two prominent international NGOs reported that the particular charges against them included the names of people who were not on their payrolls and referred to events that had taken place in towns where they had no program.

The report was anecdotal, making serious charges that could not, in many cases, be substantiated or corrected in any meaningful way. In some respects, it was more condemning of West African social mores than anything else: of girls "forced into early marriages in order to relieve families of the financial burden of supporting them." And in some cases, the authors seemed to be on a fishing expedition: "There are reports that some boys also experience sexual violence, although the response to this notion was always met with disbelief and arguments that such things do not happen in their communities." Always met with disbelief, but reported anyway.

It is undoubtedly true that some humanitarian workers were receiving sexual favors from refugees and IDPs. No matter how repugnant, the provision of favors by men in positions of power in return for sex is hardly surprising. In a region where boys often marry at fifteen and girls at thirteen, it also came as something of a surprise to many West Africans that "child abuse" referred to in the report covered anyone under the age of eighteen. Interviews with almost a dozen humanitarian organizations produced angry comments about the inaccuracy of the report, its lack of cultural awareness, and the subsequent need to include new, politically correct paragraphs in project proposals that promise to deal with a problem that is largely unseen, difficult to deter, and for which very little additional funding was available.

In the end, the UN's Office of Internal Oversight Services (OIOS) was called in by UNHCR to review the allegations. An investigation team, drawn from eight countries, included professional investigators, lawyers, refugee protection and human rights specialists, translators, and a pediatric trauma specialist. The investigation began in February

2002 and ended in July. It was unable to substantiate any of the specific cases in the original report, but it did hear of other cases and investigated them. It found two cases in which disciplinary action could be taken, but neither involved a UN or NGO staff person. The report concluded that the original report "of widespread sexual exploitation of refugees has not been confirmed, in the cases which OIOS was able to substantiate, by sufficient evidence for either criminal or disciplinary proceedings. However, the conditions in the camps and in refugee communities . . . make refugees vulnerable to sexual and other forms of exploitation and such vulnerability increases if one is a female and young."[26] This is not news. It is one of the reasons UNHCR, NGOs, and others have protection programs—or rather, it is why they request funding from donors for protection programs. The cost of the OIOS report is not known, and the scandal came and went without attention to the problem of aid agency funding and staffing.

There were other complaints about UNHCR. Many NGOs—indigenous and international—acted, as in other countries, as the agency's "implementing partners." NGO complaints included the perennially deficient allowance by UNHCR for overhead costs, but the most serious problems revolved around the reliability of a UNHCR commitment. NGO after NGO complained, especially in the latter part of 2002, that signed agreements with UNHCR were not worth the paper they were written on. NGOs try to develop longer-term relationships with their beneficiaries; they often take up the challenge of recovery and reconstruction when immediate funding for refugees ends, and because their budgets for such activities are stretched, they count on whatever agreements they have with UNHCR to cover the basic costs. But more critically, it is the NGOs that work in camps directly with refugee men, women, and children to provide the shelter, food, health care, and other necessities that UNHCR cash pays for. When UNHCR reneges on a commitment, it is the NGOs—in the camps or at the termination of a convoy, and at the end of the money chain—that are left holding the bag for what has gone wrong. Having run out of money at the end of 2002, UNHCR was, in the eyes of implementing NGOs in Sierra Leone, incompetent, contractually untrustworthy, and completely opaque in its financial management.

The real scandal in Sierra Leone was the general underfunding of all humanitarian efforts. While the NGO complaints may have a degree of validity, the problems primarily reflect a labyrinth of planning issues unseen by those on the front lines. In January 2000 at donor insistence, UNHCR introduced what it called a unified budget structure aimed at providing greater transparency and predictability in its work. The unified budget brings together all planned activities into a single annual program budget for approval by the agency's executive committee, which is made up of fifty-six governments and thirty-four observer countries and organizations. Supplementary budgets may be authorized by the UN High Commissioner during the course of a year and submitted separately to donors for funding. During 2000, for example, supplementary appeals were created for Sierra Leone, East Timor, Chechnya, Angola, and Eritrean returnees and IDPs.

The two major problems with the new planning and budgeting arrangement, as with its predecessors, are the inadequacy of funding, and the slow pace at which financial commitments are realized. UNHCR started 2000 with a planned budget of $931 million.[27] The New York donor pledging conference in November 1999 raised $168 million, and there was a carryover from the previous year of $144 million. UNHCR thus began 2000 with $312 million, about one-third of what it hoped to raise. The rest, to the extent that it would be forthcoming, could be expected during the course of the year in the form of voluntary contributions made in response to whatever supplications UNHCR might make to donors. "We have to be experts in all of the various governments' budgeting and financial arrangements," a UNHCR official lamented. "Some of what arrives is predictable, but a lot is not. Some of the money comes from Ministries of Foreign Affairs; these are often poor ministries with small budgets and a limited capacity for lobbying their parliaments. In any case, most donors fund us out of a strategic interest, not out of interest for the organization. There is no invisible hand that knits all this together into a rational whole."

By the end of 2000, the agency had actually received almost 92 percent of the requested budget, but there were two problems. First, only 20 percent of what had been received was not earmarked, which meant that higher-profile emergencies were better funded than others. Sierra Leone received only two-thirds of the $10.3 million UNHCR budgeted for the country in 2000, while income for the Federal Republic of Yugoslavia, heavily earmarked for Kosovo, came within 13 percent of the planned $107 million budget. The second problem has to do with timing—when money actually arrives. Pledges are often slow to materialize. By May 1, 2000, for example, only 26 percent of UNHCR's global budget for that year had been funded, and the agency was still awaiting payment of pledges made in previous years. The result was a critical cash-flow situation, with obvious consequences for those at the far end of the financial chain: less money, reduced services, and broken promises.

By 2002, when the NGO complaints about UNHCR in Sierra Leone were at their peak, the situation had worsened. UNHCR, like other UN agencies, was expected to include its budget for the coming year in the consolidated appeal that is created for each emergency. The 2003 CAP for Sierra Leone was completed in October 2002 and was supposed to be a comprehensive and coordinated description of the country's humanitarian needs for the coming year. The CAP has been much criticized in the past by donors as little more than a shopping list of uncoordinated and unprioritized proposals; ostensibly it had been significantly improved.

Where UNHCR is concerned, however, a complication arises. As in other UN agencies, UNHCR headquarters must develop a global plan that reflects the sum of the parts, plus regional components and costs, which are not country-specific. Country offices are expected to submit the details of their anticipated needs for the coming year in March of the preceding year. The various submissions are reviewed and trimmed according to what headquarters thinks the traffic will bear, knowing the size of a global budget that is likely to meet with donor support. The revised budget is given back to the country offices, and this is what goes into the CAP in October.

Between March and October, however, a lot can change, and in Sierra Leone in 2002, it did. The 4,000 Liberian refugees that UNHCR budgeted for in March had become 50,000 by October, and they were still flowing in. Headquarters had approved a special supplementary regional appeal for Liberian refugees in the interim between March and October but was reluctant to increase the amount again. Why? Perhaps because it might seem like too many return trips to the donor trough, or because special appeals tend to reduce general support for the agency's global budget, or even because the existing appeals for Liberian refugees were, at the end of August, still 54 percent unmet.[28] There was little point in asking for a second supplemental if the first one was only half funded. Without money to run programs, corners are cut. Protection efforts are reduced. Refugees are not repatriated, or they may be moved in military vehicles, without adequate provision for their reception and resettlement at the end of the journey. Funding for camps is cut back or terminated. And the NGOs responsible for implementing UNHCR programs will obviously complain.

The NGOs, in turn, were the subject of growing complaints from the government of Sierra Leone. In 1996 about thirty international NGOs were present in Sierra Leone; by 2002, the number had grown to ninety. The mutual antipathy between NGOs and government was increasingly characterized by open hostility. From a government perspective, international NGOs were perceived as resisting coordination; they were opaque, and they consumed huge resources in their use of expatriate staff—with the vehicles, allowances, and perks that these imply—that might otherwise have been available for direct assistance. "When they get into trouble," a senior government official said, "they come running to us. Otherwise they simply ignore us." From the NGO side, many saw a government with limited capacity, beset by problems of personnel, funding, and corruption. Members of the International NGO Forum, an informal grouping of international NGOs, found it hard to believe that there actually were ninety NGOs roaming around the countryside and suggested that the number was probably more like fifty—hardly the "swarming" that afflicted Bosnia, Kosovo, and Afghanistan.

This issue of swarming is worth examining in more detail. It was, in fact, not difficult to identify fifty-three NGOs in 2002, as these were listed in an Office for the Coordination of Human Affairs (OCHA) directory. Twenty of these were large, brand-name NGOs: Oxfam, the Adventists, Action Contre la Faim, Save the Children, World Vision, CARE, Catholic Relief Services, Lutheran World Relief, the Norwegian Refugee Council, and three permutations of MSF: Belgium, Holland, and France. Others, less well recognized in Sierra Leone, were nevertheless known commodities in the international NGO world: Goal and Concern International from Ireland, Forut from Norway, and the Marie Stopes Society from Britain, which works on reproductive health issues. Still others, like "Caritas Makeni" and "Caritas Kenema" bore known hallmarks, and a few, like Human Rights Watch and the International Crisis Group, while not NGOs in the traditional sense of delivering services, had a known provenance and track record.

About fifteen of the fifty-three were less well known. Mercy Ships International is an NGO with three ships that travel the world providing emergency and restorative health care. Its primary efforts since its founding in 1978 have been in the Caribbean and Central America. Its cash income is roughly $10 million and in-kind services provided by its medical personnel more than double this figure. Handicap International is an organization based in France but with offices in other countries, working for the past twenty years in support of the victims of landmines. Cooperazione Internazionale is a thirty-five-year-old Italian relief and development NGO with an annual cash income of about $10 million. In fact most of these NGOs could be readily identified simply by asking them for their annual report or by going to the Internet for information. Many were not large, but if they spent half a million dollars in Sierra Leone on good works, this would be no bad thing.

What about the other thirty-seven that made up the total of ninety? Many were probably "mom and pop" NGOs, started by people with a genuine concern about a particular issue. Some were small organizations initiated during the war by Sierra Leoneans overseas. Nepean Outreach to the World (NOW) has a grand name and a catchy acronym for a very small organization based in a suburb of the Canadian capital, Ottawa. Established by a retired city engineer in 1990, the agency arranged to twin Nepean and Sierra Leone's second city, Bo. Over the years and throughout the war, it raised money for rehabilitation of the hospital, market, and water system in Bo. It is not a large organization; it has no staff as such, and it certainly has no offices or white Pajeros driving around Freetown. It may not contribute a great deal in the grand scheme of things, but it does no major harm. It is not a relief organization and it is not raising its flag over refugee camps. It may not be on the radar of the government or the larger international NGOs, but for the people it has helped, it is important.

Many such small NGOs, and some of the larger ones as well, resisted government attempts to manage, control, and coordinate as strenuously as they denied such resistance. Many were on a mission, and any time spent dealing with governmental red tape was perceived as wasteful to them as their nonexistent offices and vehicles were to the government. One of the NGO thorns in the government's side developed over the issue of taxes. The government of Sierra Leone was cash strapped. After foreign aid, most of its revenue derived from import duties. So the parade of duty-free NGO lift vans and white vehicles streaming off ships in the port had, by 2001, become more than a little irksome—it had become the focus of an idea: NGOs should pay taxes! To government officials with little experience of such things, the idea may have been perfectly reasonable, and the negative reaction from NGOs might have been correspondingly understandable had it not turned into a diplomatic row. The issue became a policy matter that went to cabinet twice and was softened only when the U.S. ambassador weighed in. In the end the action protected the NGOs from a dunning, but it left government officials full of resentment.

The issue may have had something to do with the nature of the assistance provided. MSF Belgium, for example, had few complaints about government and said that it had good working relationships with the Ministry of Health. Much of its work was technical and hospital-based. In other words, its efforts were much more structured, consistent, and predictable than other forms of humanitarian assistance, and this may have led to better relations with a particular ministry. Not all NGOs gracefully accepted the fact that there was a transition period between an emergency and the wind-down into recovery. For its part, the government became more able and eager to do more, to assert itself, and to demand greater levels of authority and oversight. There almost inevitably were going to be problems on both sides of this equation. For many NGOs, the revised expectations of the government would mean a change, if not a reduction, in programming. Reductions would be difficult because they would mean staff layoffs and a decrease in some of the benefits that accrue from scale: support staff, vehicles and equipment, recognition, and status. More difficult to accept for an

NGO, however, might be ceding program and funding opportunities to a government department which it believes cannot do the job well.

꞊

For many years there has been a debate about linking relief and development: not whether to link the two programmatically but how to do it well, and how to get the money to do it at all. Emergencies do not simply end at an appointed hour; the problems of refugees and IDPs do not end when they get off a truck in the burned-out village that once served as home. Many NGOs understand the need to link emergency assistance to longer-term development but find themselves badly constrained by donor policies, or more particularly, by the teller behind the donor wicket they deal with. WFP is a perennial example in many countries, and familiar stories were told in Sierra Leone by international and national NGOs about the severe constraints accompanying WFP financing. "We are trying to build long-term relationships, and we make serious commitments to the communities we work with," said the director of a major international agency. "But WFP doesn't care about relationships, and they will often get you started and then shift the money elsewhere. . . . The UN is the most difficult donor to manage." To use WFP food "properly," most NGOs say they are obliged to subsidize the operations themselves, and few have independent income for this. CARE and World Vision balance their WFP food programs with more generously supported USAID food in order to spread the costs. Catholic Relief Services will not work with WFP at all in Sierra Leone because the twenty-five dollar fixed rate per ton simply won't cover the costs generated by the NGO.

The biggest problem for WFP and most other UN agencies in Sierra Leone, by the end of 2002, was that all of them were planning the move to recovery, but their only ready tool with which to finance the shift was the Consolidated Appeal Process. The CAP, however—depending on the eye of the beholder—was intended for emergency assistance. During 2002 there was a major debate among UN agencies in Sierra Leone about what they should include in the CAP. Some had already fudged the definition of recovery work, backing it into the vocabulary of emergencies. By talking more openly about recovery, they feared they would simply lose their donors. The CAP, they said, was read only by the emergency department in each donor agency, and unless OCHA could persuade two completely different departments in, say, CIDA, to read and contribute to the CAP, there could be problems. In fact they might simply lose the emergency departments and find nothing to replace them. The danger was thought to be even more problematic in a donor country where the split between emergency and development assistance is handled by two separate entities. In countries like Norway, where emergency assistance is not part of the development ministry at all, the risk of losing the audience is significant.

"I am very uncomfortable about putting relief and recovery into one appeal document," said the head of one UN agency in Freetown. "Recovery appeals don't work. They send a signal to the emergency departments of donor agencies that they can begin to phase out, and the development departments don't pick up the slack because recovery isn't seen as development." The risk is real and is exemplified by the attitude of the two major donor agencies in Sierra Leone. USAID said that a shift into recovery would simply lose major emergency donors like USAID's Office of Foreign Disaster Assistance (OFDA) and the European Union's ECHO. "Humanitarian agencies are not here to do poverty alleviation," the official said. "Nobody is interested in development in Sierra Leone. Development simply isn't on CNN."

This frank assessment reflects a perception of the economic forces at work within OFDA and ECHO. Britain's DFID representative, however, saw the issue differently, agreeing that the inclusion of recovery in the CAP was definitely "the way to go." The issue of what to include in the CAP had been openly discussed and debated among the UN agencies and resident donors. "The debate is not about needs," he said. "These are real and generally acknowledged. The real problem is the compartmentalization in agencies like USAID and the European Commission, where OFDA and ECHO simply represent limits on thinking about how to respond appropriately to Sierra Leone. It is a donor issue, not a technical issue."

What is the UN Resident Coordinator to do when given opinions by his two largest donors that are polar opposites? As it turned out, only a small proportion of the total 2003 appeal represented recovery assistance, but it was there, and it stood out clearly from the emergency requirements in the funding tables: red for emergency, blue for recovery. By the middle of the following year, less than 10 percent of the recovery projects had been funded. Seventy percent of the emergency food requirements, however, had been met, and 82 percent of the request for refugees had been provided.

As Sierra Leone's emergency was escalating in the mid-1990s, much of the international NGO effort was being channelled through local church organizations and the Sierra Leone Red Cross. However, many Sierra Leonean NGOs were either ignored or sidelined. Some of this had to do with their capacity and experience, but they argued that they would never develop capacity and experience—especially for the longer term—if something was not done to nurture them. One angry Sierra Leonean NGO leader asked rhetorically why it was necessary for international NGOs to come all the way to Sierra Leone to dig pit latrines. He and his colleagues questioned the accountability and legitimacy of the international NGOs, who tossed the same back at them, adding that the RUF, UN agencies, and the government itself all had legitimacy and accountability problems.

The concern about legitimacy may be important, but it is secondary to the main issue, which is that Sierra Leoneans must be able to develop their own organizations and to build their own civil society. If outsiders are unprepared or unable to help, they should at least not get in the way. Capacity for service delivery aside, the Sierra Leonean NGO community demonstrated the meaning and importance of the expression civil society in the weeks before the 1996 elections. Although weak even by African standards, Sierra Leonean NGOs—especially the women's movement—distinguished themselves in taking the lead on the issue of democracy, becoming the only evident public voice demanding elections and a return to civilian rule. Supported behind the scenes in helpful ways by a handful of donors, they braved threats and real danger, defying a nervous and unpredictable military government by openly demanding—and successfully obtaining—its resignation.

The principle of proportionality in humanitarian assistance was demonstrated by its absence in Sierra Leone. The UN appeals for the country were always low compared to those for other emergencies, and yet they rarely garnered more than half of their target. For years, overcrowding, half rations, or nothing at all was the lot of hundreds of thousands of Sierra Leoneans. And when the time for spending on recovery arrived, internal dissension erupted among front-line agencies because they knew the donors would not fund such activities. It was better to keep up the pretense of emergency as long as possible, because they feared that most donors were about to forget Sierra Leone again. Sierra Leone also demonstrated, as do many other emergencies, that the world's donor community is always prepared to spend more on remedial action that preventive measures. UNAMSIL, once it had reached full troop strength, consumed more resources in thirty-three days than Sierra Leone had received in foreign aid from all sources in the twelve months of 1990. It cost more to operate UNAMSIL for six days than all the money provided by donors to the UN for humanitarian relief in 1998. In 2002 the United Nations could obtain funding for 17,500 soldiers, hundreds of vehicles, and dozens of helicopters—but not a single donor anywhere in the world would support UNICEF's project on emergency water supply and sanitation or the World Health Organization's projects on malaria and HIV/AIDS.

The humanitarian response in Sierra Leone was fraught at various times with all the problems that plague most emergencies: poor coordination, competition for scarce resources, and acrimonious debates over the primacy of political, military, or humanitarian objectives. Often missing from the long catalog of problems, misperceptions, false starts, and mistakes is the tremendous dedication that most humanitarian agencies and workers applied to their work in Sierra Leone. The war was a terrible roller coaster of ups and downs, each down taking the country lower than the one before. It was dangerous and protracted: The conflict lasted twice as long as the Second World War. It killed at least 50,000 people. Given the nature of the war and the fact that more than a million people were on the run for years, the true figure is probably much higher, but nobody has calculated it. One way of computing some numbers is to think about the 4,000 known amputees, almost all civilians, many of them children and babies. These people had their hands and feet chopped off with matchetes and rusty axes, on the ground or against the stump of a tree. Almost none had any medical attention for days, if ever. For every survivor, five or even ten must have died. A calculator is not required to arrive at a figure of 20,000 to 40,000 deaths from these atrocities alone.

And yet Sierra Leone never really caught the attention of the international media. There was a brief CNN moment when the UN peacekeepers were kidnapped, but there were no protracted images of Sierra Leone on the television screens of Europe and North America. The so-called sex scandal received more media attention than the widespread hunger. Somalia, Rwanda, Bosnia, Kosovo, and East Timor all came and went, but Sierra Leone never really arrived as a media event. As a result, NGOs had great difficulty raising funds. Because the country had no strategic importance—historically, politically, or economically—to the world's donor nations, its decline received little attention from them. Britain and others resisted pressure to declare a country in a state of free-fall a complex emergency. Glib calls for African solutions and a peace agreement more disgraceful than Munich were the best the world could offer until, distracted by other events, the Security Council agreed to a muddled UN peacekeeping commitment. It was only when the RUF—a gang of bandits and drug-addled murderers—actually challenged the fundamentals of the United Nations itself, that one permanent Security Council member, Britain, had the fortitude to do the right thing.

In all of this, timing was everything. A year earlier there was no question of a unilateral intervention by Britain, and it is arguable that a year later it would not have happened, even if the circumstances had been the same. Sierra Leone's constant sorrows were often a matter of bad timing, but there was one instance when the timing was right. UNAMSIL might not have been created at all had peacekeeping forces not been sanctioned at the same time for Kosovo and East Timor. For once, piggy-backing onto more high-profile emergencies, Sierra Leone did not lose out to the competition. Shame and embarrassment among the donor nations may also have played a small role. A young Sierra Leonean in a badly over-crowded refugee camp in Guinea looks at the television camera. The camp is in disarray after an RUF cross-border attack. Many refugees have been killed and, behind him, people are in tears. He is holding a short-wave radio. "We hear all about Kosovo," he says angrily and in perfect English. "We hear about how you people are helping Kosovo. But what about us? What about us?"

3

East Timor—The Perfect Emergency

We were correct to think that we had no control over our destinies: to consider that resistance was futile and bravery superfluous. From the start, our fate was determined not by ourselves, not locally or by the invader even, but abroad in Canberra and Washington.
— Timothy Mo, *The Redundancy of Courage*[1]

East Timor seems to represent a tremendous humanitarian success. When a 1999 referendum resulted in an overwhelming vote for the territory's independence from Indonesia, pro-Indonesian militia began a systematic campaign of killing and destruction. In less than two weeks, however, a UN-authorized military force had landed, quelling the violence. This was followed by a UN trusteeship arrangement to mentor and train a new government for its subsequent independence in 2002. Donors were generous: East Timor received more humanitarian assistance per capita than any other major emergency up to that time, belying the charge that Bosnia and Kosovo had been well funded simply because the victims were white Europeans.

But East Timor also exemplifies many of the worst failings of donor agencies and their governments. Between 1975 and 1999, an estimated two hundred thousand Timorese died in a guerilla war, following a brutal Indonesian occupation of the former Portuguese colony. Few governments opposed the occupation, and for years little humanitarian assistance reached the island. Indonesia was too important—as a trading partner, as a pro-West buffer in the Cold War, as a member of the regional Association of East Asian Nations (ASEAN) group, and as a producer of oil—for humanitarian concerns to prevail. It was only when Indonesia stumbled, following the 1997 Asian economic meltdown and the departure of its longtime strongman President Suharto, that the international consensus began to change.

The roots of East Timor's 1999 humanitarian emergency reach deep into the fertile soil of European colonialism and Cold War politics. The country's tragedy, a quarter century of humanitarian neglect, and the eventual response were directly connected to three imperial adventures: European colonialism, Japanese expansion during World War II, and American intervention in Indochina. Portugal's first contact with the island of Timor took place in 1511. The colony gradually became a source of sandalwood, wax, and slaves who were exported to more prosperous Dutch territories in the region. Never remotely as important as Portugal's African colonies, by the mid-twentieth century Timor was a remnant of an Asian empire that had once comprised dozens of factories, forts, and trading concessions stretching from Arabia to China and Japan. Preemptively invaded by Australia and the Netherlands in 1940, East Timor was subsequently overrun and occupied by Japan between 1942 and 1945. An estimated forty thousand Timorese were killed during the occupation, and many more were used as forced labor. After the war, Portugal was able to reestablish itself on the island. The United States, while eager for British and French decolonization, had little to say about Portugal after the conclusion of a 1948 agreement in which Portugal provided the United States with an air force base on the Atlantic island of Terceira in the Azores.

With the military takeover of Goa, Daman, and Diu by the government of India in 1961, all that remained of Portugal's Asian empire in 1974 was the tiny Chinese enclave of Macau, and East Timor, with a landmass slightly larger than Israel. That year, the right-wing Caetano-Salazar government in Portugal was overthrown, and decolonization suddenly became a high priority. In Portuguese Timor there had been anticolonial rebellions and uprisings over the years, but nothing to rival the bloody liberation wars that characterized the final decade of colonial rule in Guinea Bissau, Mozambique, and Angola.

Nevertheless, in 1974 Portuguese Timor suddenly faced the prospect of independence—with an underdeveloped political class and few economic prospects. Dependent on poverty-stricken Portugal for subventions, Timor's education system, health facilities, and infrastructure were all badly stunted. The western half of the island was a province of Indonesia, a country with 132 million people, a powerful economy, and an unsavory political legacy. Its president, Mohamed Suharto, had taken power in 1966 after violent political upheavals. Military suppression of the Indonesian communist party had culminated in a bloodbath that took an estimated five hundred thousand lives.

The 1960s were Indonesia's years of living dangerously, and communism was still very much on Suharto's mind as he looked north to the collapse of pro-West regimes in Indochina in 1974 and 1975. He also watched and then promoted political confusion in East Timor. In May 1974, anticipating independence, two political parties had formed in the colony, the União Democrática Timorense (UDT) and the Associação Social Democrática Timor, which later changed its name to Frente Revolucionária de Timor Leste Independente (Fretilin: Revolutionary Front for an Independent East Timor). Although the two parties formed a coalition in January 1975, it did not last. The UDT moved closer to Indonesia and Fretilin moved to the left.

Today, fear of communism sometimes seems like a quaint historical artifact, but its influence during the last fifteen years of the Cold War cannot be underestimated. Late in 1974 Indonesia began broadcasting anticommunist radio messages into East Timor from its West Timor capital, Kupang. And it started to infiltrate the UDT. Soon thereafter, the UDT began to hold anticommunist demonstrations. Fretilin, often described today as a social democratic organization, certainly had more than an element of Marxist-Leninist ideology at its core. The independence leader Xanana Gusmão later wrote about it: "We were still dazzled by a vision of a miraculous process of human redemption" through Marxism, he said in a 1987 essay "Ideological Turnaround."[2]

Such bedazzlement in the context of 1974 and 1975 was exceedingly dangerous, and the perils extended far beyond whatever concerns President Suharto may have had. The United States was combating communist, or communist-appearing, enemies everywhere—with little success. In September 1973 it had helped to dispatch Salvador Allende in Chile, but elsewhere in Latin America the United States seemed to be fighting a rearguard action. In Africa, Dahomey converted itself into a Marxist "People's Republic of Benin" in 1974. Also that year, Somalia signed a treaty of friendship with the Soviet Union, and in Ethiopia a horrific Red Terror led to the deposition of Haile Selassie and the installation of yet another Marxist regime. Portugal's African colonies were falling to Marxism one after another: Guinea Bissau in September 1974, Mozambique in June 1975, and Angola in November 1975. The situation in Indochina was even more bleak for U.S. interests. On April 12, 1975, the Khmer Rouge took power in Cambodia. On April 30 the government of South Vietnam collapsed, and the following month the communist Pathet Lao took over in Laos. And the economic outlook was bad as well. High inflation in the West, partly the result of a 1973 OPEC oil embargo, had seen the price of gasoline in the United States rise from thirty cents to more than a dollar a gallon.

It was in this highly-charged context that Mohamed Suharto, the staunch anticommunist leader of an oil-rich nation—one that had *not* joined the OPEC oil embargo—visited the United States in July 1975. Within minutes of arriving at Camp David, in a meeting with President Gerald Ford and Secretary of State Henry Kissinger, he raised the specter of communism. He asked for military equipment from the United States and outlined his views of how events might unfold in communist Vietnam. He then raised the issue of Portuguese decolonization, saying first that Indonesia supported a process of self-determination in East Timor. There were three possibilities for the future of the colony, he said: independence, staying with Portugal, or joining Indonesia.

"With such a small territory and no resources," he said, "an independent country would hardly be viable. With Portugal it would be a big burden, with Portugal so far away. If they want to integrate into Indonesia as an *independent* nation, this is not possible because Indonesia is one unitary state. So the only way is to integrate into Indonesia." He then described the situation as he saw it in East Timor: "Those who want independence are those who are Communist-influenced."[3] On that ominous note, the conversation ended. It resumed five months later, on December 6, when President Ford and Henry Kissinger visited Jakarta at the end of a swing through Asia.

By then, the political situation in East Timor had come unstuck. In August, the UDT had mounted a coup, and for several days there was fighting in the streets of Dili between UDT and Fretilin supporters. Between 1,500 and 3,000 people were killed, until Fretilin gained the upper hand. The Portuguese governor and his little garrison decamped to an offshore island, and over the following months, battles between the factions continued. Then, on November 28, Fretilin declared the independence of the "Democratic Republic of East Timor." Eight days later, Gerald Ford and Henry Kissinger sat down in Jakarta with President Suharto, his foreign minister, the U.S. Ambassador, and an interpreter.

Towards the end of a *tour d'horizon* in which communist insurgencies in Thailand and Malaysia were discussed, Suharto said, "I would like to speak to you, Mr. President, about another problem, Timor." He said that Indonesia had no territorial ambitions, but was concerned about the unilateral declaration of independence by Fretilin, increased instability in the area, and Portugal's inability to control the situation. Suharto said it was now essential to think about what might be done "to establish peace and order for the present and the future, in the interest of the security of the area and Indonesia. . . . We want your understanding if we deem it necessary to take rapid or drastic action."

President Ford looked at Suharto and said, "We will understand and will not press you on the issue." Although the word invasion does not appear in the transcript of the conversation, it was clearly understood. Kissinger was worried about two things. "You appreciate," he told Suharto, "that the use of U.S.-made arms could create problems." The extent of the problems would depend, he continued, on "how we construe it: whether it is in self defense or is a foreign operation." The second issue had to do with the possible reaction in the United States to an Indonesian invasion. That was a Saturday. Ford would be back in Washington by Monday afternoon, which would distance him from any action and allow for damage control. "We understand your need to move quickly," Kissinger said, "but I am only saying that it would be better if it were done after we returned."[4]

But Suharto could not wait. The next day he unleashed a naval, air, and land invasion, declaring East Timor the twenty-seventh province of the Republic of Indonesia seven months later. Kissinger had asked Suharto if he thought there might be a long guerilla war. "There will probably be a small guerilla war," Suharto replied. By the time it was over, the small guerilla war would take the lives of between one-quarter and one-third of the territory's population—as many as 200,000 people in all.

Like the United States, Australia played a hard game of realpolitik where East Timor was concerned. As leader of the Australian opposition, Gough Whitlam had met President Suharto eight times before becoming Prime Minister in 1972, and they held three subsequent meetings before the Timorese situation exploded. The effort to transform Australia from a British outpost in an alien sea into an Asian good neighbor was then in full swing, and by the middle of 1975, Canberra believed that it was dealing with a "settled Indonesian policy to incorporate Timor."[5] Documents released in 2000 show that Whitlam, unwilling to tackle its most strategically important neighbor on a matter of principle, had told Suharto, "I am in favour of incorporation, but obeisance has to be made to self-determination."[6] Britain took a similar attitude. In Jakarta, the British Ambassador wrote to the Foreign Office, saying, "It is in Britain's interest that Indonesia should absorb the territory as soon as, and as unobtrusively as possible; and that if it comes to the crunch and there is a row in the United Nations, we should keep our heads down and avoid siding against the Indonesian government."[7] For the next twenty-five years, ASEAN nations and the West curried favor, oil, and economic benefit from Indonesia, while a humanitarian disaster unfolded in East Timor.

∿

The guerilla war that developed was accompanied by another issue, kept alive by the international media, civil society organizations, the Catholic Church, and a network of Timorese exiles. These stories of repression, battles, and massacres, however, were met in Washington, Tokyo, and London with little more than platitudes. Speaking at an ASEAN meeting, Canada's foreign minister stated the position clearly enough: Canada would "vigorously pursue a series of [trade] initiatives in a number of countries irrespective of their human rights records."[8] At about C$35 million a year, Indonesia was one of Canada's largest aid recipients in the 1990s, but that figure was dwarfed by two-way trade of C$1.6 billion (U.S.$1.16 billion) in 1997 and Canadian arms sales to Indonesia of C$420 million between 1993 and 1997. By the mid-1990s, Japan was Indonesia's largest investor. Twenty-five percent of Japanese exports went to Indonesia and 37 percent of Indonesian exports— mainly gas and oil—went to Japan. Britain, Indonesia's second largest investor, sold forty-eight Hawk ground attack jets to Indonesia—some used in due course against the Timorese—between 1978 and 1996. Australia, the only country to officially recognize Indonesian sovereignty over East Timor, finally won an agreement with Jakarta on oil and gas exploration in the Timor Sea in 1989, and to seal the friendship, the two countries also signed a security agreement.

Meanwhile, the guerilla war continued, flaring from time to time into open combat and fierce retaliation. The economy and the school system were Indonesianized, with some 150,000 Indonesian settlers arriving in the territory, supported by an occupying army of 20,000 to 30,000 Indonesian troops. Paramilitary forces, another feature of Indonesian control, seized, jailed, tortured, and killed dissidents and protesters at will. Tens of thousands of people were displaced, many of them held in prison camp conditions. In 1991 Indonesian troops opened fire on a crowd of mourners attending a memorial mass for a student who had been killed by Indonesian troops two weeks earlier. Some two hundred people were slain in what became known as the Santa Cruz Massacre. Writing in 1994, American activist Noam Chomsky said, "In the annals of crime in this terrible century, Indonesia's assault against East Timor ranks high, not only because of its scale—perhaps the greatest death toll relative to the population since the holocaust—but because it would have been so easy to prevent, and to bring to an end at any time."[9] On the contrary, however, Japan, Europe, and North America flooded Indonesia with military and economic aid, encouraging foreign investment, buying oil, and lauding the stability of the Suharto government.

Throughout this period, virtually no humanitarian assistance made its way to East Timor. The ICRC maintained a small unofficial and largely nonvocal office in Dili, and during the 1990s a handful of international NGOs and church organizations initiated development projects that were connected with larger Indonesia-wide programs. Bilateral donors also started projects that were part of national programs. Although the silence on Indonesian atrocities and misrule was broken more frequently during the 1990s than had been the case over the previous fifteen years, little was done to treat the underlying problem.

It is often said that without the "CNN effect," humanitarian emergencies are unlikely to achieve the prominence needed to generate meaningful international action. Where East Timor is concerned, the opposite seemed to prevail for the better part of the Indonesian occupation. Despite moments of intense media pressure, Western governments refused to respond. Before the Indonesian invasion, in October 1975, five journalists representing Australian television were killed in Timor, raising the profile of the violence and the invasion that ensued. Nothing, however, happened. Through most of the 1970s and 1980s, Australian media coverage of East Timor was steady, but it related more to partisan political debates in Australia about government policies toward Indonesia and oil in the Timor Sea than to atrocities in East Timor. In Canada, the *Globe and Mail* carried thirty-seven stories on East Timor between 1977 and 1990, fewer than three each year, while Cambodia was the subject of 570.[10] The *Los Angeles Times* ran sixteen articles on East Timor in 1975, but through the rest of the 1970s and 1980s, virtually none. Most of the stories on East Timor that did appear were written from Jakarta. Based on second-hand information, many actually praised Indonesian policies. Meanwhile, the territory remained closed to the media, diplomats, and most aid workers.

Finally, confident that it had dissent under control, Indonesia normalized the status of the province in 1989 and permitted a visit by Pope John Paul II. An open-air mass, however, soon turned into a proindependence demonstration that was quelled—with the usual violence—by the military. A visit to Indonesia by the U.S. ambassador four months later also became an occasion for student demonstrations and confrontation with the military. The Santa Cruz Massacre, however, was different, not only because of the number killed, but because at last there were foreign journalists and television cameras at the scene. Here was a "film at eleven" atrocity that could not easily be ignored. Canada, Denmark, and the Netherlands suspended their aid programs to Indonesia, and the U.S. Congress cut back on military aid. As a new member of the European

Union, Portugal—which had never renounced its authority over East Timor—was now able to garner new support in Europe for Timorese independence. Although it was soon business as usual for most of Indonesia's friends, the Timorese cat was out of the media bag. Timorese protesters now greeted President Suharto and government officials whenever they travelled abroad, and the plight of the territory was further heightened when two prominent Timorese advocates, José Ramos-Horta and Archbishop Carlos Belo, were awarded the 1996 Nobel Peace Prize.

It is unclear what might have happened in East Timor had the Asian economic crisis of 1997 not occurred. Certainly it set in motion a chain of events that finally led to what became the territory's greatest crisis—and greatest opportunity. Far away from East Timor, in July 1997, the government of Thailand devalued its currency as part of an effort to stave off an economic collapse. The crisis, brought on by a weakening economy, a burst property bubble, bad lending practices, and the collapse of dozens of financial institutions, spread like an epidemic across the region. By January 1998, the Indonesian economy was also in a state of collapse. With the rupiah in free-fall and inflation spiking, the government removed subsidies on everything and looked for any belt-tightening opportunity it could find. Food shortages and price increases soon led to rioting, and by May 1998, with the skies of Jakarta and other Indonesian cities black with the smoke of looters' fires, President Suharto was gone. Within three weeks, his successor B.J. Habibie, eager to demonstrate Indonesia's newfound democratic instincts, announced that he was willing to give East Timor a wide range of autonomy. This would, of course, occur within the context of a united Indonesia. Or so he thought.

Many organizations and individuals had worked to keep the issue of East Timor alive over the years, although some were more effective than others. The UN Security Council adopted its first resolution calling on Indonesia to withdraw its forces from East Timor within days of the December 1975 invasion. Given the winks and nudges provided by the United States, however, this meant very little. For six years after that, the General Assembly passed similar resolutions, affirming the right of the East Timorese to self-determination. But even this pro forma effort eventually guttered out, until the Santa Cruz Massacre drew public attention once again to Indonesian atrocities.

In the 1990s the European union began to take an interest, and in 1996 it unveiled a Common Position on East Timor, the first collective policy position members had taken on the issue. The policy, basically a reaffirmation of the UN position, aimed to achieve a "fair, comprehensive and internationally acceptable solution to the question of East Timor" and to improve the human rights and development situation in the territory. Despite prodding by Portugal, NGOs, and the media, however, the Common Policy was hampered by massive EU investment in Indonesia and by the eagerness with which Indonesia purchased European arms. The EU was second only to Japan in its foreign direct investments in Indonesia, with Britain, the Netherlands, and Germany leading the way.

Britain was also Jakarta's leading arms supplier, with France not far behind. Despite the ethical foreign policy of the Labour government, Britain issued fifty-six new licenses for military shipments to Indonesia within a year of Labour's 1997 election. At the height of the 1999 mayhem, Hawk jet aircraft—part of an order worth £160 million—were still being delivered. Even simple efforts to deliver EU development assistance to East Timor fumbled. An aid package worth $6.4 million was announced for East Timor in 1996, but over the following three years, not a penny actually reached the island. As one caustic review of EU achievements announced: "At the end of the day the collective might of the European Union as a foreign policy actor, committed on paper to promoting human rights and defending international law in East Timor, translated into nothing more substantial than a non-deliverable aid package. The mountain had laboured mightily and brought forth a mouse."[11]

By the late 1990s, there was a large network of civil society organizations monitoring the situation in East Timor, working with the media and lobbying their respective governments. The International Federation for East Timor, for example, had twenty-seven member organizations from Australia to Scotland. Among them were the Free East Timor–Japan Coalition, the East Timor Information Network (Malaysia), the International Platform of Jurists for East Timor (Netherlands), and the Norwegian Cooperation Council for East Timor and Indonesia. Much of the information used by international campaigners came for many years from a radio station operated illegally out of Darwin by Australian activists, and from campaigners in Melbourne and Sydney. Many of the organizations were like the East Timor Action Network (ETAN) in the United States, which was a grassroots response to the Santa Cruz Massacre. Students, veteran activists, and concerned U.S. citizens had been drawn to the East Timor issue, partly because it had been so overlooked, and partly because the United States had consistently supplied Indonesia with weapons. When some of them held a demonstration at the Indonesian Mission to the UN on Human Rights Day in December 1991, they did not intend an ongoing movement. But soon they found other individuals, organizations, and networks and began to pressure their representatives in Congress. ETAN was formed at the end of 1991 with the aim of pressuring the U.S. government to end its complicity in the Indonesian annexation of East Timor, and to press for genuine self-determination for the East Timorese. Eventually ETAN had a membership of thousands of people in every state, with chapters and contacts in many cities.

Individuals occasionally can have an enormous influence on humanitarian action, although usually they are senior politicians, aid officials, and UN luminaries. Nelson Mandela's request, for example, to meet with the jailed Timorese leader Xanana Gusmão, during a presidential visit to Jakarta in 1997, raised Gusmão's international profile and that of the Timorese cause. But ordinary people can also make a difference. In Ireland, a bus driver named Tom Hyland was one of these. One evening in 1991, a group of friends at Hyland's house watched a television program called *First Tuesday*, about a country none of them had heard of, East Timor. They sat mesmerized, watching Indonesian soldiers gunning down unarmed East Timorese in Dili's Santa Cruz Cemetery. Hyland and the others were shocked, and a few weeks later they created something they called the East Timor Ireland Solidarity Campaign (ETISC), operating out of a converted room in Hyland's house in the Dublin suburb of Ballyfermot. The group borrowed typewriters and a computer and began writing to politicians and the media. They gave talks in schools, colleges, clubs, trade unions—to anyone who would listen. Every November 12, on the anniversary of the Santa Cruz massacre, ETISC held demonstrations at the British or Australian embassies to protest of their governments' military and economic support of Indonesia. The campaign's breakthrough moment came in 1993 with a visit to Ireland by Australian Prime Minister Paul Keating. Hundreds of people demonstrated outside Dublin Castle where Keating was meeting Irish leaders. The incident received wide media coverage and was discussed on radio, TV, and in all the newspapers, bringing the plight of East Timor to even wider public attention in Ireland.

It was not all about demonstrations, however. Hyland had a special knack of persuasion and spoke as convincingly with politicians and reporters as he did with ordinary people. By the mid-1990s, Ireland had become one of East Timor's strongest champions in the European Union, and when things started to fall apart in 1999, Irish Foreign Minister David Andrews, accompanied by Tom Hyland, was one of the first high-level foreign politicians to visit the island. By then, Ireland's pro-Timorese credentials had been well established. In a speech in Toronto in 1995, José Ramos-Horta said that in terms of its influence and what it had achieved, no country had done more for East Timor than Ireland.

In 1994, Indonesia finally granted UN human rights organizations access to East Timor, and in February 1997, a month after his appointment as Secretary-General of the United Nations, Kofi Annan named a Personal Representative for East Timor, Jamsheed Marker. This prescient initiative reinserted the United Nations into the picture and provided a framework and an interlocutor for negotiations that would evolve as a result of other events. Marker, a seasoned Pakistani diplomat, was on a first-name basis with half of the foreign ministers in Asia and could not easily be dismissed as a neophyte or a lightweight. When it came,

Indonesian President Habibie's vague offer of a degree of autonomy for East Timor was part of a wider effort during July and August 1998 to reestablish Indonesia's economic and political credentials in the wake of the economic meltdown. In East Timor, dialogue was encouraged, Indonesian troop strength was reduced, and student demonstrators brandishing flags and holding independence rallies were tolerated in ways that would have been inconceivable even months before. While waving Indonesian troops embarked on ships in Dili harbor, however, others were arriving more quietly by road from West Timor. And the government was building up its militia forces as well. In rural areas, clashes between Fretilin's military wing, Falantil, and Indonesian troops were being met with fierce government retribution.

Following Habibie's autonomy announcement, the United Nations began working on a transition plan, but this was upended in January 1999 by another surprise presidential announcement. Habibie declared that if East Timor did not want to be part of Indonesia, it could leave peacefully. And in Jakarta, Xanana Gusmão was moved from Cipinang prison to a house arrest arrangement where he could communicate with his followers. Jamsheed Marker described Habibie's disposition: "capricious, idiosyncratic, replete with histrionics, imprecations and dramatic gesticulations, and with an occasional egotistical outpouring that was almost infantile in its bombast."[12] He described a bizarre dinner at Habibie's house when the elderly and ailing president sang Western pop songs for his guests, to the music of a live orchestra. But Habibie was also pragmatic and wanted to distance himself as much as he could from the politics and reputation of his predecessor.

Like other seemingly random and disconnected events—the 1974 "carnation revolution" in Portugal, the devaluation of the Thai baht, the presence of television cameras at Santa Cruz cemetery—Habibie's announcement had a profound impact on subsequent events. The prospect of a referendum, or what Indonesia preferred to call a popular consultation, long advocated by Bishop Belo and others, caught Indonesian military commanders and militia by surprise, sparking a rampage of violence. Independence activists and their supporters were arrested and tortured, and many were killed. Indiscriminate violence continued through April, when a ceasefire was finally established and an August date was set for the referendum.

Much has been written about what happened next. While it was clear to many that a peacekeeping force would be required to supervise the election and its aftermath, Indonesia's absolute refusal to countenance foreign troops prevailed. Neither the United Nations nor any of its individual members, including the United States, Australia, or any of Indonesia's ASEAN neighbors were prepared to push the issue. A small UN Mission in East Timor (UNAMET) was established to manage and supervise the referendum, but it included only 275 unarmed police. The largest part of the UN's international presence was made up of more than five hundred United Nations Volunteers (UNV), who would form the backbone of the electoral effort. In addition to the internationals, some four thousand local staff were recruited on short notice. By the time it was over, UNAMET cost $80 million in cash and kind, $50 million of it provided in the form of voluntary contributions by UN member nations. Given the timeframe, UNAMET was a remarkable feat of logistics. The agreement to establish the mission was announced on May 5, 1999. The first staff arrived in Dili before the end of the month, aiming to register voters, carry out a public education campaign, and implement the referendum by August 8. In the end, the vote was postponed to August 30, but there are few examples of such a sensitive UN operation moving so quickly and—especially under the circumstances that prevailed—so smoothly.

Among these circumstances was an organized campaign of violence and intimidation by the Indonesian military and militia against the pro-independence effort. Proautonomy rallies were attacked, students were killed, and random violence swept the entire country. By July there were some 60,000 IDPs, and many observers predicted chaos and civil war if the vote favored independence. As the day of the vote approached, with more than 450,000 people registered, the violence increased. Representations at the highest levels were made to Jakarta by the United States, Britain, Japan, Australia, and others to reign in the Indonesian military and militia, but it was no longer clear who was in charge, or what their intentions were. More than 200,000 people in East Timor, including dependents, relied on Indonesian government salaries, and many who supported the Indonesian position, including Indonesian military officers, had large personal investments in the territory.

As was the case five years earlier when the UN Security Council met to discuss Rwanda, it met too late, and did too little, to prevent or mitigate the tragedy that now unfolded. On August 27, two days before the vote, with violence spiralling out of control, the Security Council met to consider the increasingly dire reports arriving from Dili. And it approved a slight increase in civilian police, fifty police trainers, and three hundred military liaison officers. Given the warnings, given the violence that followed the elections, and given the ten thousand peacekeepers that would be sanctioned only days later, this was a triumph of hope over common sense. It was also one of many examples in the post–Cold War world of great power hypocrisy and double standards. While NATO powers had—only five months earlier—agreed to override national sovereignty in Kosovo in the name of humanitarianism, they left East Timor almost entirely to an underfunded UN, deferring to Indonesia at every turn, even though the principle of national sovereignty did not apply, *de jure*, in the case of East Timor. The Indonesian occupation had never been accepted by the UN, and only one country, Australia, had officially recognized Indonesian sovereignty. As NATO bombs rained down on Serbia and Kosovo, the governments of most NATO countries—cognizant, perhaps, of their Indonesian investments, oil and the desire for a stable, friendly Jakarta—were unable to go further with Indonesia than to "urge restraint."

Many analysts have suggested that the evidence of impending civil war was so clear that, from a humanitarian point of view, the referendum in East Timor should have been postponed. Certainly many advised this action at the time, and inveterate UN bashers have subsequently picked through the ashes, eager to assign blame. Few Timorese, however, support the Monday morning quarterbacks, even in light of what happened. Postponement might have led to cancellation and the loss of the only real opportunity there was ever likely to be for independence. The time would never be more propitious; the international community, uncertain as it was, would never be more engaged. On polling day there were 2,300 accredited observers and 600 journalists in East Timor. An astonishing 98.6 percent of the registered voters turned out, and 78.5 percent of them opted for independence.

Within hours, the punishment of East Timor began. UN offices were attacked and burned, students and priests were killed, Bishop Belo's house was razed, looting and murder became widespread, and before long, much of Dili was aflame. Journalists, observers, NGOs, and all but a handful of UN officials crowded aboard planes for the ninety-minute flight across the Timor Sea to Darwin, as East Timor descended into chaos and anarchy. Hundreds of thousands of people were forcibly moved. Or they ran for the hills or crossed the border into West Timor, creating a massive humanitarian emergency.

While in some ways the early days of September 1999 were a repeat of December 1975, several things had changed. First, the Cold War factor was no longer present. Second, East Timorese now had a voice of their own, in the form of Nobel Prize winners Ramos-Horta and Archbishop Belo, and in the newly released freedom fighter Xanana Gusmão. Behind them was an army of civil society organizations around the world. These now went to work on their members of parliament, senators, and congressmen. And although most of the journalists had fled, many were only ninety minutes away in Darwin, filing stories and waiting for the moment when they could return. The "CNN effect," which had sparked only occasionally during the previous twenty-five years, now fired its booster rockets.

It was also thought at the time that Indonesia, weakened both economically and politically, would be more pliant than was the case in 1975. In fact, however, this was not the case. Where Suharto had twice raised the issue of East Timor with Gerald Ford and Henry Kissinger, clearly seeking (and receiving) American acceptance of an invasion, Habibie and his foreign minister Ali Alatas now turned the idea of an international force down cold. But as Dili burned, the crescendo of

demands from the international NGO network grew. Media denuncia-
tions of international inaction proliferated. The Pope weighed in, and
on his way to an Asia-Pacific Economic Cooperation (APEC) meeting
in New Zealand on September 9, 1999, President Clinton said that if
Indonesia did not end the violence, it must invite—"it *must* invite"—he
repeated, the international community to do it. Kofi Annan said that
Indonesia could be held responsible for crimes against humanity. Australia had mobilized a rapid reaction force several weeks earlier, but it
would not move without Security Council approval, which was unlikely
to get past a Chinese veto in the absence of Indonesian acquiescence.
Security Council approval had not been sought for NATO's Kosovo
operation because it would never have received Russian sanction. Here
it was deemed important, in part to revalidate the Security Council,
which had been bitterly divided over Kosovo. And Australia's foreign
minister, Alexander Downer, showed none of his East Timor worries
when it came to sending Australian troops to the nonstrategic, oil-free
Solomon Islands in 2003. He spoke then of a new doctrine of intervention in the Pacific. "Sovereignty in our view is not absolute. Acting for
the benefit of humanity is," he said. But where East Timor was concerned, Indonesia was the issue, not humanity.

Politics, morality, public pressure, and humanitarian concerns all
having failed, the big gun was at last rolled out: money. World Bank
President James Wolfensohn wrote to President Habibie that donors
would have difficulty with future support for Indonesia if peace was not
restored and if the referendum outcome was not honored. On September 9, as East Timor burned for a tenth day, the IMF put a Jakarta-
bound mission on hold, to signal that a resumption of lending—critical
to Indonesia's economic recovery—was part of the equation. The
United States and Britain announced a boycott of arms sales two days
later, and the European Union followed soon after. A September 11
Security Council meeting that lasted well past midnight saw delegate
after delegate take the microphone to demand action. Finally, on September 12, Indonesia consented to an international peacekeeping force.
Its bloody, quarter-century occupation of East Timor was at an end.
Five days after the Security Council mandated the creation of the International Force for East Timor (INTERFET) on September 15, the
force established its presence in Dili and, within a month, every Indonesian soldier and official in the territory was gone.

Viewed one way, the liberation of East Timor was a twenty-four-year
international disgrace. The lives of some 200,000 people were lost, and
during a period when fifty other countries received their independence—
already well after history's great period of decolonization—East Timor
suffered under a brutally repressive regime, stunted culturally, politically,
and economically. Sacrificed to cold war expediency and diplomatic pragmatism in 1975, the eventual peacekeeping, relief, and reconstruction

effort cost the United Nations and its member nations well in excess of a billion dollars in 1999 and 2000 alone. The 1975 assumption that an independent East Timor might lead to regional instability resulted in an annexation that—in the long run—led not just to great regional instability, but to the greatest regional crisis in a generation. Australian political scientist Rodney Tiffen castigates the pragmatists of 1975: "Like many who decide to forsake principle for pragmatism, they found themselves in a deepening mire. Rather than a quick, neat, painless takeover, the Indonesian operation was prolonged, clumsy and bloody. . . . Policymakers had seriously underestimated the strength of East Timorese nationalism and had failed to recognize that a huge majority of the population adamantly opposed forceful incorporation into Indonesia."[13]

Viewed another way, the East Timor outcome can be seen as a UN success story. Once the go-ahead was given for the referendum, it was carried out efficiently, effectively, and without serious complaint in less than three months. The United Nations has supervised many elections, but East Timor's was only the third it had managed on its own, and the achievement was commendable. Slow as the Security Council was to act on warnings of imminent disaster in September 1999, it did act, and it did so within the systems designed for such action. And it certainly didn't hurt that the Pope, the World Bank, the IMF, Tom Hyland, the international media, and the world's NGOs all pressed for action. Without them, the United Nations might not have intervened. But they were there, and the United Nations did intervene. It was also convenient that Australia was nearby and that it had mobilized a troop contingent ready to go on September 8. But even then, it was a remarkable feat to actually have troops on the ground only five days after the Security Council made its decision on September 15.[14]

By the time the first INTERFET troops arrived, three-quarters of the 850,000 people who lived in East Timor had been displaced, 250,000 of them dispersed in makeshift camps across the border in West Timor. An estimated 70 percent of the country's limited infrastructure had been destroyed. Most skilled personnel and a large part of the commercial sector had left. But the death toll from the events of September was surprisingly low, and the worst aspects of the security problem were extinguished in a short time. Human Rights Watch estimated that a thousand people had been killed, although the numbers who died as an indirect result of the fighting and dislocation were probably much higher.

The immediate issues revolved around emergency assistance and reconstruction, although rebuilding to the country's previous low development levels was not a standard at which aid agencies could in good conscience aim. Per capita GDP in 1997 had been less than $400, and half the population lived close to the poverty line. At fifty-six years, life expectancy was low. Only 41 percent of the population was literate, and few had access to potable water, electricity, and health care. As a World Bank report put it, "East Timor is different from other post-conflict situations in one very important respect. There is no apparent need for pacification between different ethnic, cultural, or religious segments of the population. The need—and it is enormous because the destruction was premeditated, thorough and massive—is for reconstruction."[15]

There were, however, immediate humanitarian needs, and the UN Office for the Coordination of Humanitarian Affairs (OCHA) was quick to respond. The head of the Geneva office, Ross Mountain, was sent to Darwin, the northern Australian town closest to East Timor. There he had a few days with other UN agencies, NGOs, and the military while the final approvals were being sorted out with Jakarta. An independent evaluation later found that OCHA performed well in East Timor because, unlike other emergency situations, it was first off the mark, landing in a vacuum where there was no authority, no organization, no donors, no NGOs, and no facilities. It sent experienced, senior staff who knew the UN system and the world of NGOs; it had a strong vision of what had to be done; it was able to seize opportunities as they arose; and it managed to override internal UN procedures and systems that often block effective and efficient action. It was, in a sense, the "perfect emergency."

OCHA can perhaps be faulted for the absence of a prereferendum contingency plan, but neither the United Nations nor the donor agencies had anticipated the violence that would occur. On September 12, OCHA had issued a standing order to its UN Disaster Assessment Team (UNDAC), and with assistance from Britain and Sweden, two support modules arrived on September 18, only three days after what was later referred to as "entry." These helped give OCHA the relevance and credibility required when the first NGOs began to arrive on September 25. Sectoral working groups were established and an intensive planning exercise, started in Darwin, was completed on September 27. Although refined over the following month, the document produced during the planning exercise was, in effect, the basis for a UN Consolidated Appeal (CAP), helping generate donor funds in the immediate aftermath of the destruction. The CAP estimated needs over a nine-month period at $183 million for East Timor and $6 million for operations in Indonesian West Timor. Evaluators would later criticize the document because of confusion over its purpose: Was it a planning document, a fundraising tool, or an expression of strategic intent? NGOs were critical because it failed to dislodge funding from the UN system for them. But for those 150 NGO workers and UN officials sleeping on concrete floors and in UN tents at "Camp OCHA," such critiques lay in the future.

That OCHA could organize seats on aircraft and provide satellite phone services, food, water, and latrines made it the only game in town. It created a register of NGOs, held information meetings every day, and provided general advice, trouble-shooting services, and orientation for newcomers. Much of this took place within a context of grave uncertainty about security and a lack of experience among the Australian military in dealing with civilian emergency operations. These relations were also coordinated by OCHA, as were relations with bilateral donors. A donor group from the United States, Britain, Japan, Sweden, and Thailand arrived in Dili on September 22, and OCHA's grasp of the situation helped facilitate rapid funding of some of the most urgent needs. During the first month of operations, "safe haven camps" were created for displaced people, food was distributed, and emergency non-food items such as blankets, clothing, and household items were distributed to 64,000 people. Sixty food convoys were sent to rural areas, and ten hospitals and health facilities were reopened. Within three months, 125,000 refugees had returned from West Timor.

By the end of December 1999, the worst aspects of the humanitarian emergency were over, and by April 2000, OCHA was gone. In the end, an estimated $200 million was provided by donors for emergency relief, although not always to the areas identified by OCHA, and certainly not with the alacrity needed. Donors committed $156 million through the CAP and spent another $40 to $50 million through NGOs and other non-UN mechanisms. Two months after the launch of the appeal, at the beginning of December, only $37 million had actually been received, almost half provided by the United States and the European Community Humanitarian Office (ECHO), with most of the balance from Australia, Japan, Britain, and Portugal.

The medium-term donor response to the challenges in East Timor, however, was very different from what prevails in most postemergency situations. In October 1999, the UN Security Council established a UN transitional administration for East Timor (UNTAET), which assumed all executive and legislative authority for the transitional state until formal independence could be granted. UNTAET, essentially a colonial authority, was to have a planned budget of $700 million, drawn from the assessed contributions of member states. In other words, its funding was not dependent upon the interests, priorities, and whims of donor countries. Also in October, the World Bank fielded a fifty-five-person Joint Assessment Mission to identify reconstruction needs. The timing was fortuitous, not because the Bank had been quick off the mark but because the mission had been planned months before the trouble began and could now be operationalized. In December, the Bank established a Trust Fund for East Timor, which it would administer. Shortly afterward, at a meeting in Tokyo, fifty donors and international agencies pledged $523 million for the reconstruction of East Timor over the following three years. Much of this would be channelled through the Trust Fund for East Timor, but donors also created another pool of money, the Consolidated Fund for East Timor, managed by UNTAET to cover the running costs of the fledgling government-in-waiting.

By mid-2000, UNTAET had replaced a small Timorese advisory council with a larger body that began to act as an informal parliament. Xanana Gusmão won the presidential election held in April 2001, and in August, elections for a constituent assembly followed. Full independence was achieved on May 20, 2002, and in September of that year, East Timor—now Timor Leste or Timor Loro Sae (Timor "where the sun rises")—became the first state to join the United Nations in the new millennium. The economic prospects for Timor Leste were not bad. Although the country is primarily dependent on coffee as a cash crop, oil revenues are expected to be approximately $7 billion in the two decades after 2004, a remarkable windfall for a tiny country that has suffered so badly in the past. Where oil is concerned, Timor's biggest challenge will be to diversify the economy and to use the oil revenues wisely. The immediate challenges include creating a competent and responsible civil service, developing effective education and health services, and working toward human development policies that can help eradicate the country's deep-seated poverty.

Almost from the beginning, there was a thinly disguised rivalry between the World Bank and "the rest"—UN agencies and NGOs. The World Bank arrived early, and its Joint Assessment Mission became the basis for much of the early postemergency planning. The Bank's Trust Fund for East Timor was at once a matter of necessity and a stroke of genius. Because there was no government and no real UN administrative structure when the Tokyo pledging conference was held in December 1999, donors needed a focal point for their contributions. In meeting this need, the fund also became a de facto coordinating mechanism for donors, managed by a single agency (with the Asian Development Bank handling some aspects). This was a notable, if accidental, achievement, reducing the donor cherry-picking and earmarking that characterizes so many emergencies. With the UN running the government and the World Bank handling much of the reconstruction fund, donor coordination was better in East Timor than in perhaps any other emergency in recent memory.

Such coordination came at a cost, however. The World Bank's heavy reliance on consultants, its endless assessment missions, its detailed planning requirements, and its distinct ideas about how things should be done created considerable unhappiness among many UN agencies and NGOs. The fledgling Timorese administration itself asked for a reduction in the endless string of consulting missions. The Trust Fund for East Timor absorbed a lot of the funds that, under other circumstances, might have been channeled through UN agencies and NGOs. The Bank, in fact, found itself in something of a core-competency quandary, operating in a country where the government-in-waiting had no intention of borrowing funds. ("A mistake," said Bank officials, eager for clients to spend now and pay later.) And so the Bank, which frequently reminds critics that it is a bank and not an NGO, soon found itself devising and running NGO-type efforts: a community empowerment project with revolving loan funds and community radio programming; a $500,000 community employment project; a small enterprise project; a microfinance development project (administered by the Asian Development Bank). While many of these projects did involve UN agencies and NGOs, the World Bank was very much in the driver's seat, attracting visibility and earning political mileage from its newfound role—while actually spending only $5 million of its own funds.

Before 1999 there was only a handful of international NGOs—ones that the Indonesian government considered safe. Some were obliged to operate from a national office in Jakarta, while others operated in East Timor in a semiclandestine manner. Between September and December 1999, 49 international NGOs arrived and more came later; within two years the number had grown to more than 250. Many of the internationals that arrived in Dili in the immediate aftermath of the crisis did so with good intentions and perhaps some real skills, but many brought very little money with them. In other words, they came looking for both work and money, and in the immediate postemergency period, many were successful in both areas, obtaining grants from USAID, Japan, DFID, Portugal, the European Union, and others.

Transnational NGOs had real advantages over one-country NGOs. CARE Canada was the lead member for CARE International in East Timor, for example. Logically, it was seen by the Canadian International Development Agency (CIDA) as a Canadian NGO and received more funding from CIDA than any other Canadian NGO. But to other donors it was simply an international NGO. ECHO funded it via CARE GB; AusAID channeled money through CARE Australia, and other donors used the same approach. The Oxfam family arrived with more than a mix of donors; they came with a mix of skills and mandates. As the Australian Oxfam member, Community Aid Abroad was geographically the closest and had a mandate for relief as well as longer-term development. It was therefore the most likely to stay on. The British Oxfam came with its preprogrammed capacity for providing water, sanitation, and public health. And NOVIB, Oxfam's Dutch family member, sent funds to support local NGOs instead of doing things itself. This collection of agencies brought a mixed approach to relief and recovery: the immediate and the longer term, direct action and building local capacities.

As in other emergencies, NGOs were used by UN agencies to deliver food, to help repatriate refugees and to rebuild schools and clinics. But when the immediacy of the relief period wore off and donors began to turn their attention to reconstruction and longer-term development, there was considerably less money available locally than most NGOs were used to, especially with so much of the reconstruction funding tied up in the World Bank's Trust Fund. World Vision had three hundred staff at the height of the emergency but within two years was down to forty, facing closure if new contracts did not soon become available. When it began in East Timor, it had fifteen donors, but by that time it was down to three. In standard new operations, a World Vision office will have money for emergency spending and some startup operations, but it needs a base of child sponsorship in order to sustain a program. East Timor was not ready for this. So the only alternative was to design projects and market them to donors, or bid on projects designed by donors. Some NGOs wound up chasing small embassy grants, while others decided that the emergency was over, and left. Action Contre la Faim, the International Rescue Committee, and MSF all left within two years, although many of their peers felt that the haste was unseemly and had more to do with an absence of money than a lack of need for their services. The Irish NGO GOAL and SCF U.S. left because the few available local contracts were insufficient to cover the core costs of running even a minimal program.

As the country moved from relief to recovery mode and as the fledgling government began to assert itself, new issues arose for NGOs. In the early days, thousands of foreigners had come and gone at will. This was understandable because they were *helping*. Now the government began introducing visas and work permits and, as was the case in Sierra Leone, even suggested that NGOs should pay taxes. This was considered by many to be inconsiderate and ungrateful. Speaking with some bitterness, however, a government official put forward a different view: "Other people sell our product and we get a commission," he said. He was referring, of course, to the political economy of humanitarianism—the aid "tied" to use of a donor country's product, the expatriate salaries, and the administrative costs associated with the effort—and how little of it trickled down to the local economy.

It takes an hour and a half to fly from Australia to Asia in a two-engine EMB-120 Brasilia. The plane leaves Darwin in a lull between tropical downpours and flies over the Timor Sea—water the entire distance until the clouds that loom over East Timor come into view. The island is long and narrow, with a series of ridges and low mountains running along its spine. The plane crosses the island, heads out over the sea again, circles, and then lands at the airport west of the city. A few children and touts hang around the exit, but they are polite compared to those at most airports, and soon lose interest in the disembarking passengers. A few chairs and tables off to one side are occupied by a group of New Zealand military, two of them women. All are wearing sidearms, carrying automatic rifles, and drinking Sprite.

The drive into town at dusk is depressing. Dili looks like the small provincial backwater it was under Indonesian administration. Set on a bay with the hills and mountains behind, it has potential for beauty, but little is evident to the first-time visitor. The rich built their homes along the waterfront on the road in from the airport, but even the grandest of them is modest. Many buildings on the eastern outskirts were burned by militia or departing Indonesians in 1999. In the center, the destruction is worse. But Portuguese memorials—to five hundred years of colonial rule; to an obscure governor in the first half of the last century—have survived the Indonesian occupation and have been newly refurbished. A large park in the center of town celebrates the Indonesian liberation of the colony: a grotesque rendition of a man brandishing a weapon and a broken chain. A cow forages beneath it in the overgrown grass.

The main administrative buildings have been reconstructed, first for UN use and later for the new government, but much of the city has been wrecked. Downtown, a flourishing service industry of small hotels, shops, and restaurants has grown up to serve the expatriate community. The Galaxy Hotel offers a room with a fridge, hot and cold running water, and BBC World Service television for U.S.$45 a night, including breakfast. Next door the City Café, with tables on the sidewalk under an awning, serves Italian food and cold Portuguese beer. It might well be Lisbon, for all the Timorese in view. But in Lisbon, the buildings across the street would probably not be burned and gutted shells. In the evening boys appear, selling bad copies of the most recent American films and "jiggy-jig movies" on disc.

Some of the UN offices are at the Obrigada Barracks, a motley collection of portables, sheds, and jerry-rigged barracks, with a small PX, a bar, and a restaurant where soldiers and UN civilian police eat and drink beer. Many sidearms are in view. Inside the gate are the "Kiwi Lines" barracks and the "Pakistan Lines" barracks on either side of a small garden. A plinth has been erected bearing the words of the Pakistan national anthem, in English and Urdu, a clue for future archeologists as to the make-up of the peacekeeping force. A UN administrator complains about having to construct a $71,000 wall around the residence of the SRSG, not because of any inherent security risk to the UN, but because the house is close to the U.S. embassy and there could be fallout if it is attacked. There is concern about al Qaeda infiltration from Bali. Recently he had to repatriate the body of an eighteen-year-old New Zealand peacekeeper, who shot himself when he got a "Dear John" letter from his girlfriend at home. Now he keeps twenty-five plywood coffins on hand, because every time there is a military incident or an incursion from West Timor, the UN must carry out autopsies in order to determine what kind of weapons were used, a clue as to the origin of the perpetrators. At first, he says, the bodies were returned to the families in body bags—it was messy. The UN is expected to do better, hence the coffins. Past the restaurant, on the road that runs along the waterfront, a policeman—perhaps Thai or Singaporean—aims a radar gun at passing cars: He is operating a speed trap. Farther on, a large Caucasian policeman in shorts, a small Canadian flag on his shoulder patch, is leading a team of Timorese trainees on bicycle patrol: community policing.

The costs of the military, relief, and reconstruction efforts in East Timor are difficult to calculate. Some of the numbers appear in UN statistics, but many do not. In gross terms, the INTERFET military operation cost Australia, for example, almost A$3 billion (U.S.$1.8 billion) alone, although after deducting contributions from the UN and calculations for what would have been spent by the military had the East Timor crisis not arisen, the additional *net* cost to Australia was more like A$215 million (U.S.$127 million) a year.[16] Japan contributed $100 million to enable troops from developing countries to participate in INTERFET. UNTAET, which included the cost of peacekeeping, managing a large stable of expatriate bureaucrats, and creating a new government for the country, cost $574 million in 2000 and approximately $690 million in 2001. UNTAET and its successor organization, United Nations Mission of Support in East Timor (UNMISET), consumed an additional $454 million in 2002 and $292 million in 2003. Nearly thirty countries sent troops to participate in peacekeeping. In contrast to their general reluctance to send troops to Africa, thirteen industrialized countries sent military contingents. In many cases UN reimbursement rates did not cover the actual costs incurred by these troop-sending countries, requiring additional expenditures and hidden costs.

In addition to its $100 million contribution to peacekeeping, Japan committed an additional $130 million to relief and reconstruction over three years, much of its spent through UN agencies and NGOs, or through the two trust funds. The United States committed $98 million, Portugal $91 million, the European Union $68 million, and Australia $44 million. In short, the generosity was outstanding, not least in comparison to humanitarian spending elsewhere in the world. While precise numbers are impossible to obtain, some estimates place humanitarian spending in East Timor at $241 per capita (figure obtained by dividing $189 million by 800,000 people). Relief spending was probably considerably more than $189 million, as noted above. And in fact, the cost could be calculated differently, dividing 800,000 into the $3 billion cost of the entire relief, peacekeeping, and reconstruction effort during the first three years of post-Indonesian rule: a figure of $3,750 per capita.

A closer look at the political economy of all this generosity, however, reveals more cynical, self-serving motivations. If East Timor was going to separate from Indonesia, security in the region and the longer-term national integrity of Indonesia were of keen interest to Europe, the United States, and all members of ASEAN. It was essential that the emergence of an independent East Timor not herald the breakup of Indonesia. The separation had to be achieved in as orderly a fashion as possible, and with the greatest level of acquiescence that could be obtained from Jakarta. Acquiescence in hand, the new country then had to be stabilized as quickly as possible, to ensure an end to violence and an orderly transition. A key area in which transition was most urgently required, of course, was in the oil and gas sector. This transition was of greatest interest to Australia, the only country in the world to have officially recognized Indonesian suzerainty over East Timor, not incidentally because of the huge petroleum reserves lying beneath the Timor Sea.

The Timor Gap, between Australia and East Timor, is thought to be the world's twenty-third largest oil field, with estimated reserves of five billion barrels of oil and fifty trillion feet of natural gas. Although it took some years, in 1991 Indonesia and Australia finally signed a treaty, dividing the spoils. It was therefore essential, as Indonesia faded from the scene, that this political embarrassment be extirpated, and that Australia make new friends in Dili as soon as possible. Happily for Australia, a treaty on the division of oil and gas reserves was negotiated between UNTAET and Australia in 2001 and ratified by the independent government of East Timor in 2002. When East Timor's prime minister said on the day after independence that he expected negotiations on unresolved petroleum sector issues to continue, Australian Prime Minister Howard told reporters, "I was not the least surprised by what he said. I expected him to say something of that kind. We'll talk to him, we'll listen to him, but we think the way we've conducted ourselves has been fair and reasonable and we'll continue to be like that."[17]

Japan also had an interest in the Timor Gap. Japanese firms Osaka Gas and Inpex bought into the new arrangements and, in the years ahead, much of the gas from the Bayu-Undan field will go to Japan via Tokyo Gas and the Tokyo Electric Power Company. For Japan, there were other concerns in East Timor, not least the matter of face. Having brutalized the territory in the first half of the 1940s and having then engaged in a doting collaboration with its oppressor from 1975 to 1999, Tokyo had some catching up to do. Although few Timorese today are old enough to remember the Japanese occupation, there is a collective historical memory and an oral tradition, and books are available to remind students that a prominent Japanese motto during the 1940s was "Nippon: the brother, the protector, the master of Asia." At the Japanese embassy, officials readily agree that Japan's "historical background" in East Timor "cannot be denied." The twenty thousand Japanese soldiers posted there had "a certain impact on the people," an official says.

Japan's Self-Defense Force was another issue. There is a constitutional prohibition in Japan against the defense force serving abroad. Japan did, however, contribute financially to the first Gulf War and it sent troops to Cambodia, albeit unarmed, and then to Goma in Zaire. East Timor was an opportunity to push the envelope a bit further, by sending a nine hundred-man engineering battalion. This was protested as vigorously in Japan as it was in East Timor, where students saw it as an insult added to the injury of half a century. And while generous in overall terms, Japanese funding for reconstruction was tied directly to the use of Japanese goods and services, regardless of the fact that open tender arrangements would have saved a great deal of money. This tied aid is a common practice among donors when they are managing their own projects. It is less common to tell an agency such as UNDP that it can have $31.89 million for the rehabilitation of roads, water supply systems, and power stations, but only on the condition that Japanese firms be engaged for the work. This takes donor earmarking to a new high in self-interest.

As the world's largest economy, the United States' assessed contributions to the United Nations meant that it paid for about a quarter of UNTAET's budget. The United States also provided $36 million in food aid, with additional spending to support NGOs, the Combined Fund for East Timor (CFET), and efforts to rejuvenate the coffee economy. Local and international NGOs were supported for work in civil education and election monitoring, reconciliation and human rights, media training, and combatant reintegration. USAID's Office of Transition Initiatives was able to establish itself within four months of entry, and within nine months had made 129 small grants, mainly to civil society initiatives. The influence of the pro-Timor civil society movement in the United States was felt at budget time. USAID asked Congress for a $10 million allocation for East Timor in 2000 and got $25 million; in 2001 the agency asked for $19 million and again got $25 million—more than was being spent in Vietnam or Cambodia.

An interesting feature of U.S. involvement, although not part of its official aid calculation, was something called the United States Support

Group East Timor (USGET). USGET represented an American military presence in East Timor separate from United Nations Mission of Support in East Timor (UNMISET) until the end of 2002. With about ten military personnel, it "coordinated U.S. military activities in East Timor and the rotation of U.S. forces through temporary deployments." These included regular U.S. Navy ship visits and deployments of military medical and engineering teams that provided humanitarian and civic assistance, including engineering projects as well as medical and dental programs. According to the Web site of the U.S. Pacific Command, USGET installed plumbing in schools, painted and installed windows at orphanages, and renovated youth and education centers. U.S. sailors from the guided missile destroyer *USS Decatur* installed plumbing, electrical wiring, electrical fixtures, and a water tower for the Morris birthing clinic in Dili. "USGET has a long established record of support to East Timor. With over 10 ship visits, 70 community relation projects, 27 medical and dental team visits, and 30 major engineering team visits, USGET has played a significant role in providing humanitarian relief and will continue to do so while deployed to newly independent East Timor."[18] While the adjective "significant" may overstate the case, USGET cost about $11 million a year, considerably more than the Office of Transition Initiatives (OTI) budget and—averaged out over the ten USGET personnel—a pretty hefty $1 million per person. UN volunteers, of whom there were hundreds in East Timor, cost the UN $35,000 a year, everything included. USGET was not recorded, however, as part of the official American aid package.

Certainly the most anachronistic aid operation was that of Portugal. To its credit, Portugal never accepted the Indonesian occupation of East Timor and always maintained the brave fiction that Lisbon was somehow in charge of matters. In some ways, as it turned out, it was. Portugal kept the Timor issue alive in the United Nations and then in the European Union after it joined in 1986. It rallied all of the Lusophone countries against the Indonesian occupation and was a leading force in efforts to negotiate a settlement with Indonesia as new writing began to appear on the wall in the late 1990s. Portugal's total foreign aid budget in 1999 was only $289 million, half of it in the form of debt relief—a polite way of saying that it cancelled, that year, a lot of defaulting loans to former colonies. Its $91 million commitment to East Timor over three years was therefore a remarkably significant contribution in relation to its global effort. One of the great ironies of the post-1999 period is that there were more Portuguese soldiers and police officers serving with the United Nations in East Timor than at almost any time in the five hundred years of Portuguese engagement.

Considerably more than half of the Portuguese contribution, however, was for the propagation and advancement of the Portuguese language.

Brazil also established an aid program with heavy emphasis on cultivating the Portuguese language. By 1999, Portuguese was a forgotten language in East Timor. Beyond the elderly, few spoke the language and even fewer could read and write it. Tetum, the local language, was largely unwritten, however, and could not accommodate the requirements of governmental administration. Indonesian Bahasa, widely spoken, was politically unpopular, and English—although the language of the closest large land mass—was unknown. But when the new government adopted Portuguese as the official language of the country, jaws dropped. Members of ASEAN, in which English is the lingua franca, asked if Timor Leste was serious about being part of Asia. Others feared that the choice planted the seeds of further civil strife, because it gave the best jobs in the new administration to returning exiles, disenfranchising those who had stayed and fought the occupation for twenty-five years.

The problem in all of these political calculations is not so much that governments might have interests in the allocation of their aid but that their professions of humanitarian concern are so wildly divergent from reality and, from a political perspective, that they actually result in so little political bang for the buck. Humanitarian emergencies continue (largely unaddressed) in Aceh and elsewhere in Indonesia, and the country's political future is likely to be anything but quiet. Japan garnered little influence and less applause for its heavy-handed tied aid. Portugal may add a speck in the Timor Sea to its invisible Lusophone commonwealth, but at some cost to Timor's standing as an Asian nation. Timorese may not say much about the historical role played by Britain, the United States, and others, but emergency assistance does not erase memory. Australia, the most cynically political over twenty-five years, did the most to mend fences and appears to have gained the most for its efforts. Time will tell whether this is the case.

Twenty-five years late in awakening to the inevitability of East Timorese independence, the donors, in particular the humanitarian machinery, had moved very quickly. Although Indonesia was strong-armed into withdrawing, it did so voluntarily. The first peacekeeping troops arrived only days after the Security Council sanctioned their intervention, and the civil strife—which could have been much worse—was minimized. The first emergency assistance moved quickly and was well coordinated by the United Nations. Many of the Jakarta-based donors already had experience with East Timor, and the proximity of Darwin, a major service port, proved invaluable. There was widespread understanding that significant funding would be needed for reconstruction, something neglected in many emergencies. Reconstruction funds, too, moved more quickly than in other emergencies, in part because several of the donor representatives based in Jakarta had visited East Timor during the late 1990s and were familiar with the territory.

The United Nations took full responsibility for running the country during the interim period, using UN assessed contributions rather than voluntary contributions. Donor cherry-picking was thus reduced significantly. In Sergio Vieira de Mello, the United Nations found the perfect governor for the interim period. A Brazilian, he brought development, humanitarian, and language skills to the job. He had good knowledge of the United Nations and donor systems and just the right proportions of polish, humility, and disdain. The World Bank provided an important coordination role in the reconstruction effort, again something missing in most postemergency situations. The funding was adequate, and with oil and gas revenue on the horizon, donors could see that their contributions would not have to be open-ended. And throughout the emergency and reconstruction period, donors had a relatively free hand. There were no warlords, no cranky ministers to appease, no government apart from themselves. Donor coordination was simple, the country was small, and much of the work was easy—cleaning and building. East Timor: the perfect emergency.

Of all the complaints that eventually emerged—as complaints always do—about the emergency effort and the immediate postemergency period in East Timor, the most common is that the donors, the NGOs, UNTAET, and all those who came to help actually did little to build local capacities. East Timor, it is said, was set on the path to independence without adequate preparation. A detailed study produced by King's College London in 2003 said, for example, that "UNTAET left the institutions traditionally responsible for oversight of the security sector—Parliament and its committees, the relevant ministries and civilian-led national security coordination agencies—underdeveloped and incomplete."[19] The same, it said, was true of the security sector itself and the judiciary.

The implication is that international agencies rushed around doing things themselves; UNTAET could and did operate in what some thought was an imperial manner, because there was no structure in East Timor after September 1999. There was no government to work with, to support, or to get in the way. There were no local organizations, no local capacities, no professionals. This picture, of course, is only partially true. A broad coalition of political parties and individuals known as the CNRT (*Conselho Nacional de Resistencia Timorense*–National Council of Timorese Resistance) had been created, with Xanana Gusmão at the helm. With his return to Dili in October 1999, there was in fact a body with which UNTAET could have worked. But Gusmão was also the leader of Fretilin and its fighting arm, Falantil. As in Kosovo, where the United Nations had deliberately excluded the Kosovo Liberation Army from transitional structures in order to avoid prejudice in later election outcomes, the CNRT was sidelined in the initial months. As one observer put it, "With hindsight the lack of consultation is really shocking; but it also would have been impossibly complex to bring all the different Timorese interests to the table as well. In a way, the fact they were inaccessible made it much easier. It was hard enough to deal with the existing variety of views among Member States. It was almost easier for UNTAET to set up from this ground zero position with little local politics to worry about."[20]

Beyond the CNRT, there were also other local organizations, but almost none of the expatriates who arrived spoke Tetum and few spoke Bahasa. It took a long time for the lessons of misplaced urgency, arrogance, and hubris to start sinking in, and by then, many of the agencies and aid workers were on their way home. "Building capacity" is a vague term that contains at least as much potential for hubris and error when it is taken seriously as when it is not. Capacities cannot be built overnight; they are not like boxes of Ikea furniture to be assembled by amateurs over a leisurely weekend. Time, in any case, was never a luxury in East Timor. Of all the platitudes in aid manuals, project proposals, and evaluations of humanitarian action, the need for capacity-building is one of the most common. But of all the things that need doing in emergencies and postemergency situations, capacity-building is probably the least well understood and the most difficult to do well.

As the UN flag was lowered on the night of May 19, 2002, East Timor set out on its voyage of national discovery, its "tryst with destiny" to use Nehru's expression on a similar night in India, fifty-five years before. Timor Leste did so, equipped with the lessons of an intense and bitter experience in global realpolitik; with enormous amounts of newfound international goodwill; with a better-than-average portfolio of aid projects offered by donors exhibiting fewer of their inefficiencies and pathologies than usual. The nation was debt-free and could look forward to a healthy flow of oil and gas revenues in the near future. "What a lucky country!" a UN official says, gazing out of his window across an expanse of burned-out buildings awaiting reconstruction. "What a lucky country!"

4

Afghanistan: Back to the Future

Twice the British had launched campaigns against the Afghans . . . repeated scares and crises kept the northwest always on their minds. . . . Sometimes they had thought the actual possession of Afghanistan necessary. Sometimes they had settled for a policy that would merely keep the Russians out of Kabul. . . . Roads were built, boundary posts set up, forts established. . . . The tribespeople, though, deeply resented the new interference. A holy man known to the British as the Mad Fakir, and described by Winston Churchill as "a priest of great age and of peculiar holiness," travelled around inciting them to rebellion. He was helped by the news just reaching those distant provinces of Muslim triumphs elsewhere in the world. . . .
—James Morris, *Pax Britannica*, 1979[1]

As with Sierra Leone and East Timor, the humanitarian crisis in Afghanistan has festered for decades, surfacing only now and again on the radar screen of the wider world. But the on-again, off-again pattern of international concern for the country and its people is more indicative of the fluctuating mindset and attention span of the outside world than it is of the steady-state problems of Afghanistan itself. Adding insult to injury, the ongoing work of assistance and protection has benefited more from shadows than from the light. Ironically, too, the humanitarian enterprise has acquitted itself better when its fundamental principles have come under direct challenge—as, for example, at the hands of the Taliban—than when humanitarian action has been commandeered by muscular donors with specific political agendas.

The historical record since the invasion of Afghanistan by the Soviet Union in December 1979 confirms the close interaction between politics and aid.[2] That was the case during the Cold War period and in its aftermath (1979–1992), during the civil war years (1992–1996), during the Taliban era (1996–2001), and during the struggle against terrorism (from late 2001 onward). In each era, humanitarian action has had political patrons who have influenced the shape, contents, and outcomes

79

of efforts by the outside world to provide life-saving succor and to protect basic rights. Even the high-profile humanitarian effort after September 11, when Afghanistan once again received top international billing, failed to shake the politicized aid reflexes of earlier years and to get things right. As the corrosive impacts of power and politics and the resistance of the humanitarian apparatus to fundamental change show, the latest "humanitarian" endeavor has learned little from the past.

War has been a constant in Afghan life since the Soviet invasion in late 1979. A study undertaken by the International Committee of the Red Cross (ICRC) notes that "Afghans have endured an endless succession of wars: the 1979–1989 fight to drive out the Soviet Union military forces; three years of armed conflict between the mujahideen and the Soviet-supported communist government; two years of civil war among Afghan factions; and since 1994, the fighting between the Taliban and the Northern Coalition. Only suffering and destruction have remained constant, as the players, goals and battlefields have shifted time and again." The ICRC places the twenty-year toll of this bloody history at 1.7 million deaths, two million persons permanently disabled, and five million displaced. Violations of the basic human rights of civilians, including women, have been endemic.[3]

During these decades, international perceptions of Afghanistan and the Afghan people have changed dramatically from one period to the next. At one time or another, the Afghans have been viewed as "resistance heroes against Soviet aggression, drug-dealing warlords and bandits, the arena for proxy wars, victims of Taliban oppression, and unwilling hosts to international terrorism."[4] It goes without saying that such fluctuating perceptions have influenced policy, especially regarding the alleviation of human suffering.

The invasion by the Soviet Union in December 1979 turned Afghanistan overnight into a major front in the global war between communism and the West. President Carter responded by suspending a multiyear grain agreement and applying a series of other financial and commercial sanctions. On his watch, President Reagan grouped Afghanistan with Cambodia, Angola, Mozambique, Ethiopia, and Nicaragua as countries in which the United States would halt the advance of international communism. In addition to waging wars through proxies, a series of U.S. administrations and their allies harnessed assistance programs into the service of overarching cold war objectives. The spirit was epitomized in a 1985 editorial in a Washington, D.C. newspaper: "Anyone who examines the historical record of communism," opined the *Washington Star*, "must conclude that any aid directed at overthrowing communism is humanitarian aid."[5]

From the overriding and all-consuming objective of beating back communism, the line is a clear and direct one to politicizing aid intended for people in need. U.S. assistance efforts on behalf of Afghans during the Cold War concentrated on the 3.5 to 4 million refugees in camps across the border in Pakistan, just as refugees in camps neighboring other Reagan Doctrine countries became a focus of U.S. aid in other cold war cockpits. The refugee camps, observes MSF's Fiona Terry, "provided a military sanctuary in which combatants could receive protection, food, medical attention, and security for their families [and] a shield behind which the Pakistani government could channel military aid and training to the mujahideen fighters."[6] Clandestine aid was also provided by the United States and by Pakistani intelligence services directly to resistance fighters within Afghanistan. Authoritative estimates place the value of U.S. economic and military assistance to the mujahideen during the 1980s at some $3 billion, ostensibly a major factor in their successful war against Soviet occupation.[7]

Reviewing a time when the blatant politicization of humanitarian aid went largely unremarked upon and unquestioned, a 1990 study noted that during the previous decade, some 265 NGOs had been involved in efforts to assist Afghanistan, through refugee camps in Pakistan (more than 100 agencies), cross-border operations into Afghanistan itself (77 agencies), and advocacy efforts in the region or in donor capitals (about 70 agencies).[8] Aid efforts in the camps included provision of food, health services, and income-generation opportunities.

UNHCR, which provided massive resources, and NGOs, which offered an array of services, emphasized the humanitarian aspects of their work. However, such aid was politicized at a very local level—many refugees were issued ration cards only after registering with a political party. And armed resistance fighters, who could have been disqualified under existing refugee law, were registered right along with bona fide refugees.

Cross-border activities mounted by NGOs from Pakistan were part and parcel of the Cold War political landscape and agenda. Most of the private American groups received funds from the U.S. government. The United Kingdom, France, Germany, Sweden, and Norway were also major donors to NGOs from their countries. The clandestine nature of such work made impacts hard to evaluate, and the obstacles encountered were considerable. Aid agencies negotiated access with the local political or military Afghan leadership, who often engaged in bidding wars to attract resources from groups seeking entry and then took their own cut of what was provided, planting their own people on NGO staffs in the process.

Individual NGOs, anxious to enjoy a piece of the action, made their own arrangements with different commanders, largely undeterred by negative effects of their deals on national cohesion or aid accountability. The NGOs tendency to work in reasonably secure areas left the most exposed and vulnerable people to fend for themselves or to be reached by other relief organizations. The illegality of these operations also exposed NGOs to bribery and extortion from Pakistan authorities and others along the entire supply chain. In a kind of humanitarian blowback, the mujahideen commanders on the receiving end of international aid in the 1980s would again play a controlling role in the post-September 11 period.

Most NGOs that engaged in advocacy efforts promoted the cause of the mujahideen (warriors of god) or, in cold war nomenclature, "freedom fighters," and explicitly or implicitly opposed the Soviet occupation. The advocates and their counterparts in the region were composed, notes one account, largely of "a close-knit web of right-wing organizations, which includes think tanks, funders, activists, church representatives, university intellectuals, soldiers of fortune, retired U.S. generals and high government officials . . . [A]nticommunism is the glue that holds these groups together."[9] Just as American NGOs supported U.S. policy geared to aiding resistance to the Soviet occupation, many European NGOs played a similar role vis à vis their own governments, which by and large followed Washington's lead. Human rights monitoring and advocacy were equally politicized: Abuses by the Soviets and the Soviet-sponsored regime in Kabul received close scrutiny while the mujahideen largely received a free pass.[10] The United Nations was also tarnished by its lack of even-handedness in the human rights domain.

The political naivete of the U.S. NGO community at the time was particularly stunning, contrasting sharply with the political savvy that some NGOs have since developed during the post–Cold War period. During the Reagan years, many of the aid agencies that accepted U.S. government resources to work on the frontlines of the Cold War were unwilling to acknowledge the political nature and implications of their involvement. "We do not have a political agenda ourselves," they insisted. "We are simply helping people who happen to be victims of Communist regimes." NGOs viewed their humanitarian mission as self-legitimizing and beyond question, somehow disembodied from the otherwise evident politics of the situation. Politics were in everybody's portfolio except the humanitarians.[11] Only the ICRC managed to work on both sides of the conflict during the Soviet occupation, mounting programs of emergency food distribution among vulnerable groups, providing medical services to the wounded, visiting prisoners, and monitoring prison conditions.

Assistance through the United Nations was also politicized during the Cold War years. Prior to the April 1988 Geneva Accords that ended the war, UN programs were largely concentrated among Afghan refugees outside the country. A token UN presence in Kabul sought to implement selected development programs but was able to do so only in areas under government control. Only a few small NGOs and the ICRC were present in Kabul. However, the 1988 Geneva Accords laid the groundwork not only for Soviet withdrawal but also for a large-scale United Nations-led assistance effort, Operation Salam, under the direction of Prince Sadruddin Aga Khan. Promoting the concept of "humanitarian consensus," Sadruddin won the consent of the parties to allow international humanitarian activities to expand. Attention shifted from concentrations of refugees in Peshawar and Quetta to Kabul. Benefiting from the ebbing of East-West conflict, UN agencies began to tackle the monumental task of postconflict Afghan reconstruction and development, initially through cross-border operations and eventually using Kabul-based staff.

Following the 1988 Geneva accords and the withdrawal of Soviet troops in early 1989, the political-military—and also the humanitarian—lay of the land changed drastically. The cohesiveness of the mujahideen, a movement that had begun to emerge even before the Soviet invasion and then had coalesced to force Soviet withdrawal, soon began to fracture, leading to a period of outright civil war from 1992–1996 in the newly declared Islamic state. Fighting was intense and brutal among various warlords, each with his own ethnic constituency, geographical base, military contingent, system of patronage, and sometimes even civil infrastructure. Fighting between mujahideen factions laid waste the city of Kabul in 1992.

Responding to the prevailing state of lawlessness, the Taliban emerged in 1993–1994, composed of fundamentalist clerics and students largely from ethnic Pashtun areas of Afghanistan and from the refugee camps and towns across the border in Pakistan. After taking Kabul in 1996, the Taliban eventually consolidated control over some 75 percent of the country against an increasingly unified Northern Alliance of mujahideen commanders. Violence among various mujahideen factions and then between the Alliance and the Taliban was ruthless. Widespread human rights abuses by all parties were well documented. However, in a throwback to Cold War double standards, the abuses of the Taliban generally received greater attention than those of the mujahideen.

During the civil war years of 1992–1996, Afghanistan and its problems receded from the international limelight. As the country lost its geostrategic importance, assistance and protection activities became more distant from political agendas. Principled action became more possible and while aid levels were reduced, a cadre of more established and professional agencies came onto the scene, replacing the grab bag of organizations that had stepped into the Cold War breach.[12]

Yet humanitarian work was anything but divorced from its historical roots. Afghan factions sought to perpetuate the earlier leakage of aid resources and to maintain the upper hand over the community-based leadership that might have offered a more equitable distribution of aid. International aid groups were reluctant to work in areas controlled by the Kabul authorities or to be particularly collegial with those who did. The U.S. government resisted UN efforts to bring food and other relief supplies to government-held areas. Extraction and expropriation on the mujahideen side, patchwork programs on the aid agency side, and donor and host government manipulation repeated a pattern established during the Cold War.

However grievous the behavior of the various regimes and warlords and however welcome the return to a modicum of law and order that they provided, the Taliban affronted the most elementary standards of humanitarian succor, human rights protection, and even fundamental human decency. In an ostensible effort to protect the integrity and health of women, the Taliban forbade their employment and restricted their education and their appearances in public. They also required that woman wear head-to-foot clothing. Men were required to wear beards of a certain length and to pray five times daily. Humanitarian agencies' access to women and girls was severely restricted, as was employment of women and use of female expatriate staff. The Taliban's administrative style created nightmares for aid agencies, who found themselves forced to negotiate with an idiosyncratic and inconsistent set of interlocutors at a variety of levels. Relief and rights groups began in 1997 to develop community-wide activities in response to such blatant challenges to humanitarian principle and practice.

The United Nations took the lead in developing a strategic framework to guide interactions with the Taliban. This framework sought to move efforts by UN agencies and NGOs beyond a patchwork of individual, localized projects into a more national, inclusive, and cohesive approach. The framework also addressed recurring tensions between the provision of emergency aid in accordance with core humanitarian principles of neutrality, impartiality, and independence, on the one hand, and, on the other, the desire that such assistance contribute to the broader task of peacebuilding, development, and justice. The framework was designed to present a common front among the agencies in negotiating with the Taliban and to protect humanitarian activities from subordination to "political, operational and other conditionalities." Humanitarian actors were at long last raising some of the essential political questions they had studiously avoided during the Cold War years.

The framework ultimately failed to achieve its objectives, though analysts disagree as to why. There were differences among the aid agencies and donor governments regarding whether to engage the Taliban authorities or to isolate them. In articulating core principles, agencies found they had a multiplicity of them, many in uncertain relation with each other and subject to varied interpretation. In the absence of more system-wide UN leadership and greater interagency solidarity, the Taliban succeeded in playing the agencies off one another. There was also a lack of buy-in to the framework from the UN's political side, which had its own agenda and seemed less convinced of the contribution of humanitarian action to the broader processes of peace and justice. "The fundamental problem," said one aid official in 1997 in a rare moment of candor, "is more with the United Nations than with the Taliban, and we have control over that."[13]

Over time, the Taliban became increasingly resistant and arbitrary in response to international pressure, making people in need of assistance and protection less, rather than more, accessible. Some analysts saw the Taliban polity devolving from one of a "failed state" to a "rogue state"; others saw the failed state nomenclature itself as a label of convenience to justify the strictest possible conditioning of international assistance, whatever the humanitarian consequences. The Taliban's cavalier approach to human rights also became an increasing problem for aid agencies.[14]

For their part, donor governments tended to resist the idea of programming within a strategic framework, preferring to plan and implement their work unimpeded. As frustrations with the Taliban mounted, donors became more and more circumspect in their approach to aid, specifying more objectives and more restrictive terms. The growing politicization of aid created problems for aid organizations and their humanitarian principles. Relations between international aid agencies and the authorities became further strained with the August 1998 U.S. bombing of al Qaeda bases in eastern Afghanistan in response to the bombings of U.S. embassies in Nairobi and Mombassa.

In the end, the political economy of aid and its institutional inertia proved the undoing of the strategic framework, despite its innovative strides toward greater coherence. Individual agencies proved to be wedded to traditional ways of doing business, resisting the idea of more tightly integrated UN presence and programming. Meanwhile, donors who seemed willing to support a unified assistance program and who, under the circumstances, might even have settled for greater authority on the part of a UN coordinator, were nevertheless reluctant to have activities funded out of a common pot. The objective of greater coherence between the UN's political and humanitarian work was also stillborn. Had the strategic framework succeeded, the humanitarian enterprise would have been in a better position to respond to new political circumstances, when the trickle of resources would once again become a torrent.[15]

The Taliban era ended with their defeat at the hands of the Northern Alliance, actively supported by the. U.S. military. Following the attacks by al Qaeda against U.S. targets in September 2001, the United States launched war against al Qaeda and its political hosts in October. Teaming up with the Northern Alliance, the United States succeeded in winning back most of the area controlled by the Taliban, including the city of Kabul, which fell in November.

Overnight, aid agencies that had been functioning in relative anonymity in their dealings with an isolated group of religious radicals found their activities of sudden interest to a U.S. administration launching a war against terrorism. The names of Kabul and Kandahar, Mullah Omar and the Taliban, seldom heard in Washington, now became household words on Pennsylvania Avenue. The U.S. president made overturning the Taliban and destruction of al Qaeda central elements in the embryonic war against terrorism. The immediate fallout from 9/11 in Afghanistan, however, was the withdrawal of expatriate aid staff in anticipation of a U.S. counterattack and reprisals against international aid workers.

The terrorist acts against the World Trade Center and the Pentagon led to an outpouring of international sympathy for the United

States. Initially, the U.S.-led war against al Qaeda enjoyed wide political support in the United States and at the United Nations. In the Security Council, all five permanent members were supportive, and in the General Assembly, virtually all member states concurred. Overnight, the mujahideen were back in the limelight, sharing the stage as born-again allies. Cautionary flags were raised, however, regarding new alliances of convenience, particularly where human rights violations were concerned. "While there is increased optimism for a political settlement," an MSF gathering in November 2001 warned, "it should not be forgotten that the parties controlling large parts of the country are the same actors as in the period 1992–1996."[16] However, the egregious abuses of the mujahideen were once again overshadowed by their perceived military-strategic value as allies in a new Western political-security project.

Framed by the broader global counterterrorism effort, the humanitarian work of aid agencies also assumed heightened importance. "In its renewed involvement in Afghanistan," wrote one analyst with a keen eye for historical parallels, "the United States is again turning to humanitarian action as a key component of its strategy. Again, it is calling upon U.S. NGOs to be agents of its foreign policy."[17] Humanitarian efforts represented a visible means of demonstrating that the U.S.-led anti-terrorism initiative was not an attack against the long-suffering Afghan people. Aid efforts were hurriedly accelerated to assist people in their own villages and thus avoid the destabilizing effect of a mass out-migration to neighboring countries. A major humanitarian catastrophe among those who remained in Afghanistan would also undercut the broader political objectives of the evolving global counterterrorism initiative.

Confirming the view of cynics that "quiet humanitarianism" is an oxymoron, President George W. Bush announced that the White House would be ready to receive direct donations from the American people for its own Afghan Children's Fund. Aid groups opposed the fund, both because it was seen to politicize aid to Afghanistan and because it represented unwelcome interference in their own fundraising. From the administration's standpoint, however, the need to put a compassionate face on its war against the Taliban and al Qaeda was all-important. As one analyst has noted, "Vociferous concern about the rights of Afghan women when the Bush administration was mobilizing support for its bombing campaign was paralleled by military, financial, and political support for lawless factions that have again killed and raped women and girls with impunity in Afghanistan."[18]

The largest donor to post-9/11 humanitarian efforts in Afghanistan, the United States was also the single largest aid donor to the country across the previous quarter-century. Yet from the standpoint of effective aid delivery and constructive results, its off-again, on-again interest represented a distinctly mixed blessing. "The good news is that a lot of high-level U.S. policy makers are interested in Afghanistan," observed one senior aid official in Washington in late 2002. "The bad news is that a lot of high-level U.S. policy makers are interested in Afghanistan. If Afghanistan were Liberia, we'd have a lot easier time managing the crisis."[19] In fact, there is "a negative correlation between international politics, understood as direct superpower involvement, and the ability of the international system to engage with [humanitarian] crises in a relatively principled manner."[20] Principles, it seems, are what guide action when no more important considerations are at stake.

There was a striking parallel between the impact of government engagement on aid activities and on the operation of the international media. "During the Taliban era a small number of Kabul-based corre-spondents mainly set the news agenda for Afghanistan," reflects a BBC reporter looking back on her then-lonely beat. "After the September 11 attacks, mightier players came onto the field: the United States, military and political public-relations machines, news editors back home, and, to a lesser extent, the United Nations and the aid industry." Like the aid apparatus, which had enjoyed functioning in relative anonymity, the press felt pressure from its institutional stakeholders and from govern-ments back home to accentuate the positive. "Getting positive report-ing of a conflict is a military necessity," the BBC's woman on the spot would later comment.[21]

U.S. government involvement complicated the humanitarian scene in Afghanistan in two specific respects. First, although the administra-tion waited almost a full month after September 11 before initiating bombing strikes, once launched the war took its toll against civilians as well as humanitarian operations and personnel. "Tens of thousands of people were displaced," reported one concerned aid group, "as the [U.S.] military actions took place and [as its Afghan partners,] the Northern Alliance, advanced through major parts of the country as part of an aggressive and intensive military campaign."[22] In one incident, two well-marked ICRC warehouses were hit by U.S. bombs; in another, Afghan national staff who had volunteered to stay behind to protect UN demining equipment were killed by coalition bombs. The U.S.-led military strategy played to mixed reviews among humanitarian groups. Some held that the military campaign had met the test of proportion-ality and complimented the Pentagon for its careful selection of targets. Others criticized the loss of aid property and the interruption of humanitarian operations.

Second, and perhaps of ultimately greater import, neutrality was compromised by the conduct of the war, which blurred the lines between military and humanitarian action. U.S. military aircraft dropped human-itarian daily rations (HDRs), deceptively similar in their yellow packag-ing to cluster bombs. Some NGOs believed that HDRs made their own relief work appear to be an extension of U.S. political-military policy and also criticized the military for including in its packets food items unfamiliar to Muslim populations. Of still greater concern was the practice by U.S. military personnel, wearing civilian clothes but bearing arms, of distributing aid as part of a wider effort to win local hearts and minds. Challenged to require soldiers to wear clothing identifying them as soldiers, the Pentagon initially protested that this would jeopardize the troops' security. Though anxious not to have its troops share what it discovered to be the vulnerability of professional aid workers, the military command eventually agreed to have U.S. soldiers wear some clothing or other sign of their identity.

Meanwhile, humanitarian efforts were being promoted in the United States as an integral part of the war against terrorism. "American policy makers must not think of the humanitarian campaign as an afterthought or charity work," wrote Professor Graham Allison of Harvard. "It should be regarded as a genuine second front."[23] Secretary of State Colin Powell took the instrumentalization of private aid efforts to new heights, observing that he and his colleagues at the State Department were "serious about making sure we have the best relationship with the NGOs who are such a force multiplier for us, such an important part of our combat team."[24]

As in the earlier periods, aid agencies responded in a variety of ways. Some NGOs agreed to work within the framework that Powell articulated, using resources provided by the U.S. government in whatever humanitarian space was made available to them. Others opted not to seek or to accept U.S. government funds for activities in the region, to limit their work to areas outside of Afghanistan, or to rely exclusively on private or UN resources. Agencies would face similar choices the following year in Iraq, made more difficult there by the absence of the Security Council imprimatur that had blessed UN-led efforts in Afghanistan.

United States NGOs bore a special burden. Members of international NGO federations found their European counterparts far more ready to criticize U.S. policy and far more chary about taking funding from their respective governments. On October 17, 2001, Oxfam International and five other agencies urged that the bombing "be suspended to allow food to be delivered in safety and at sufficient quantities to sustain people through the winter." A few days earlier, the UN High Commissioner for Human Rights, Mary Robinson, warned of the impacts of the bombing on aid work. The Commission's special rapporteur on the right to food condemned food drops by the military as "catastrophic for humanitarian aid" and for the "extraordinary work" that aid agencies were doing.

The UN system was heavily involved in both political and humanitarian roles. It sponsored the talks in Bonn in December 2001 that formalized the change of regime and it specified the process by which power would be transferred to a representative elected government. The United Nations promoted a Tokyo ministerial meeting the following month that produced pledges of $4.5 billion in funds for reconstruction. In March 2002, the Security Council created the United Nations Assistance Mission in Afghanistan (UNAMA), which had both political and assistance tasks.[25] UNAMA is discussed in greater detail in the following section.

Despite the successful regime change through the application of military force, pockets of Taliban and al Qaeda continued to resist the authority of the new government and its international backers. The target of various U.S.-led military operations in the coming years, these two groups would pose an ongoing threat to the security not only of Afghan civilians but of international and Afghan aid operatives, whom they frequently targeted. During an eleven-day stretch in February 2004, for example, nine murders of NGO personnel took place.[26] More than two years after the presumed defeat of the Taliban and al Qaeda, a sizeable swath of the Afghan countryside was patently unsafe for humanitarian operations. The operatives mounted by the international operatives in the wake of the war are described in detail below.

In their ongoing attempt after 2002 to snuff out a rear-guard action by Osama bin Laden and his followers, U.S.-led coalition troops focused on the isolated and religiously conservative areas of northwest Pakistan where bin Laden was thought to be sheltering. "The virulent fundamentalism in the tribal areas, which are governed directly by Pakistan's federal government," noted one newspaper account, "is the product of decades of government neglect and the anti-Soviet jihad of the 1980s, according to Pakistani analysis. The United States indirectly helped pay for hundreds of hard-line religious schools that produced anti-Soviet fighters. Today, the same schools appear to produce anti-American fighters."[27] However compelling the Cold War strategies and tactics may have appeared at the time, "The short-sightedness of the U.S. policy has now been well documented."[28] In historical perspective, the U.S. agreement to allow warlords and their protégés a significant role in the Karzai government may once again risk undermining long-term U.S. interests.

Indeed, as analysts begin to connect the dots between politics and humanitarian action during this turbulent period of Afghan history, the impacts of political objectives on humanitarian principles and practice are clear. The fact that the most hard-line mujahideen commanders received the most substantial U.S. support during the 1980s came back to haunt the United States after September 11, 2001, when mujahideen commanders such as Gulbuddin Hekmatyr and his Hezbi Islami movement turned U.S. weapons, provided in abundance during the Soviet occupation, against troops of the U.S.-led coalition and resisted the authority of the Hamid Karzai regime. In earlier years, the United

States, along with Saudi Arabia and Pakistan, also had ties to Osama bin Laden, a Saudi national who, based in Pakistan, recruited volunteers and funds for the "holy war" against the Soviet invaders and infidels—and then their successors.[29]

Each of the four periods of recent Afghan history—the Cold War, the civil war, the Taliban years, and the post-9/11 era—has challenged the international aid enterprise. The divisive politics of the Cold War period continued through the country's civil war, affecting perceptions about the integrity of humanitarian activities. The ascendancy of the Taliban provided opportunity for a more principled approach during a period of lowered international profile, although the aid community had difficulty orchestrating concerted action. Finally, the war against terrorism and, in this instance, against Afghanistan and al Qaeda, took the aid effort back to the previous state of affairs, with humanitarian and human rights principles subsumed within a high-profile security agenda.

Toward the end of 2001, the international mood about Afghanistan was decidedly upbeat. In the opening salvo of the newly declared war against terrorism, the Taliban and al Qaeda had been routed in a well-targeted military operation led by the United States. Troops from some twenty nations ultimately joined Operation Enduring Freedom. Armed with a UN Security Council mandate, an International Security Assistance Force (ISAF) had set up shop in Kabul. A new government was installed, a cabinet selected, and a process established to produce a democratically elected regime within two years. Megaresources had been identified for the daunting tasks of relief and reconstruction. The United Nations's multiple roles were clear. The clouds on the horizon seemed manageable.

It was only natural, perhaps, that the leaders of the Northern Alliance, an ally in the military victory—including unsavory characters with old as well as fresh blood on their hands—would resurface in the cabinet of Hamid Karzai. Reining in the warlords and extending governmental authority and services to the hinterlands would tax the new regime, but it seemed doable given the scale of outside political and financial support. The fact that Osama bin Laden had not been captured and the possibility that al Qaeda might mount a serious rearguard action were acknowledged but discounted. The impacts of the prevailing insecurity on aid operations and the eventual targeting of aid personnel were not anticipated as major deterrents.

The prevailing hopefulness was shared by the humanitarian enterprise, albeit with some apprehension. In early November 2001, a group of NGOs meeting in New York, at a time when military pressure from

the coalition was taking its toll on the Taliban, accentuated the positive.
In contrast with the obstacles encountered in dealing with the Taliban,
an opening for humanitarian action was clearly in the offing. But how
much space would be available? "At this early stage in the 'war' against
terrorism, with no clear template for humanitarian action established,"
the group committed itself to learn from earlier experience in Afghanistan and elsewhere in order to "do it right" this time around.[30]

Its eagerness to swing into action notwithstanding, the international aid apparatus—tarnished by many previous lackluster passes at
Afghanistan—felt as though it were on trial. "A decade-long destructive
war with the Soviet Union and the subsequent civil strife for nearly 13
years have devastated infrastructure in agriculture and other sectors of
Afghanistan's economy," wrote the FAO of the looming challenge.
"Thousands of hectares of prime agricultural land have been taken out
of production due mainly to lack of irrigation and the presence of millions of landmines. . . . During the past three years, the country has witnessed a devastating drought which compounded the impact of years of
conflict and brought a large section of the population to the brink of
starvation." Indeed, the aid agencies had a lot riding on how well they
acquitted themselves in this particular crisis. "Perhaps Afghanistan is
more important as a 'last chance' opportunity for the international aid
institutions," observed one practitioner in a particularly telling remark,
"than international aid is for the future of Afghanistan."[31]

A group of professional aid evaluators was less sanguine. They
identified nine recurring themes from earlier crises to guide donor government policies and programs for the Afghan emergency. "The current
climate, characterized by a justified sense of urgency among aid agencies to maximize the impact of aid and avoid the recurrent problems of
the past," they reminded donor governments, "provides a real opportunity to put into place effective mechanisms for getting the relief and
rehabilitation effort in Afghanistan 'right.'"[32]

A number of the policy challenges they identified would indeed
materialize in the coming months. These included a coherent policy
framework to protect humanitarian space; being clear about coordination structures and foregoing the temptation to insist on flying the
national flags of donor countries; limiting external military forces to
security and protection chores rather than dispensing aid; and using and
strengthening local institutional capacity. Since the final item proved
perhaps most pivotal to the evolution—and, in a worst-case scenario, the
eventual failure—of aid efforts in Afghanistan, it deserves citation in full.

"Unmanaged influxes of aid agencies—multilateral, bilateral and
NGOs—are an increasing feature of high profile international political-
military-aid interventions," the evaluators observed. "Such influxes
drive up office and housing rents, draw good local staff away from their

normal roles/jobs, spur 'bidding competition' among organizations, and create the perception that the agencies are benefiting more than the local population." But the challenge does not end there. "The heightened cultural/religious sensitivities in Afghanistan reinforce the need to limit the number of international agencies and personnel and ensure the equality and training of those agencies and staffs operating in Afghanistan." What should be done? "The most efficient way to contain the problems of expatriate dominance and disruption is to prioritise the identification and engagement of local and national emergency and rehabilitation actors, even where national and governmental structures remain weak or not fully legitimate. The significant skills and capacities within Afghanistan and the Afghan diaspora should be recognized and harnessed."[33]

This cautionary note was hardly revolutionary. In 1997, a new paradigm for assistance to Afghanistan had urged a more demand- and field-driven approach that would help reduce the decidedly foreign character of aid activities and inputs. "An approach which featured augmented responsiveness to Afghan needs might involve reduced externality in international presence and activities and find more significant connections with local institutions and values." It might also take the enterprise off a collision course with the Taliban.[34]

Crystallizing late in 2001, recommendations like these came to be known as the "light footprint" approach. Secretary-General Kofi Annan sounded the theme at the Tokyo fundraising conference in January 2002. "Our challenge is to help the Afghan people," he said. "Neither the United Nations nor anyone else can be a substitute for a functioning state with popular support. Afghanistan's course must be determined by Afghans. It must be led by Afghans and implemented by Afghans."[35] An amen chorus of senior officials from UNDP and other UN agencies joined in, with donor governments and NGOs not far behind. The Security Council itself specified that international assistance be routed through the Afghan Interim Administration. As time would tell, however, the institutional weight of the international aid apparatus requires more than solemn pronouncements in Tokyo and Bonn or, for that matter, in Kabul or Kandahar if it is to avoid trampling local institutions and initiatives.

Within a few short months after September 11, 2001, the bloom was off the rose and events were carrying the humanitarian international NGOs back to the future. The NGO group that had found much to be hopeful about in November 2001 was sounding far more negative by April 2002. "The optimism that had characterized last November's meeting—at that time, the opportunity to 'do things right this time' beckoned—had given way to seemingly inevitable obstacles." The disarray among aid actors on the ground represented "a step back: back to problems in former Yugoslavia and Kosovo in dealing with international military forces, back to Goma in the jockeying for positions among agencies on the ground, back to the Caucasus in terms of lack of respect for humanitarian actors, and to Somalia in terms of the rough edges between the UN's political agenda and humanitarian activities." The group's despondency reflected not only the recurrence of all-too-familiar pathologies but also the sense that "the options in Afghanistan grow more limited with each passing week."[36]

For their part, the Afghan authorities were increasingly alarmed by what they viewed as their own marginalization at the hands of the aid enterprise. They had begun speaking out early in 2002. The head of the Afghan Assistance Coordination Authority, Dr. Ashraf Ghani, a former World Bank official, urged that "donors respond to our priorities and not their own. Only through this coordination can we fulfill the common goal of creating government capacity and moving to reduce Afghanistan's reliance on the aid community."[37]

By November 2002, the sore was festering almost beyond redress. Comments from Kabul and the countryside suggested the depth of the animosity. Articulating his frustration at the international aid system, one knowledgeable and respected government minister decried "the continued operation and 'business as usual' of the parallel policy, delivery, information and coordination structures [which] undermines the sovereignty, legitimacy and rebuilding of competent state institutions. . . . From the legitimacy perspective, it is painful to be unable to respond to our constituency and refer them to the mercy of the UN and NGOs." The aid enterprise, in his icy judgment, was proving to be more imposition than facilitation.

Such views were reinforced by events in the field. A UNHCR official met with a group of Afghans who, wishing to return from Pakistan, had requested plastic sheeting, cooking utensils, and some food and funding to tide them over the transition period. The official explained that the UN pipeline had been interrupted and that these items, while part of UNHCR's standard refugee resettlement package, would not be available for several weeks. The leader of the group replied, "If this is the best the UN can do, we don't want the UN." An Afghan observer, hearing the UNHCR interpreter soften the comment in translation, insisted that the statement be rendered with full force.

What had gone wrong? Why the undisguised impatience and scorn for the international system, at whose mercy the government found itself? Why had the number of agencies and expatriate personnel not been limited in order to nip in the bud the perception that "the agencies are benefiting more than the local population"? There were three major difficulties, each going to the heart of the political economy of aid: the absence of mutual trust, the freewheeling aid marketplace, and the politicized nature of the interactions.

First, there was the internationals' evident lack of trust in the Afghan government, a sentiment the Afghan officials reciprocated in full. The special historical circumstances—a new and untested government with embryonic administrative capacity and limited authority outside the capital—predisposed donor governments to channel aid multilaterally and through NGOs rather than bilaterally. This is typical of most humanitarian emergencies. Bypassing the government, however, played a role in poisoning relationships with the authorities. It reflected a narrow understanding by international actors of the role of the state in promoting economic and political reform.

The decision to detour around the authorities was negative inasmuch as aid flows would be key in priming the pump for economic and political recovery. One observer sympathetic to the Afghan government's viewpoint noted that "the international community *made* this government. It is disingenuous to put people into power for reasons of stabilization and then to throw up your hands in despair when they're not performing." The fact that by April 2002 the authorities had drafted a coherent and impressive National Development Framework did little to overcome donor reluctance. As late as November 2002, a bilateral aid official wanted to retain control over basic needs assessment and resource allocation, in the interests, she said, of protecting these functions from political manipulation. Behind the rhetoric of facilitation was a reluctance to relinquish control.

Afghan government officials, bristling at the implication that the most representative ministerial group in Afghan history somehow lacked understanding of and commitment to its own people, saw the issue as one of power and authority. "The UN and NGOs for the last two decades have been used to ruling the relief and development processes in Afghanistan," commented a senior official with evident passion, "and now they find it difficult to give up that power." He acknowledged some legitimacy to international concerns about corruption and capacity, but after a certain point these become tired rationalizations for "business as usual" by the aid enterprise. Why should an internationally recognized and supported regime be treated like its Taliban predecessors, who were recognized only (for a while) by Pakistan, Saudi Arabia, and the United Arab Emirates? The new regime should be allowed to build a new future.

Tensions between the Afghan authorities and the aid internationals coalesced around the policies and person of Ashraf Ghani, whose succession of key positions in planning and finance thrust him into daily dealings with the international agencies. His knowledge of their missions and mandates, procedures and accountabilities was at least as grating for the agencies as his assertive, acerbic personality. He relished turning the tables on those who felt the new Afghan authorities were on trial. As a critic of donor UN agencies, NGOs, and contractors, his institutional literacy was downright intimidating.

The agencies and donors used an October 2002 visit by Clare Short, Britain's Minister of Overseas Development, to appeal to President Karzai for the donors and agencies to be treated with more respect. Like an earlier visit by Emma Bonino in 1997—a feel-good victory for outsiders but a setback for practitioners and activities on the ground—Short won the battle but lost a good part of the war. The authorities eased their confrontational approach with UN officials, but aid programs themselves did not change significantly. Indeed, her visit underscored the unsustainable externality of the aid enterprise.

Government animosity was not limited to the United Nations. The head of the International Council of Voluntary Agencies (ICVA), visiting Kabul in April 2002 on a trouble-shooting mission, reported, "There are repeated rumors of hostility, or at least resentment, from [Afghan] government representatives towards NGOs. These feelings may have been fed by the fact that for more than a decade, NGOs have been able to operate in Afghanistan in a vacuum, bypassing the central government, and sometimes even working against [it]."[38] Clearly the Afghans were not the only actor with a history.

The issue of trust will be considered in more detail in Chapter 9, which posits that the humanitarian enterprise at large is marked by a climate of mistrust and a lack of transparency. Afghanistan is Exhibit A in that thesis. Distrust among all the actors, international and national, governmental and otherwise, was so palpable and pervasive during the first two years of the revived international aid effort after 2001 that potential synergies were lost and important opportunities were missed.

A second factor in the demise of the apparently best-laid international plans: as soon as the political situation stabilized, the Afghan aid marketplace quickly opened for business. Arriving on the scene were not only emergency aid experts but also reconstruction and development practitioners, contributing to confusion over whether the problems were longer or shorter term. The humanitarian apparatus came with its own history, prescriptions, and modus operandi, doing things the way they were "always" done. For all the novelty and idiosyncrasies that confronted them, humanitarian officials had a strong sense of institutional pride which, particularly when challenged, was laced with a sense of infallibility. They were confident that they could make the aid system work for the Afghan authorities and people, as long as their hands weren't tied.

The UN agencies were peopled by seasoned veterans of crises elsewhere. That was, in fact, one of the lessons taken to heart by the system. Frontline field duties are too important to be left to recent university graduates and itinerating tourists, however well-meaning and energetic. The old hands arrived early from agency headquarters and other field postings, set up shop quickly, adapted to the fragile security situation, and proceeded to identify government counterparts and design aid programs. (One critical exception was the delayed arrival for several months of the head of the UN's "assistance pillar.") By fall 2002, UNICEF alone had more than three hundred expatriates in the country. They and other international agencies established relationships with senior ministry officials, keeping expatriate involvement largely behind the scenes.

What struck observers, however, was the extent to which UN agencies were on automatic pilot. In the initial round, their plans, moving on a fast track to agency headquarters, were routed only at the last minute past Afghan authorities, at the insistence of Ashraf Ghani. "What have you done this past year to promote livelihoods?" the head of the UN Voluntary Fund for Women in Afghanistan was asked at a government review session. WFP came to town with its standard food-for-work programs (the largest single element in all international aid transfers to the cash-starved government). But the Kabul authorities had a different idea. They held out for cash-for-work as more suited to local needs, audaciously threatening to take the dispute, if necessary, to WFP's executive board for adjudication. "I felt bruised, along with the pride of the organization," reported a senior WFP official after a particularly grueling session.

As time passed, the UN system began to hear the authorities' message: patented remedies that may have worked elsewhere were not welcome. In their Year 2 operating plans, several UN agencies reduced the number of expatriates. Habitat, apparently to its own surprise, built three thousand homes on the Shomali plain in three months, meeting a timetable dictated by the government. Other UN agencies were also taking notice. "Normally we give our ministerial counterpart a couple of Landrovers and let it go at that," conceded one UN country director, acknowledging at the same time that such an approach wouldn't fill the bill in Afghanistan.

In retrospect, UN agencies, NGOs, and donor governments were undoubtedly stronger due to pressure from the Afghan authorities to perform effectively and responsively. UN officials conceded privately that Ghani's pyrotechnics did indeed enhance performance. In fact, he may well have extracted the kind of coordination that the UN, left to its own devices, would have had difficulty delivering. Only in Eritrea, UN staff mused, had government expectations been so taxing.

For their part, private relief groups entered the high-profile post-9/11 period feeling like jilted lovers. Surveying the landscape in mid-2002, one analyst concluded, "NGOs feel increasingly beleaguered and unappreciated by a donor community and UN system that has, from the NGO point of view, almost totally depended upon NGO courage and ingenuity to deliver programmes throughout years of conflict."[39] While NGOs had paid their dues and were still needed, the ground had begun to shift beneath them as a new Afghan government, recognized for the first time in years by the international community, asserted its authority and began to discuss "controlling" them.

NGOs were accustomed to greater decision-making independence and programming freedom than the authorities—in need of visibility themselves—were willing to grant. One NGO official, who had held her agency's ground throughout the Taliban years, said she found the Taliban easier to deal with than the Karzai regime. The NGO picture was muddied by the fact that the NGO community, whose ranks had swollen into the hundreds, included fly-by-night outfits, long-distance runners, indigenous commercial groups fronting for special interests, as well as authentic human rights and civil society organizations. In other words, the NGO crowd in Afghanistan looked pretty much like it does in any other emergency.

In addition, there was uncertainty among NGOs about their relations with donors and the United Nations. Many NGOs that prided themselves as agents of social change were "offended by the assumption that they are simply implementing partners of official aid donors or UN agencies," reported one observer. Yet much of their funding came from donor governments, themselves an independent and profile-conscious lot. The go-it-alone approach of governments that pay the aid bills, the observer continued, creates "a donor market place in which NGOs can go shopping for support for their favored projects. There are many moments when the donors talk as if they were members of a cartel, but few occasions when they actually behave as one."[40]

Harnessing international organizations and resources to priorities identified by the government and people themselves was an explicit objective of the Karzai regime. President Karzai himself laid out the ground rules: "The [Afghan] government is the policy maker; implementation is undertaken by NGOs or the private sector, with selection through competitive bidding. Procurement, monitoring and supervision of the projects will be conducted by international consulting firms in partnership with government staff." The final feature was designed to assure skeptical outsiders of the new regime's accountability.

But, NGOs asked uneasily, how would the new process be implemented? What performance criteria would be used? Would the playing field be level? The best quality at the lowest price, NGOs said among themselves, is hardly a criterion that favors us over commercial or military suppliers. Activities geared to empowering local communities and leadership, which may initially cost more than quick-impact projects by the military, might over the longer haul prove more durable and cost-effective. Small wonder that NGOs feared that their role as implementing agencies might be living on borrowed time. At work here was a recurring NGO tension between acting as a service delivery vehicle and playing a wider range of roles.

The donors who drove the humanitarian apparatus had their own needs, whether for visibility, accountability, or a sense of engagement in the process. Some—the Dutch for example—made it clear that they were not interested in "flag-flying" but were happy to provide the United Nations with resources that would not be further identified as Dutch. "If you are a reliable and effective donor," said a Dutch official in Kabul, "you gain a lot of respect, including unsolicited compliments from recipient countries. We abstain from planting our flag, but others plant it for us. After all, quality counts. The less publicity about what you're doing, the more respect you gain." This approach, though unusual among donors, was music to the ears of the Afghan authorities.

The Japanese took a more typical position. "We are very much interested in seeing our flag," noted one official, who then produced a sample of the signs being placed at regular intervals along the Kabul to Kandahar road, where reconstruction was proceeding—haltingly, given security incidents—with major support from Tokyo. The sign featured the Afghan national flag, with UNDP and Japanese logos on either side. Tokyo also set up a special trust fund to which only Japan could contribute, creating something of an embarrassment for the World Bank, which administered it.

The two aid hegemons—the European Community and the United States—were more like the Japanese than the Dutch. "The European Community is the worst flag-flier around," confessed one EU official in a moment of self-criticism, adding that despite all the self-promotion, "still nobody understands us." The Americans, who contributed some 80 percent of all the international humanitarian resources to post-9/11 Afghanistan, were not known for their modest and self-effacing ways. In Afghanistan, as elsewhere, food commodities provided under U.S. Public Law 480 were labeled, bag upon bag, "Gift of the People of the United States." The issue of "badging" was not simply about the identification of contributions; it also reflected competition among donors themselves.

For the Afghan government, the issue of bilateral flag-flying had a special political dimension. "Flag-flying itself," said one minister, "is not a problem. In fact," he continued, "the government does not in principle object to the sources of aid being publicized. At a certain point, however, excessive donor visibility undercuts government legitimacy." For a government whose future turns on successfully establishing its bona fides with its own people, the issue is one of uncommon sensitivity.

Unless the authorities are *seen* to be improving the quality of Afghan life, the government's credibility will suffer. A political liability at home, the absence of an improved standard of living and enhanced security can also create problems on the outside. "Frequent trumpeting of overwhelming donor generosity and inflated claims of UN and NGO impact," notes one analyst, "are almost the sole diet that feeds public opinion concerning the international aid effort in Afghanistan."[41] The needs of the authorities and the aid apparatus thus pull in different directions. Small wonder that the political authorities in crisis settings are ultrasensitive to the profile of external aid efforts—or that the international aid enterprise itself, driven by its own perceived needs, is frequently associated with delusions of grandeur. Granted the difficulty of striking a reasonable balance of interests within the political economy of aid, the agencies and their donors have more to gain from the success of host government authorities than from external perceptions of their own contribution to that process.

In Afghanistan, as elsewhere, donors wrapped themselves in a mantle of coordination but then proceeded according to their own likes. Sensing the need for genuine coordination among the multiplicity of actors, in 2002 the Afghan authorities created a series of program groups and secretariats keyed to the country's national development framework (for example, return and reintegration, health and nutrition, water and sanitation). But this innovation met resistance from donors, reluctant to limit their activities to three or four groups or to conform to the processes envisioned. Instead, decisions were based on "HQ determined priorities, NGO nationality, bureaucratic definitions, length of funding of a project, [and] personal knowledge of the agency and project."[42] To complicate matters further, donor decisions reflected apprehension about which local groups were trustworthy to work with. Once again this suspicion soon became mutual.

All in all, the swarming of UN agencies, NGOs, and donor governments that comprised the aid marketplace in Afghanistan was not only an irritant to the national authorities but also an embarrassment to many of those directly involved. During a three-week period in early 2002, one Afghan NGO reported that sixteen of its staff had been offered jobs by the UN while an international NGO doubled local staff salaries twice within two months to prevent defection to larger organizations.[43] The government made no secret of its own frustration. Commenting on the wide differential between expatriate and national pay scales, President Karzai insisted (in vain) on a similar ratio of productivity. If expatriate aid workers were paid ten times as much as local staff, he said, they should be ten times as productive. "What about *your* capacity?" a senior government official would routinely and sarcastically inquire of NGOs who came to him with earnest offers to build the capacities of his ministry. "Do you speak Dari or Pashtun? Learn it and then come back to us and ask for 'counterparts.'"

Thus the light international footprint soon gave way to a heavy tread that proved difficult to alter, even though improvements were made over time. While aid agencies had legitimate concerns, it is difficult not to sympathize with the Afghan authorities. Personalities aside, why should they not insist that the international aid apparatus deliver what their country needed, as they themselves understood it? While members of the new regime were clearly not paragons of human rights virtue, dialogue on critical issues of public policy is preferable to international fiats and retroactive humanitarian hand wringing. "Putting recipient governments in the driver's seat" had become a common donor objective—or at least a common donor refrain—at the end of the 1990s. In Afghanistan, the authorities heard the words, and they were not wrong in believing that their new government, whatever its weaknesses, should not be relegated to side-car status.

In addition to mutual distrust and the jostling aid bazaar, politics also took a toll on the humanitarian system in Afghanistan after 2001. Conceptually, emergency assistance was well shielded from extraneous political considerations. UN Security Council Resolution 1401 of March 2002 drew a careful distinction between unconditional emergency assistance and conditional longer term aid. "[A]lthough humanitarian assistance should be provided wherever there is a need," the resolution stated, "recovery or reconstruction assistance ought to be provided through the Afghan Interim Administration and its successors, and implemented effectively where local authorities contribute to the maintenance of a secure environment and demonstrate respect for human rights."[44] That is, the distribution of aid not considered life-saving may take into account other issues such as compliance with human rights norms, but humanitarian assistance was to remain neutral, impartial, and independent.

The distinction recalled the language of the earlier strategic framework, which had sought to bring "politics, human rights, and international assistance together in a coherent and mutually reinforcing manner in the interests of promoting peace."[45] Yet that framework had failed to make structural changes in the management of UN activities in Afghanistan that would preserve the nonpolitical nature of emergency aid while capitalizing on the potential of other contributions to peace-building. The renewed attempt at coherence in 2001–2003 also largely failed.

In fairness, the problem was larger than Afghanistan. The coherence agenda has been a chronic conundrum for international policy makers for more than a decade. As analyst Mark Duffield puts it, "Rather than a failing of the UN in Afghanistan, the relationship between aid and politics represents a major unresolved and inadequately analyzed issue between donor governments."[46] In fact, the distinction made in the Security Council resolution offers a promising approach: protecting the independence of emergency assistance while expecting reconstruction and development inputs to reinforce a broader political framework. Elsewhere, too, there had been confusion about whether the protection of human rights should be given a prominent place in a peace strategy or deferred for a later stage of nation-building.

In the Afghan context, the political agendas of donor and host governments alike worked to subvert the intended distinction between emergency and reconstruction assistance. Humanitarian activities, which were to be unconditional, were interpreted broadly and blurred into other forms of postconflict aid that were subject to human rights and political criteria. Donors were clearly reluctant to fund reconstruction and development rather than emergency programs, which were less attractive to their publics and required greater involvement by the national Afghan authorities and greater integration into the national development plan. But the regime itself was anxious to move beyond emergency and on to reconstruction challenges.

The allocations of international aid showed a clear preference for NGOs and UN agencies to act as delivery channels rather than government ministries, which received only 20 percent of all available aid in Year 1. In one case, the U.K. Department for International Development (DFID) refused to fund the ministry of health as recommended by UNICEF, saying it would fund UNICEF itself, or use the money for something else. Donors also preferred short-term efforts of three to six months rather than for more extended periods. As elsewhere, they wanted quick impact projects, often not caring whether they were delivered by civilian aid agencies or the military.

Tragically, Afghanistan is a centuries-old graveyard of fast-paced efforts by outsiders, hell-bent on accomplishing this or that laudable goal in a hurry. Given the politicized history of all the aid efforts over the years, it would have been remarkable had activities after September 11, 2001 been insulated from the high-profile politics of the moment. USAID is perhaps the best case in point. The United States frequently sent out conflicting signals, perhaps reflecting the plethora of U.S. government officials involved. In fall 2002, a new director of the USAID program in Kabul told a group of NGOs that U.S. policy sought to have nothing to do with the Kabul government. Its preferred funding vehicles would be NGOs and the UN.

Weeks of embarrassment followed this apparent rebuff of the regime that the U.S. itself had installed. American views were subsequently clarified by then-Secretary of the Treasury Paul O'Neill. In Kabul for a brief visit—the length of such visits seemed inversely proportional to the rank of the official—O'Neill underscored President Bush's "commitment to 'help build a civil and just society.'" The president wanted more funds to be provided, O'Neill said, directly to the government of Afghanistan "rather than to international bodies and non-governmental organizations, in order to bolster the government's stature and credibility with its own people."[47]

The Provincial Reconstruction Teams (PRTs) provide another example of the infiltration of political objectives into assistance activities. The idea behind the PRTs was that groups of U.S. officials from a range of government agencies—civilian and military, aid, agriculture, and intelligence—would be deployed, beginning in 2002, in selected Afghan provinces. By the end of 2003, the PRTs had been extended to eight provinces, several of them managed by the militaries of other donor governments. The task, the United States said in explaining the original concept, was to identify human needs in selected nearby villages, to assist where possible using civic action funds provided by the Defense Department budget for quick impact projects, and to provide security for PRT personnel and associated activities, including intelligence-gathering. PRT interlocutors were the local authorities, including warlords, themselves often a source of local instability and human rights abuses. Defending their approach to local leaders, U.S. military officials explained, "It is more important to engage them than confront them." The Pentagon described the PRTs as engaged in "combat humanitarian work."

The PRTs raised difficult issues for both the United Nations and NGOs. Afghanistan, said a colonel in charge of civil-military affairs, represents "the first time in years that the U.S. military has had money and supplies to provide humanitarian relief on the ground." His use of the term "humanitarian" was a sore point within the aid community. "What's going on here," observed one NGO official with alarm, is a distortion of humanitarian affairs that "could redefine humanitarian work globally." While the United Nations sought to liaise with the coalition military, it was careful not to become directly associated with PRT activities, the purpose of which, coalition personnel made clear, was "to garner support for U.S. military objectives." Many NGOs also kept their distance, even from the USAID personnel who were colocated with other U.S. officials in PRT compounds. One concern among aid agencies was that PRTs did not vet their work with the Kabul authorities, placing their activities outside the national development framework and Afghan central government purview.

Problems notwithstanding, other countries began to examine the PRT idea, not least because President Karzai asked them to. In 2004, a group of Canadian military officers, NGOs and CIDA officials met to discuss the possibility of a Canadian PRT somewhere in Afghanistan. Interestingly, the most reluctant in the group were not the humanitarians (who *were* decidedly reluctant) but the military. They foresaw enough trouble protecting themselves, quite apart from having to look after do-gooders with a different agenda.

A comparison can be made between the PRT model and the fortified hill towns of fifteenth-century southern France and Spain. At that time, the rich and the middle classes stayed inside the town walls, venturing out only by day to travel and to supervise the farm work of peasants. The towns were walled for good reason—the peasants, who lived in abject poverty, were wont to rebel, burning crops and rampaging across the countryside. As governments and the church began to see that a system based on enclaves, with a few rich and many poor, was unworkable, they also began to appreciate that self-interest properly understood required a more inclusive vision of society and a time frame that went beyond the immediate planting season.

By early 2004, Afghanistan's government ministries had been strengthened and essential social welfare undertakings, such as vaccination campaigns and education activities, had been mounted. Capacity-building efforts were beginning to shift from the national ministries in Kabul to needs at the provincial level. But the government was still having difficulty exercising authority in the hinterlands, and there was continuing confusion over whether the major challenges were humanitarian or structural.

The "light footprint" had deepened, as it did later in Iraq, with growing official and popular discontent over the heavy expatriate presence, unaccompanied by serious improvement in the quality of everyday life. NATO had assumed responsibility for the International Security Assistance Force, which had been authorized to try its hand at security outside of Kabul, although it had been slow off the mark. Responding to a growing number of violent incidents that targeted civilians and aid workers, the coalition was forced to redeploy some of its forces from provincial reconstruction to military operations against die-hard Taliban and al Qaeda remnants. Aid personnel were arguably more vulnerable for their association with a struggling national government and unpopular international policies.

In hindsight, many of these developments were predictable. The past quarter-century in Afghanistan, combined with the recent history of the humanitarian enterprise elsewhere, have come together with considerable negative synergy. Afghans familiar with the permutations of aid across their complex history have confronted an arthritic aid apparatus managed by people with limited knowledge of the local terrain and sensitivities. The interplay between two sets of relatively immovable objects has affected both, leaving each bloodied but largely unbowed. By most accounts, the Afghan authorities have enjoyed some success in pressing the international aid apparatus into the service of their own objectives. The aid apparatus, however, has made distressingly few structural changes to offset the weaknesses that are likely to recur in future crises.

"Afghanistan comes with a history," note two seasoned observers. "Having survived years away from the spotlight of international attention, Afghans might be forgiven for being confused at the haste with which decisions are now being made about the future of their country. Afghans might not have much left, but they do have their memories."[48]

5

Alarums and Excursions

We say we are going to stay the course, when we are always looking for the exit. Nation-building could be an exercise in solidarity between rich and poor, the possessors and the dispossessed. Too often, it is an exercise in mutual betrayal.

—Michael Ignatieff[1]

At the end of December 2003, a 6.6 magnitude earthquake struck the town of Bam in southeastern Iran. Estimates of the death toll reached 50,000, with untold losses to property and livelihoods. Within days, relief teams and supplies had arrived from two dozen countries, including Russia, France, Italy, Jordan, and Ukraine. The United States sent a team of sixty doctors and twenty logisticians, setting up a field hospital near Bam. Bill Garvelink, deputy assistant administrator of USAID's Bureau for Humanitarian Assistance, went to Iran and held talks with Iranian ministers, the first U.S. official to do so in twenty-five years. "We don't focus on political issues," Garvelink was quoted as saying, and Iranian President Mohammad Khatami thanked Washington for its assistance. The United States agreed not to fly the American flag over its tent hospital.

It did not take long, however, for the humanitarian effort to turn political. On New Year's Day 2004, the White House suggested that it might send Republican Senator Elizabeth Dole, a former president of the American Red Cross, to Iran with a further shipment of relief supplies. A member of President George Bush's family might possibly accompany her. Clearly, this was not going to be a forgotten emergency. Iranian State Radio, widely regarded as a mouthpiece for the country's conservative clergy, ramped up the political stakes, saying, "The Americans, by publicizing their aid to Iran, have ineptly tried to implement their duplicitous policy of creating a rift between the Iranian nation and government."

Chapter 2 on Sierra Leone demonstrated the fine art of "forget-ting" serious emergencies when there are no political issues at stake and when a country has no geopolitical importance to major aid-giving donors. It also calculated the high cost of remedial humanitarian and peacekeeping action when an emergency—which would certainly have cost much less to address earlier in its evolution—can no longer be ignored. Chapter 3 on East Timor showed how humanitarian assistance actually *can* work when donors are prepared to sing from the same song sheet, even if they were twenty-five years late and even if their motives were mixed. But Chapter 4 on Afghanistan demonstrated not just the relentlessly political perversion of humanitarian assistance. It also revealed the more generalized inability of the humanitarian system to function coherently, even when it makes the most conscious effort in a decade to do so.

This chapter touches briefly on four other humanitarian emergen-cies, examining both recurring themes and issues raised in earlier chap-ters. For decades, humanitarianism in the Sudan has acted as a substi-tute for serious political engagement, sustaining not just human life but aid agencies and possibly the conflict itself. Operation Uphold Democ-racy and the attendant humanitarian operations in Haiti during the mid-1990s reiterate problems of time and timing—the consequences of short-term thinking, exits without strategy, and aid unremittingly tied to donor purse strings. An examination of relief modalities in Bosnia demonstrates the hollow core at the center of pontifications about the importance of building local capacities and civil society. And a review of the Southern Africa drought of 2002 revisits the issue of needs assess-ment and evaluation. The chapter ends with a brief reflection on the role of frontline workers in crisis situations.

The Sudan: Aid in Conflict

In a particularly bloody and inhumane period of world history, the Sudan must rank near the top in the list of countries most inhospitable to the fundamental human rights and day-to-day survival of its people. Drought-related famine and conflict-related distress are implicated in generations of widespread suffering, and the policies of government and insurgent groups have caused or compounded the misery. A persistent theme throughout a fifty-year period has been the proximity of and uneasy interplay between politics and humanitarian action.

Civil war from 1955 (shortly after the Sudan became independent) until 1972 between the largely Arab and Muslim North and the predomi-nantly Christian, animist, and black south claimed many lives and dis-placed even more people. After a decade of relatively peaceful coexistence,

the country experienced searing drought and widespread famine during 1983–1985 and erupted once again into civil strife. During 1988 alone, war-related deaths claimed the lives of an estimated 250,000 persons. A period of on-again, off-again conflict throughout the 1990s and into the new millennium brought additional death and displacement to civilians, north and south alike.[2]

Against this backdrop of suffering, several generations of relief activities have been mounted. In the spring of 1972, the United Nations, donor governments, NGOs, and the Red Cross Movement acted quickly to capitalize on the return of peace to launch a program that would assist refugees returning to the south from neighboring countries to restart their lives. In 1984–1986, the United Nations mounted a large antifamine effort, largely in the north, run by the Office of Emergency Operations in Africa, a new institutional construct designed to circumvent the established UN aid bureaucracy. In 1989, the UN launched Operation Lifeline Sudan (OLS), extracting commitments from the Khartoum authorities and the Sudan People's Liberation Army (SPLA) in the south to core humanitarian principles, including access in both government- and insurgent-controlled areas of the country.

The magnitude of international resources provided for use in the Sudan after the inauguration of OLS in 1989 placed Sudan in the middle of the aid recipient countries. In 2001, its humanitarian aid levels made it the eighth most generously funded country by DAC donors, receiving less than Afghanistan and the Balkans but more than Sierra Leone and Mozambique. The UN Consolidated Appeal for 2004 alone requested $465 million in "humanitarian relief for 3.5 million people and transitional aid to support the peace process in Africa's largest country, wracked by 20 years of civil war and 'a vicious cycle of misery.'" The funds were to underwrite 160 projects "proposed by 13 United Nations relief, development and human rights agencies and by 25 non-governmental and international organizations."[3] Country pledges by donors in 2004 were once again expected to be substantial, making the Sudan one of the world's larger humanitarian operations.

The Sudan's half-century of woe has also witnessed numerous peace initiatives. The Addis Agreement in 1972 successfully brought down the curtain on postindependence civil strife; another agreement in Addis in December 1988 stemmed the bloodshed of that year. To address resumed violence, later peace talks have taken place under a variety of auspices, including the Organization for African Unity (OAU), the Intergovernmental Authority on Development (IGAD), and concerned states such as the United States, United Kingdom, and Kenya.

Peace negotiations between the Khartoum authorities and the SPLA were set to resume once again in early 2004. Anticipating their success, the announcement of the 2004 UN financial appeal noted that negotiations were "at a critical stage. A comprehensive agreement promised to bring 'unprecedented opportunities as well as challenges for the people of Sudan in a fragile, transitional period.'" The aid request included "capacity building and quick start, quick impact programmes designed to start up as soon as a peace agreement is signed." The senior UN official involved observed that "early peace dividends" from such activities could "help sustain the collective will to give peace a chance." The likely opening presented by the advent of peace had boosted the overall level of aid requested.

The Sudan's experience with aid and peace would seem to be largely positive. But upon closer examination, it becomes evident that the political economy of war and the ripple effects of international assistance have conspired against the achievement and maintenance of peace. For the past fifteen years—a long time as relief operations go—OLS has been the major point of internationally managed interaction between north and south. OLS has provided the framework within which most NGOs have functioned. Its priorities, reflected in the annual consolidated appeal, have been the focal point of donor government support. Its management and monitoring have been the task of a never-ending succession of high-level UN officials, virtually none with prior experience in the country or even elsewhere on the continent. The turnover of more junior aid officials, and, for that matter, of donor government ambassadors, has been almost as rapid. A tour of duty in the Sudan, nowadays a frequent entry on aid worker resumes, has a certain cachet.

As a focal point for overall international engagement with the Sudan, OLS has proved a rather uncomfortable fit. An early indication of problems surfaced during its first year, when an increasingly heavy international footprint emphasized the movement of relief supplies through agreed "corridors of tranquility" rather than on nurturing and extending the fragile peace arrangements on which activities in the north and south were premised. In one telling encounter, OLS pioneer James P. Grant, UNICEF director and Special Representative of the UN Secretary-General to the Sudan, was approached during a visit by a delegation of Nairobi-based religious and peace groups, who asked that more attention and resources be directed to peace concerns. Grant understood the urgency of their appeal but told his visitors that he regretted not having peace in his mandate.[4] The incident provides an early example of the lack of coherence between the political and diplomatic aspects of the United Nations and its aid activities that would continue to perplex the system, both institutionally and operationally, for years to come.[5]

With each passing year, the belligerents' commitment to the humanitarian principles they had agreed to in 1989 became more tenuous and contested. The Khartoum regime strafed civilian targets and then used the ensuing insecurity to deny access by air and ground to aid personnel. The insurgents placed major government-held cities in the south under siege, denying access of life-sustaining essentials and relief workers. Both sides used food—much of it internationally donated—as a political weapon. Commanders on both sides scorched the earth when it served their military or political purposes. Increasing the observation of international norms—one of the objectives of OLS—seemed to elude the international community. Each side committed with impunity a series of attacks that killed and wounded aid workers.[6] To be sure, the Sudan had been the first country to sign the Convention on the Rights of the Child when the international conference convened in New York in fall 1989. Yet back at home, where commitments were tested against military exigencies, behavior flaunted humanitarian norms.

By 1996, seven years into OLS, there had been some fifteen diplomatic missions and six renegotiated agreements on humanitarian access. More than once, the program almost closed. Yet however ornery the belligerents and however egregious their violations of commitments, the program's trajectory over the years was remarkably constant. "The default option for any foreign initiative to do with Sudan," notes one study with evident exasperation, "is 'let's maintain OLS."[7] In fact, the vulnerability of relief efforts in the Sudan has its roots in the pre-OLS mid-1980s, when the belligerents displayed a cavalier attitude toward international aid and toward their own responsibilities to allow humanitarian access and monitoring.

A major OLS study commissioned by the United Nations and released in July 1996 devoted three hundred pages to data and analysis
but only a single six-line paragraph to what it considered the successes
of the program.[8] The once innovative and promising international initiative had become, it concluded, a prisoner of the conflict itself. A second but more independent study, published in May 1997 by African
Rights, a tough-minded research and advocacy group based in London,
noted that the official OLS review had yet to produce meaningful
change and challenged those responsible to introduce major reforms.

Where the UN-commissioned report had noted that "humanitarian
assistance closely follows the dynamics of the conflict," the independent
study found, "As the years have passed, OLS (along with other humanitarian activities in the war zones) have become closely integrated into
the conflict itself."[9] Where the official review observed the emergence
of "two markedly different contractual regimes" operated by the United
Nations from Khartoum and Nairobi, African Rights saw the basic
humanitarian principles of neutrality, impartiality, and independence
violated by the compromises that OLS administrators had made to keep
operations afloat north and south. The independent study was refresh-
ingly hard-hitting and critical, asserting that the earlier review process
had been "controlled by governments and the UN, and therefore
remained hostage to their own priorities and institutional interests."[10]

If the impacts of aid on conflict have gone largely unaddressed, the
blame must be shared not only by aid officials and diplomats but also by
evaluators and researchers. Social scientists, too, have beaten a path to the
Sudan, many of them in the employ of governments and agencies, often
with graduate students—the next generation of aid evaluators—in tow.
But report writers and academics have, unfortunately, little to show for
their labors in the way of institutional change. There is, it seems, a political economy of research paralleling the political economy of humanitarian action, which itself has many givens that undercut the identification
and implementation of necessary reforms. The two Sudan studies not
only confirmed the problems of aid in conflict but demonstrated the relative strengths and weaknesses of independent versus in-house reviews.

The cottage industry of humanitarian research that has flourished
in recent years has not succeeded in producing commensurate improvements in relief and rights operations. In fact, some commentators have
observed that "the range of humanitarian evaluation work is rapidly
expanding, and the gap between practice and guidance is *growing*."[11]
The notion that their labors are not contributing to significant improvement in humanitarian operations is as unsettling to evaluators as
is the charge against practitioners that their efforts are fueling conflicts.

The humanitarian enterprise, even when confronted by solid evidence, whether from internal or external reviews, that it is being abused

by belligerents or contributing to conflict, takes little remedial action. The idea of terminating program operations in the Sudan in order to extract greater compliance from the warring parties was seldom seriously considered, although in July and August 2000 the United Nations suspended WFP/OLS flights for eight days until it received an apology, requested by the secretary-general, from the president of the Sudan for strafing incidents that targeted a UNICEF vaccination team, an ICRC plane, and WFP aircraft on a humanitarian mission that had been pre-approved by the Khartoum authorities. This, the first OLS suspension in eleven years, was done to sustain the continuity of operations over the longer haul.

OLS also provides some dramatic and not-so-positive examples of the aid marketplace in action. One such is the growth of Lokichoggio in northern Kenya. In 1989 a small landing strip with a few houses, "Loki" is now a major town with the infrastructure needed to sustain multi-faceted relief operations throughout the enormous territory of the southern Sudan. From a management point of view, the evolution may be positive and even cost-effective. As a demonstration of the undue emphasis on material resources of a major relief operation, however, the scene comes across far more negatively. The Khartoum authorities, who make regular overflights, have compared Loki to a scene from Graham Hancock's *The Lords of Poverty*, a scathing critique of the work and life-styles of aid workers.

In reviewing the influence of political economy factors on humanitarian action, the steady-state profile of the Sudan at a relatively high level of international engagement across the past decade is noteworthy. "The problem is not the lack of attention," concludes the African Rights study, "it is lack of knowing what can be done. Almost every international instrument of pressure has been applied to Sudan except military intervention or all-out trade sanctions. They have simply failed to work." (Following the U.S. bombing of suspected terrorist training camps in 1998 in the wake of the attacks on U.S. embassies in Nairobi and Dar es Salaam, there is now one less arrow in the international quiver.) The Sudan hardly constitutes a forgotten emergency, only a maddeningly persistent one.

In fact, OLS over time has taken on a life of its own. Earlier on, those who felt that the relief effort was contributing to the conflict had an obligation to make the case for the cessation or suspension, reduction or recalibration of international assistance. Over time, however, the tables have turned. The burden has now shifted to those who believe that OLS *should* be continued, chronic side-effects notwithstanding. In 1997 it was noted that OLS had "become an institution in its own right, determined to preserve itself. Its donors are also determined to see it continue, for a range of reasons."[12] With the eventual advent of peace,

relief work may morph into a reconstruction and development effort—
but without ever having examined the extent to which earlier infusions
of material aid over numerous years had played a role in sustaining the
war. It would be distressing if future efforts remained uninformed by
lessons identified from earlier involvement, as was the case when the
level of aid activity in Afghanistan increased following the demise of the
Taliban and the arrival of the Karzai government.

The toughest question faced by humanitarians during these years of
human agony in the Sudan was whether to curtail or discontinue operations in response to abuses of assistance by belligerents. "At no point
over the fifteen years could we say, 'Let's stop,'" recalls one senior UN
program manager. "There were always people desperately needing
assistance. Yet over the fifteen years of OLS, large numbers died and
enormous numbers were displaced. At the same time, the UN did build
up a capacity to effectively help people in need. Without OLS, the suffering would have been greater, the turmoil worse, the possibility of
engagement lost." The aid official's logic is as compelling as it is
humane. Yet the contrary view must also be taken seriously: that the
relief of suffering cannot be pursued in a political vacuum, unreinforced
by diplomatic efforts to end the causes of the bloodletting.

There is, then, a certain irony to the world's massive humanitarian
endeavors in the Sudan. A creative humanitarian initiative with global
ramifications, OLS soon became a force implicated in sustaining a conflict, which in turn generated suffering for which the United Nations
then appealed for resources. Discussions about reducing or refocusing
activities were discounted as unfair to vulnerable groups; yet sustaining
the lives of vulnerable civilians as an end in itself seemed shortsighted
and devoid of the necessary context provided by the ongoing war.
Where positive synergies between aid and peace had been foreseen,
negative synergies actually resulted. An NGO, reviewing the mounting
operational problems encountered by the highly acclaimed relief effort,
concluded rather disconsolately, "The principle is the best part of
OLS."[13] After millions of deaths and countless abuses of international
humanitarian and human rights and refugee law, principles actually
seemed to count for very little.

Haiti: Nation-Building Lite

Haiti, one of the poorest countries in the world, was beset by corruption and violence for the better part of the twentieth century.[14] More
clearly than most countries, Haiti exemplifies the merry-go-round
nature of bad governance, degenerative change, conflict, and external
intervention. Events during the 1990s also demonstrate the challenges

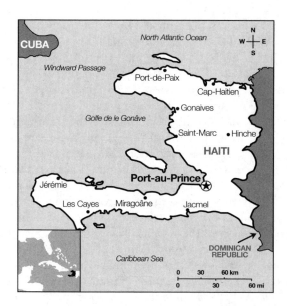

faced by external relief and rights agencies in attempting to break the repetitive cycle. The experience underscores the extent to which donor-driven policies—in this instance, nation-building on the cheap—can exacerbate suffering and human rights violations.

With the demise of the Duvalier family regime in 1986, there ensued a five-year struggle for power between the old autocratic elite and those seeking fundamental change. The election of Jean-Bertrand Aristide in 1990 looked like the winds of change at last were blowing over Haiti, but a military coup in September 1991 put an apparent end to hopes for democracy and good government. Over the following three years, Haiti was subjected to Organization of American States (OAS) sanctions, a worldwide fuel and arms embargo, and finally, in July 1994, military intervention authorized by a UN Security Council Resolution. GDP—already low—fell by 17 percent in 1992–1993 and by an additional 10 percent in 1994. Agricultural production and exports declined dramatically and the economic and social infrastructure, such as it was, fell apart.

During the three-year arms and oil embargo, Haiti became a full-fledged humanitarian emergency. Violence, political suppression, and hunger stalked the land. Between three and five thousand people were killed, and at one time as many as three hundred thousand were displaced. So desperate were people to escape their plight that tens of thousands took to the sea in makeshift boats, hoping to reach Florida— or anywhere. In 1991, the United States was feeding fifteen thousand

Haitian refugees who had been picked up by the Coast Guard and relo-cated to the U.S. military base at Guantanamo Bay in Cuba. In one day, July 4, 1994, the U.S. Coast Guard picked up 3,200 boat people. The next day it intercepted 2,800. Haitians were taking their plight to sea, and to the nightly television news across America. A smallish inter-national security issue was now becoming a major media event.

Finally, after months of negotiations and the imminent threat of a full-force military invasion, the military government stepped down. In September 1994, a U.S.-led multinational force entered Haiti. As some-one put it, the force was "no more multinational than the Republican Party is multicultural,"[15] but that was beside the point. Operation Uphold Democracy, with twenty thousand U.S. troops behind it, restored the Aristide government to office, in much the same way as British military intervention had preserved the Kabbah government in Sierra Leone.

Both the immediate and long-term needs in Haiti were enormous. Productive capacity had been severely damaged, and there was an urgent need for tools, seeds, animals, working capital, and infrastructure devel-opment. In January 1995, Haiti received donor pledges of $1.2 billion in reconstruction support, to be disbursed over the following eighteen months. But the role of the primary interlocutor, the U.S. military, was not nation-building. Long-time Haiti watcher Bob Shacochis describes the policy this way:

> Except for letting the army's engineers tinker with the existing electri-cal and water infrastructure, there were not going to be any community projects in Haiti assigned to the military. No nation building . . . an order direct from the White House. Instead, the idea was for the troops to hand the ball off to the NGOs and the PVOs, and the tree-huggers would dig the place back out of the grave. But by the end of the first week in October [three weeks after the military arrived], the Special Forces started looking around and grumbling—the NGOs and PVOs, vaunted and saintly, were no-shows.

One problem for NGOs, "vaunted and saintly" or not, was money: Who would write the necessary checks and for what purpose? During the three-year military government, some humanitarian assistance, much of it in the form of food aid, had arrived in Haiti. The largest provider of food was USAID, followed by Canada and the European Union. WFP, too, programmed food, much of it also originating in the United States. As much as 75 percent of the food provided by USAID was delivered by three NGOs—CARE, the Adventist Development and Relief Agency, and Catholic Relief Services.[16] Altogether, food aid programs were feed-ing between six hundred thousand and a million people a day.

One Canadian NGO took a slightly different approach to food, more out of necessity than anything else. The Centre canadien d'étude et de la coopération internationale (CECI) had been obliged by the government of Canada to withdraw all of its expatriate staff from Haiti. But the NGO's Haitian staff came up with an innovative proposal. They would combine imported Canadian relief food with local food purchases. They would mill the grain locally and develop a local distribution network. Negotiations with CIDA were no simple matter, not least because the organization has a standing rule that 90 percent of its food aid must originate in Canada. But in this case, buying locally injected cash into the economy and gave farmers work. Milling locally provided jobs, and using local trucking firms did the same in a place where most foreign NGOs maintained their own vehicle fleets in order to reduce the risk of corruption.

In the end, the project injected more than $2.25 million into the economy, creating jobs and feeding six hundred thousand people at the height of the crisis. It also built local capacities to plan and deliver an assistance program that was humanitarian and developmental at the same time. A CIDA evaluation was positive, and in 1996 CECI was recognized by the FAO as one of ten organizations in the world to have made an important contribution to improving the food security of developing nations. The Haiti project was singled out as an example of special innovation.

With the immediate emergency over, however, CIDA was no longer interested in innovative food delivery programs in Haiti, at least not innovations that breached the 90 percent Canadian content rule. Writing about CECI's frustrations, Kathy Mangones, a seasoned NGO worker, said, "It is ironic that just at the moment when the program should have been able to expand its operations and systematize its approach, CECI was obliged to do new gymnastics in order to comply with donor requirements adapted more to the needs of the donor country than the needs of the recipient."[17] Those who pay the piper call the tune.

Gradually, as Shacochis puts it, "in the diffusing contrails of the invasion, the humanitarians had begun to appear, isolated sightings and then a great fluttering on the horizon, like a migration of monarch butterflies."[18] However, most of them, like CECI, were tied to the purse-strings of bilateral and multilateral donors. Several donors initiated employment programs aimed at rehabilitating or reconstructing basic social and economic infrastructure: roads, irrigation and drainage, schools and health centers, potable water systems, erosion control, and soil conservation projects. With an expenditure of at least $100 million, more than one million person-months of work was created for unskilled and low-skilled workers throughout the country up to December 1996.[19] Income was earned, hundreds of kilometers of road were rehabilitated, hundreds of schools and clinics were rebuilt, and thousands of acres of erosion-threatened slopes were protected. In this respect, the efforts were generally effective.

But a 1997 evaluation looked beyond the immediate outputs and found that many of the projects had been hastily planned. "As a result, not enough time was dedicated to ensure proper participation and involvement of beneficiary communities and local authorities. There was not enough consideration for post-project operation and maintenance; and in practice those maintenance considerations—if ever planned (in a few best cases)—have not been implemented thoroughly."[20] The evaluation said that labor-intensive public works and infrastructure rehabilitation were not only valid, they were a high priority. But tied to their emergency origins, they lacked the required development perspective and the time frame needed to do the job properly. As a result, they failed to generate lasting employment that might have occurred by promoting small contractors and sustainable community improvement committees.

This is not a new type of finding, nor was it new in 1997. Many possibilities for doing aid differently have been well documented and well-known for years. A successful CIDA-supported school reconstruction project in postwar Nigeria documented the same lessons in community management, local employment creation, and the construction of durable buildings and furniture as far back as 1972.[21] Mary Anderson and Peter Woodrow documented many such examples in *Rising from the Ashes*, a 1989 book well-known to aid practitioners.[22] All the lists at the end of all the evaluations and studies of postwar reconstruction say the same thing: Projects have to be part of a coherent plan that is based on sound knowledge of the people, their culture, and history. Take the time to do it properly and to ensure that there will be ongoing support if this is required; involve local authorities and communities at all levels of planning and implementation; and don't start, no matter what the pressure, until they are fully on board.

Under political pressure from donors to make a difference quickly, however, institutional memory tends to develop amnesia. Quick impacts may not be long term, but they are impacts. "It's better to have a working road for four months than not at all," said one aid manager in Haiti.[23] Given the resources available and given the events of the previous ten if not one hundred years, this was not an attitude that Haiti needed at the moment of its greatest development opportunity.

There is more. USAID's Office of Transition Initiatives (OTI) was created in 1994 as a separate office within the Bureau of Humanitarian Response to serve as a distinct operating unit that could carry out "overt political programs in crisis-prone countries in transition from war to peace. OTI's goal is to enhance development prospects in priority, conflict-prone countries by empowering the citizenry of a country so that they can move towards democratic self-rule."[24]

In its first three years, OTI became operational in Angola, Bosnia, Haiti, and Rwanda and initiated activities in Liberia and Sierra Leone. It funded radio and print media programs, projects run by civic groups aiming to bridge communal divisions, projects promoting human rights and democratic political processes, and projects aimed at training and reintegrating demobilized soldiers. One such project involved the demobilization of the entire Haitian army (Forces Armées d'Haiti– FAd'H) to neutralize the short-term threat it posed to peace and to U.S. peacekeepers in Haiti, to prevent possible further security disruptions over the longer term, and to lay a foundation for reintegrating former soldiers into Haitian society.

Some 5,482 former soldiers were processed through a program that provided career counseling, vocational training, stipends, tool kits, and a job referral service. In some respects the program was remarkably successful. Despite difficulties with government, it was well coordinated, appropriately funded, and sufficiently flexible to deal with unforeseen problems as they arose. Good quality training was provided to the 4,867 men who graduated from the program. Most received tool kits, and most participated in the job referral service.[25] A second evaluation, conducted several months after the program had concluded, found that the primary objectives had been met. Engaging the former soldiers in a training program had helped protect U.S. military forces and had contributed to short-term peace and security. By continuing the program over two years, a longer breathing space had been secured for political, security, and economic transitions. There was only one glitch: "Although the demobilization program gave the former FAd'H some of the skills required for employment, full reintegration is not occurring because of the lack of progress in other areas."[26]

This positive-sounding conclusion, which must have been laboriously vetted around conference tables in Port-au-Prince and Washington, rather understates the problem. Of the 4,867 men trained, only 304 had found employment, 28 of them as security guards—not a job for which training had been provided. The "lack of progress in other areas" that prevented 94 percent of the men from finding jobs included low economic growth—hardly surprising, given Haiti's economic history— and the possibility of social stigma attached to former soldiers. But, the evaluation observed, employment was only "a tertiary objective of the program" (and in some ways more a hope than a real goal).

It doesn't matter, then, that 1,790 men were trained as auto mechanics, probably doubling or even tripling the number of mechanics in Haiti, or that 602 men were trained in computers for a job market that could realistically employ only a tiny fraction of them. Even as this expensive and rather cruel hoax was being perpetrated on men who, in their previous lives, were hardened and sometimes brutal soldier-policemen, a new national police force was being created. The same evaluation rated the new force as small, ill-equipped, undertrained, badly paid, and composed of officers too young and inexperienced to handle the job they had been given.

In its "Results Review for 1996 and Resource Request for 1998," OTI noted some of the lessons learned in its first three years. One was that exit strategies need to be flexible enough to respond to changes in circumstance, and that the two-year limitation on an OTI country operation might not be realistic. The problem of linking real people, who pose real threats, to real opportunities that will keep them out of serious trouble—the fundamental development challenge—is not mentioned. As a step on the transitional path between emergency and development, the Haiti Demobilization and Reintegration Program can perhaps be regarded "more as a hope than a real goal." "More a hope than a real goal"? "Better to have a working road for four months than not at all"? With friends like these, who needs enemies?

A dozen years after the coup and almost a decade after Operation Uphold Democracy, Haiti remained by far the poorest country in the hemisphere, beset by human rights abuse, electoral fraud, a shrinking economy, and hunger. Jean-Bertrand Aristide stepped down in 1996 after his term in office, as the constitution required, but he was reelected in 2000. Vote rigging caused some donors to withhold development assistance, while journalists, judges, magistrates, and opposition politicians were harassed and arrested. Police brutality was commonplace.

Two-thirds of Haitians still live below the poverty line. Half the population remains illiterate and every health indicator in the country is moving in the wrong direction. One child in four under the age of fifteen has no parents, is disabled, works as a domestic servant, or lives and works in the street. In 2003 the United Nations sent out a special $84 million appeal for Haiti to focus attention on what it called Haiti's "silent, chronic and forgotten crisis." Few donors stepped forward with cash. On January 1, 2004, Haiti celebrated two hundred years of independence from France. Not far from where the dignitaries were making speeches, the police used tear gas and clubs to disperse antigovernment demonstrators. Two months later, Aristide was gone and a new international peacekeeping force had arrived.

During the 1990s, three years of OAS and UN resolutions, threats, bluster, much negotiation, an economic blockade that increased the suffering of an already damaged population, and finally the imminent threat of a full-scale military attack caused a bad military regime to step down. A democratically elected government was restored to power, a good thing. During those three years, humanitarian assistance, provided mainly by NGOs and UN agencies, took a slight edge off the tragedy. When the opportunity at last arrived to "uphold democracy," however, there was little to uphold. Almost everything in Haiti had to be built, not rebuilt, and nation-building was not what donors had bargained for. The rush of ill-conceived projects was exacerbated by too much, rather than too little, money. Or too much too soon, and for too little, time. Paralyzed during three years of military rule, donors were now in a hurry to declare victory and return to business as usual. Not surprisingly, on the rocky ground of Haitian politics and history, Nation-Building Lite stumbled and then fell.

By 2004, Haiti was looking much as it did fifteen years earlier. With most development assistance frozen, the country was left once again to the best devices of peacekeepers and humanitarian agencies, and to whatever they could raise from unresponsive governments.

Bosnia: The Importance of Local

Before the breakup of Yugoslavia in the early 1990s, the part of the country that became Bosnia-Herzegovina lacked a tradition of civil society institutions. When the country emerged from the 1995 Dayton Peace Agreement, one of the challenges was to reorient the thinking of government officials toward the nascent nonprofit sector. Officials did not understand what an NGO was or what the establishment of an independent sector might mean. They grouped NGOs with political parties, for-profit associations, service deliverers and with businesses, which paid heavy payroll and social security taxes. Aid projects were

thus vulnerable to high rates of taxation at first. The growth of non-profit as well as private sector institutions was one of many elements in the broader transition from a command to a market economy, a complex process that would hardly happen overnight. In 1993 only a handful of local NGOs had been involved in relief and reconstruction work; by 1996, the number had risen to ninety-eight.

Into this institutional vacuum descended the international humanitarian apparatus. From the outset, it overshadowed nascent local institutions and even fledgling national and local government entities. Newly arriving aid agencies were the embodiment of intense interest in the region, particularly in Europe. And Bosnia-Herzegovina was the first post–Cold War conflict that could be reached from western Europe by plane in an hour or by road in a day. It was the first conflict to which European youth and other adventurers could easily hitchhike. Geography as well as human interest and solidarity thus ensured that as the bloodletting and ethnic cleansing surged in 1992–1993, ad hoc groups in European cities from Stockholm to Strasbourg sprang up to collect relief items, rent trucks, and head for Tuzla or Sarajevo. This freelance humanitarianism, while a barometer of international concern, would complicate the tasks of the traditional aid agencies and their dealings with local institutions.

The initial wave of international NGOs arrived in Bosnia-Herzegovina in 1992. Their numbers went from 65 in March 1993 to 126 in September of that year. Of this group, a score became implementing partners of UNHCR, providing an array of social welfare services to the region's large refugee and displaced population—estimated at 1.3 million persons in Bosnia-Herzegovina alone. UNHCR itself in November had 678 staff (226 expatriate and 452 local) in thirteen offices around the region. The ICRC had almost one thousand staff (202 international delegates and 790 local employees) in its twenty-nine offices. In a rare departure from its normal procedures, the International Council of Voluntary Agencies (ICVA) set up coordination and liaison offices in both entities of Bosnia and Herzegovina.

One early order of business for the internationals involved finding or developing counterpart organizations. This was not difficult for NGOs that already had numbers on the local scene: faith-based NGOs—Catholic, Orthodox, mainline Protestant, and evangelical—and the Red Cross movement. The Bosnian Red Crescent Society already had working relationships with its counterparts in Geneva. Many aid groups did not, however, and they scoured the landscape for partners. In some instances, international agencies found preexisting groups; in others, they created them.

A second order of business was to establish programs. A very high proportion of the local NGOs were formed to deal with the psychosocial problems of the communities in which they lived: widows, orphans, the elderly, the handicapped, and those traumatized by war, violence, and the loss of their homes. The widespread use of rape as a weapon of war lent added urgency to psychosocial programming. Through 1994, 1995, and much of 1996, social services represented the overwhelming priority in the country and were the locus around which many indigenous NGOs were formed.

Over time, however, new priorities came to the fore. The reconstruction of houses and public infrastructure such as schools and clinics was an area of need that attracted greater donor attention. The World Bank placed increasing emphasis on the economy and microenterprise development. By about 1998, donors were placing top priority on facilitating the return of refugees and IDPs to their homes. As funding for psychosocial work declined, however, serious problems emerged. Many, if not most, local NGOs had been formed to deal with this specific problem. Many of their workers and volunteers were psychologists, social workers, and generalists who sought to help those traumatized by war. They felt that changing donor priorities ignored the continuing problems facing the tens of thousands of people who made up their case load, at a time when, in many instances, the possibility of doing real psychosocial healing was only just beginning.

The problem was not that the need for social services had diminished, but that available international funds declined, and neither the NGOs nor their supporters had devised a coherent medium-term plan to deal with the problem. Moreover, because so many of the NGOs and their workers had a social welfare orientation, they were unequipped for, and in some cases uninterested in, working on reconstruction and microenterprise development. Because funding had dried up in one programming area, however, they were drawn into new areas in which they had no special expertise, simply to survive.

A third task was to build capacity. Nurturing the development of private domestic institutions made good sense, and most international aid bodies had capacity-building as a stated priority. Some nontraditional donors became involved as well, including the Open Society Institute funded by financier George Soros and his New Bosnia Fund. However, capacity-building represented a very small proportion of the funding actually going to local NGOs. For the most part, capacity-building took the form of training, not so much in how to develop and advance independent action but in orientation to the requirements and procedures of international agencies and donors. For many groups, the problem was not so much how to write a report for donors, but how to write six reports, in English, in six different formats every quarter, or even every month.

In a broader sense, the capacity-building objective, however narrowly understood, existed in tension with the need for urgent delivery of social services. Faced with the trade-offs, most donors and expatriate organizations opted for service delivery. While they characterized their interest in supporting local NGOs as an investment in a strong, pluralistic, socially integrated civil society, in their funding of local NGOs they essentially sought—and found—cheap service delivery. Despite its good intentions in channeling funding through local NGOs, UNHCR was perhaps the most prominent international culprit in setting up such groups for a fall. The largest source of NGO funding for a number of years, the refugee agency's restrictive approach to determining allowable management and administration costs helped create a community of organizations that lived a hand-to-mouth existence.

During the 1990s, tensions within the wider NGO community soon became evident. By 1993, there was no single community but the beginnings of two separate NGO groupings, one local and one international. Local NGOs did not feel particularly welcome in the meetings of international NGOs, held on UNHCR premises, and so they formed their own association. The cultures of the two sets of actors were also quite different. One was primarily western, Judeo-Christian, and international; the other was local, Islamic, and indigenous. While some organizations made efforts to straddle both worlds, the two groups remained distinct. Some local entities—primarily solidarity organizations, consciousness-raising groups, and grassroots organizations at the community level—went their own way altogether, some of them with quite positive results.

Tension also existed between international and indigenous agencies on matters of quality control. The rapid growth of the local NGO sector, driven by donors with money to dispense, was inherently risky from a management and performance standpoint. Some local NGOs were funded far beyond their capacity for good management. Organizations less than a year old were charged with managing project portfolios in excess of a million dollars, a supply-driven situation that represented little more than opportunism on the part of both donor and recipient. On the part of the donor, it resulted from a search for executing agencies, no matter how new, fragile, or competent. For their part, NGOs, anxious for security and employment, were unable to say "no" in the face of need, opportunity, and optimism.

As the decade wore on and the levels of funding from donor governments began to dwindle, outright competition between international NGOs and local institutions became more evident. Like the international NGOs they emulated, many indigenous NGOs also fell into competition with each other, vying for donor attention and funding. "Donor governments frequently complain about the plethora of local NGOs, the duplication of activity, lack of cooperation and so on," notes analyst Mark Duffield. "However, it is their own insistence on funding public welfare and social reconstruction projects through NGOs on a project basis that helps produce this situation. The general under-funding of the local NGO sector . . . has encouraged competition between members and a culture of secrecy concerning funding sources that works against cooperation."[27]

The consequences of emphasizing service delivery over the creation of an independent civil society were far-reaching, extending well beyond the humanitarian sector. As one study puts it, "By treating local NGOs as cheap executing agencies and by ignoring what it would take to strengthen the sector properly, donors not only threatened the emergence of a genuine civil society but stood to lose their executing agencies as well."[28] It is telling that as of the beginning of the new century, Bosnia had some 1,000–1,500 civil society organizations, far fewer than in other countries in eastern Europe that were making the same transition from command to market economies.

Part of the problem was donor naivete about the NGO reality in Bosnia, but some of it was simply opportunism: using local organizations as cheap delivery mechanisms, regardless of the longer-term societal cost. International NGOs were not exempt from such criticism, especially those that transformed their projects into a local organization before heading for home. Having done precisely this, one prominent international organization reviewed the progress of its progeny in August 1996 and found an organization that was—not surprisingly—fighting for its financial life, despite its good programming reputation. "Having invested in the creation of local NGOs," the evaluation states (possibly a year too late), "we now have a responsibility to support them through their transition to a sustainable independent sector. Given the crucial role played by a strong NGO sector in democratic society, we should all consider this a serious issue that constitutes a threat to the future of a multi-party, democratic Bosnia and continue to invest energy and resources into supporting local NGOs."[29]

Many local NGOs had indeed been formed as conversions of projects established by international NGOs, wanting to "leave something behind," or by the local staff of these organizations, wanting to strike out on their own. Other organizations formed spontaneously to deal with particular problems and to take advantage of special funding made available by donors. Apart perhaps from indigenous human rights NGOs, many of these organizations had little understanding of their place in civil society or of tasks beyond service delivery, including advocacy. Few developed out of community spirit, and many operated without boards of directors or anything resembling the sort of constituency that western NGOs take for granted.

On a more positive note, the fact that outside relief efforts encountered so many obstacles in Bosnia-Herzegovina—political, programmatic, logistical, and procedural—put a premium on self-help efforts by local communities and individuals.[30] A number of international and indigenous NGOs worked creatively with community leaders to arrange administration and transport of relief material to otherwise inaccessible locations. They encouraged communities to take responsibility for their own welfare and to arrange their own transport, making minority populations more accessible to relief supplies. Another encouraging development was the 1997 creation by international NGOs of a Bosnian NGO Foundation, which sought to strengthen the capacity of nine indigenous NGOs. Yet it failed to attract any funding for its endowment and survived on the same project treadmill as its member organizations.

As the humanitarian response in Bosnia-Herzegovina evolved over time, it acquired the features of the global aid marketplace: competition among agencies, dependence on external donors, a fast-paced approach with unrealistically short time frames, frictions between expatriates and domestic officials and institutions, and expatriate departures unrelated to missions stated or accomplished. As at the global level, there was no "invisible hand" to ensure proportionality or quality control. International NGO activities were concentrated in Sarajevo and Tuzla rather than dispersed more evenly throughout the republic. Aid efforts in Bosnia-Herzegovina were disproportionately high when contrasted with activities in Serbia and in the Republika Srpska. In Bosnia-Herzegovina, as in other countries moving from command to market economies, there was uncertainty about whether humanitarian initiatives should retain a narrow focus or should become, in effect, a wider social safety net for the general population.

In one respect, the role of local institutions played out differently in Bosnia-Herzegovina than in several other high-profile emergencies. In Afghanistan, Iraq, and in Haiti during the sanctions, the importance of local institutions was heightened when expatriates departed because of growing insecurity. In such circumstances, UN organizations and international NGOs were able to point with pride (and relief) to the continuation of humanitarian endeavors in their absence. In Bosnia-Herzegovina, the exit of international actors was born not of lethal violence and widespread intimidation but of a general decrease in perceived urgency and reduced donor attention. One lesson from Bosnia-Herzegovina is that donor-driven institutional development is only as durable as aid agencies make it.

Much has changed in Bosnia-Herzegovina since the mid-1990s, but the legacy of weak civil society organizations remains. The high-water mark of donor funding has come and gone, with interest and resources shifting to other crises such as Kosovo and Afghanistan, where the importance of being local would once again be affirmed upon arrival but honored only in the breach.

Like the global humanitarian enterprise, the political economy of humanitarian action in Bosnia-Herzegovina said more about donors and expatriate practitioners than about vulnerable populations. The frustrations were summed up by a local NGO representative at a meeting in Sarajevo in 1996. "They came here, not for us, but for them."[31] Visiting Bosnia several years later, historian Michael Ignatieff agreed. "The Western need for noble victims and happy endings," he writes, "suggests that we are more interested in ourselves than we are in the places, like Bosnia, that we take up as causes."[32]

The Southern Africa Drought of 2002

It should not be imagined that so-called natural disasters are any more free of complexity and calculation than those caused by human agency. The southern Africa drought of 2002 offers a case in point. The basic facts are these: Lower than normal maize harvests in 2001 were followed by a drought and much worse harvests in 2002, exacerbated by massive human devastation from HIV/AIDS. By the middle of that year, disaster was looming, and on July 1, the World Food Program launched a regional emergency operation covering six countries: Lesotho, Malawi, Mozambique, Swaziland, Zambia, and Zimbabwe. It was estimated that some 12.8 million people would require 1.2 million metric tons of cereals to carry them over into the 2003 harvest period. By the end of 2002, WFP was reaching fewer than 50 percent of the people it had targeted, but during the more critical months of January to March 2003, performance dramatically improved. In the end, a disaster of biblical proportions was averted, and the great Southern Africa drought of 2002 slipped into history.

In fact, the story is much more complex. Highly professional early warning systems failed to draw attention to the issue until late in the day, and not until NGO fundraising campaigns had reached a fevered pitch (for which they were to be criticized later). Donor compassion was compromised by tardiness and by misgivings about the corruption and mismanagement of several African governments, creating a serious possibility that starving people might be made to pay the ultimate price for their governments' ineptitude and venality. As if this was not enough, commercial and ideological issues exploded into the midst of the emergency, in the form of a debate about genetically modified (GM) food.

In October 2001, Save the Children UK began to warn of serious food shortages in southern Africa. Even earlier the Famine Early Warning Systems Network (FEWS NET), a USAID-supported operation, said that southern Africa maize production in 2001 had been the lowest in six years. No disaster was predicted, however, because it was thought that reserve grain stocks held by governments were high enough to cover the problem. For the lean period of late 2001 and early 2002, this was true, but by the end of 2001, the crops then in the ground

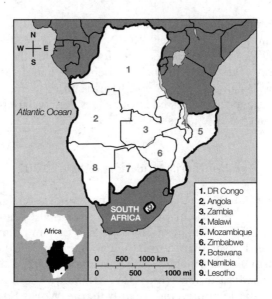

were already suffering from a lack of rain. On December 12, 2001, FEWS NET reported that high levels of food imports would be needed throughout the region in the year ahead, but there was still no suggestion of disaster. The following day, in almost direct contrast, WFP launched an appeal for $54 million to feed more than 550,000 rural Zimbabweans who faced severe food shortages. A 24 percent drop in the country's main season crop had created a food deficit of nearly half a million tons of grain. In Canada, CARE—worried about impending food shortages—requested funding from CIDA for a nutritional survey in Zimbabwe. The request was turned down "due to competing budgetary priorities and scarce resources."

One of the reasons for CIDA's reluctance to consider a nutrition survey—or any other form of assistance for Zimbabwe—was the Zimbabwean government's thuggish behavior leading up to national elections set for March 2002, its repression of the rights of the opposition, and the confiscation of land from the country's white farmers. In 1999, agriculture accounted for 20 percent of Zimbabwe's GDP, but a year later it had fallen to only 11 percent. Corn production fell nearly 70 percent and winter wheat was down 40 percent. Some of this was drought-related, but mostly it was about the Mugabe government's confiscation of productive white-owned farms, and the subsequent collapse of the farming sector. Bilateral aid agencies were not inclined to provide any support to Zimbabwe that might indicate approval of its farming policies, and they were reluctant to provide food aid if it might be diverted to political purposes before the election.

On April 2, 2002, John Watson, CARE Canada's executive director, returned to Ottawa from a field visit to Zambia and Zimbabwe and wrote to CIDA: "I spent a significant amount of time in the rural areas talking to farmers involved in CARE programming. The situation is desperate. There is a complete loss of this year's maize crop in many parts of both countries." A week later the FEWS NET issued a less emotive statement than Watson's, saying that production shortfalls were "imminent" and that there would have to be a concerted effort by governments, donors, UN agencies, and NGOs "to avoid a potential humanitarian crisis." Still, the crisis was only a potentiality.

It would be another five weeks before crop assessments came in, and even then FEWS NET was restrained, reporting "serious production shortfalls" and saying that these "could evolve into humanitarian crises" if appropriate and timely action was not forthcoming. By then, however, a full-fledged panic had developed among front-line agencies. In the middle of May, WFP approved emergency food operations for Malawi and Mozambique. On May 24, Save the Children ran an ad in the London *Times* saying that "Southern Africa is in the grip of a food crisis. Millions of people who already live in desperate poverty now face the very real threat of starvation." The same day, UNICEF ran an ad saying that "Time is running out for the people of Southern Africa. . . . Adults and children in Malawi, Zimbabwe, Mozambique and Lesotho are all being affected by one of the world's worst food shortages in decades." On June 1, World Vision ran a full page ad in the *Globe and Mail* saying, "10 million face starvation. . . . Without immediate emergency aid, millions could die!"

Zambian President Levy Mwanawasa declared a national food disaster, warning that four million Zambians faced starvation. He said that the country would run out of food in July or August, and he appealed to international donors for help. On June 1, USAID added $18.9 million worth of food to the $49.5 million it had already earmarked for the region earlier in the year. And finally, on July 1, WFP launched its region-wide emergency operation, aimed at delivering 1.2 million tons of grain to an estimated 12.8 million people in need.

If the political situation in Zimbabwe had put a damper on donor enthusiasm, it was to get worse in Malawi and Zambia. In May it was revealed that the last of Malawi's grain reserves had been sold off the year before. The government said the IMF had told them to do it; the IMF denied any involvement whatsoever. Several investigations later, it remained unclear where the proceeds of the sale had gone, but it was not to the government. A more thorny issue developed in Zambia and then went regional: the largest food aid donor, the United States, was shipping GM grain. One by one, the governments of Zambia, Zimbabwe, and Mozambique refused to accept the grain. With the food already in ships bound for Africa, the debates became louder and more polarized. Some Zambians claimed that GM food was poison, that it would make them blind, that it would destroy local biodiversity and agriculture. Even if the grain was milled before distribution, it was said that some might fall off trucks before milling and ruin local agriculture. NGOs such as Greenpeace and ActionAid agreed that GM food was problematic. The word "genocide" was thrown about in raucous coordination meetings. The Zambian government was accused of courting the starvation of its people by denying imports for some esoteric principle, while the right-wing Washington-based Cato Institute lashed out at everyone:

> There is no way the U.S. maize could be certified as GM-free, nor is there any food safety reason why it should be. The fear of African leaders in the region is less one of food safety than it is that some of the donated grain would end up being planted, making future exports to Europe when the rains return difficult to certify as being GM-free. The EU is using the NGO scare campaign to require GM or GM-free labeling of all grains as a means of protectionism for its agriculture industry, which it already subsidizes at the rate of $1 billion a day.[33]

The debate was no longer about humanitarianism or even science, it was about politics. And, while the Cato Institute may not have said so, European import certification and agricultural subsidies in the United States itself were also factors influencing donor behavior. In September 2002, an NGO worker in Zambia described the scene:

> The situation is grim, and getting grimmer. I think we are about a month away (maybe two) from a major, major problem. The elderly, mothers and female-headed households are already not eating for days sometimes. And the general population in a few of the areas where we work can no longer find fruits, nuts, anything. They are weak and they are hungry . . . and with the GM-food debate, the food for October and November is nonexistent. . . . Donors first wouldn't talk about [food aid] until we had crop forecasts, and then they wanted, and still want, nutritional stats, which are trailing indicators. By the time you get those and get the food in, [it will be too late] . . . all in all, it is quite depressing. I am beginning to think that donors have to see people half dead before they begin to move. The Americans were actually the exception. They put ships on the sea before they knew where they were going—that's quite exceptional.[34]

In the end, it is not clear how many died, and how many were saved. In fact that question may conceal a larger one: How many became so badly malnourished that they later died from something else? What long-term damage was done to the physical and mental development of babies and children? The hidden disaster may have been worse than the more obvious one. By December 2002, only 266,000 tons out of a target of 620,000 tons had actually been distributed, considerably less than half. By the end of March 2003, when the new and improved harvest was coming in, the pipeline had received about 76 percent of what had been requested, but one-third of what had been pledged was still undistributed.[35] In the end, Zambia never accepted any GM food, milled or otherwise. Surprisingly, given the frenzy required to get the food operation started, a WFP evaluation said that starvation had been rare, as was acute malnutrition. "At no point in the operation was famine a reality, but the situation reflected high degrees of poverty and deprivation over several years."[36] By February 2003, international NGOs were actually pushing to get the WFP pipeline closed down, for fear that incoming food would depress agricultural prices during the new harvest.

Why was there no starvation? A first possibility is that everyone got the numbers wrong—that the situation was never as bad as NGOs and UNICEF had made out. An evaluation published in 2004 found, for example, "The crisis was overstated in terms of the threat of famine, but at the same time the chronic roots of the crisis were understated."[37] Maybe the fundraising claims *were* overstated, but on the ground in 2001 and 2002, there was no major dispute about the numbers. They had been real, and they had been high. And given the casino economy of humanitarian assistance and the potential loss of life if an appeal fails, it is *always* better to overstate the need than to understate it.

A second possibility is that people's coping mechanisms were underestimated, although when the worst of the hunger arrived, everything— bush oranges, nuts, wild okra—was simply gone; there was nothing in the cupboards and there was nothing left to scavenge. In retrospect, some reports say that there was a poor understanding of people's ability to cope, for example, to forage for "wild food and milk," but this ability, in fact, had been carefully examined, at least by the professional NGOs and UN agencies on the ground. A third answer is that enough relief—even at 50 percent of target—arrived to prevent the megadeaths that had been predicted. It was not enough overall, but it reached the worst areas—thanks to donors, WFP, and the front-line agencies—and made a difference.

A fourth answer—and this should be most worrisome to those concerned about southern Africa's long-term future—is that when the numbers of those facing starvation were calculated, they were "calculated for normal." In other words, they were calculated on the basis of the calories needed by a normal individual to sustain a healthy life. Nobody received anything like normal rations. The stunting rate in Zambia is 59 percent, one of the worst in the world. But as one NGO worker notes, donors respond to wasting (i.e., starvation), not hunger, stunting, or any of the lesser indicators. "There is nobody fat out there today," she says. This answer is the most troublesome, not just because it suggests that the relief effort failed to deliver enough, but because it means that a large part of southern Africa's population remains undernourished and will be, most likely, unfit and unable in the years ahead to rise above what is becoming a deeper and more chronic poverty. Stunting, of course, is not an emergency issue; it is a long-term developmental problem requiring more attention than humanitarian agencies can provide.

At the end of 2002, there were simultaneous exultations from the U.S. government and WFP about famine having been avoided. The United States could take some satisfaction from its diversion of food aid on the high seas, getting it to the drought areas early, and from having lobbied other donor governments to become involved. With Catholic Relief Services, CARE, and World Vision, USAID also established a unique consortium approach to food deliveries in the region for the following three years. WFP helped orchestrate an international response and persuaded countries like the Netherlands and Switzerland to pay for milling U.S. food aid once it arrived in southern Africa, thus resolving one major political issue. But other political factors in the region and economic considerations regarding markets and commercial interests collide with the apparently less important issue of human needs to mute any great sense of humanitarian victory.

As humanitarian agencies were closing the files on the drought of 2002, they began to open new ones on problems looming for 2004. The rains failed again in 2003, putting an estimated six million people at risk. In July 2003, WFP launched an appeal for $311 million, but was still short $100 million, more than six months later. Hungry WFP recipients went on half rations and people once again turned to eating wild fruit, roots, and bugs. In a January 2004 article on the drought, Reuters/AlertNet used the words "urgency" and "desperate" several times, noting the HIV/AIDS pandemic had made people even more vulnerable. The report also reminded readers that humanitarian agencies had been criticized for overstating the need in 2002.

People

Chapter 7 will discuss the influence that individuals can have on a humanitarian effort. Some of these individuals—ministers of state, heads of aid agencies—have the weight of their governments behind them. Some, like Bob Geldoff and Bono, have a popular following that they can draw upon for support. Others, like Irish bus driver Tom Hyland and the many other anonymous individuals like him, manage by the force of determination and hard work to galvanize public support and resources for emergencies that governments are prone to ignore. This book touches only indirectly, however, on the individuals who populate the front-line agencies—those who work in the refugee camps, hospitals, and feeding stations, often under difficult and dangerous circumstances, and those who hold the fort in capital cities and agency headquarters, providing logistical support and raising the funds needed for work in faraway places.

It is sometimes thought that people are the largest problem in sorting out the humanitarian puzzle: inept do-gooders, poor administrators, and hapless political appointees. There is certainly some truth in this view. Greater transparency in the system, better evaluation, and less political meddling would go a long way in alleviating the problem. It is worth noting, however, that for every bumbling administrator, there are a dozen working long, hard hours to ensure the necessary coordination of activities, expedite the ever-present paperwork, and meet genuine human needs. Outside of the humanitarian hothouse, and even inside it, most of these people and the tasks they tackle every day are completely unknown, and few receive the recognition they so richly deserve for their efforts.

An incident in 2003 highlighted the contributions, and the vulnerability, of individuals working on the front lines. On Tuesday, August 19, a suicide bomber detonated a truck with 1,500 pounds of explosives outside the headquarters of the United Nations in the former Canal Hotel in Baghdad. The blast claimed twenty-two lives, sixteen of them UN employees, including Sergio Vieira de Mello, the UN Secretary-General's Special Representative in Iraq. A Brazilian, de Mello had been on the job since June 1. He was on leave from his duties in Geneva as UN High Commissioner for Human Rights for this special high-profile, four-week assignment that had dragged on for many more. He had served as a senior UN official in peacekeeping and reconstruction operations in Cambodia, the former Yugoslavia, and East Timor. But he began his career like most others in the humanitarian system, living in rugged conditions in the new Bangladesh and the southern Sudan and later working in the salt mines of the bureaucracy in Geneva and New York. His task in Iraq was to provide high-level liaison between the UN and the U.S.-led Coalition Provisional Authority and to oversee the UN's humanitarian and other activities. Fatally injured in the blast detonated three floors below his office, de Mello lived for several hours before succumbing. He is reported to have told rescuers not to let the incident lead to the withdrawal of the UN from Iraq.

Two days later, BBC World Service television showed de Mello's casket being loaded aboard a transport aircraft for return to Geneva. On the same newscast, there was film of an unarmed New Zealander, Ross Mountain, negotiating his way past Liberian rebel checkpoints to discuss access for food shipments with combatants in a highly-charged atmosphere that had dragged on for weeks, awaiting the arrival of peacekeepers. A major humanitarian emergency had developed in the interim, and while U.S. President Bush pondered the possibility of sending in the marines (later declining to do so), it was UN and NGO workers who represented the front line of international presence, under the most dangerous circumstances. Mountain, OCHA chief in Geneva, began his professional life in the NGO trenches and had served in some of the world's most difficult assignments: Afghanistan, Iraq, Haiti, Lebanon, and a previous stint in Liberia. Ironically, he had laid the groundwork for de Mello in East Timor, setting up the initial humanitarian response, as described in Chapter 3. For his efforts, in December 2003 UN Secretary-General Kofi Annan appointed Mountain to succeed de Mello as his Special Representative for Iraq.

6

Foreign Policy Imperatives

*All nations make decisions on self-interest and then defend them in the name
of morality.*

—William Sloane Coffin[1]

Foreign policy interests inevitably intrude on the humanitarian response to emergencies. The interaction can have positive outcomes;
it can also deflect humanitarian attention and resources away from
those most in need. And as the chapters on Sierra Leone, East Timor,
and Afghanistan have demonstrated, the imposition of political agendas can weaken the humanitarian impact of an intervention while at the
same time achieving very little in the political realm—producing, in
effect, the worst of both worlds. Humanitarian principles stress proportionality in the response to need, but time and again, disproportionate
spending flows to emergencies that are close to donor countries, or
which, when politics leapfrogs geography, have greater political import
for those providing aid. Some conflicts are simply off limits to international humanitarian involvement altogether.

Old-fashioned superpower politics as a driver of, or damper on,
humanitarian work has declined since the end of the Cold War. Yet political calculations still result in disproportionately large levels of international humanitarian activity in areas where the interests of powerful
countries are at stake. To the distress of humanitarians, the post-9/11
emergencies in Afghanistan and Iraq drew humanitarian attention, expertise, and funding away from other crises, reflecting the distorting impact of
superpower politics. Humanitarianism can also become a substitute for
other forms of action. Thus, for several years the Bosnian crisis was
treated as a humanitarian, rather than a political and military, problem.

Foreign policy interests, or lack thereof, are implicated in what the
humanitarian enterprise has come to call "forgotten emergencies."

Because they provide no compelling reasons for action beyond humanitarian need, some crises are essentially ignored in the competitive world of politicized emergencies. At the hour of their greatest humanitarian need, Liberia, the Democratic Republic of the Congo, the 150,000-plus internally displaced Tindouf and refugees in western Algeria received little attention in comparison to other emergencies, or in relation to need. Other emergencies are forgotten because amnesia may serve a foreign policy objective. Ongoing emergencies in Afghanistan were selectively forgotten by several donors who, after 9/11, suddenly remembered the country with a jolt.

These egregious disproportionalities, while not new, are the reasons that multilateral humanitarian institutions and the Red Cross movement were created: to provide an anchor against the prevailing political winds and to reduce the influence on humanitarian action of unilateralism and of bilateral political agendas. Today, however, the foreign policy interests of donor countries exercise growing influence on the humanitarian behavior of UN agencies and NGOs, skewing their efforts and muting their advocacy on behalf of victims. And while "the donor made me do it" can become a convenient rationalization for the managers of implementing agencies, both UN and NGO officials have good reason to believe that the anchor is beginning to lose its hold.

This chapter reviews the roles foreign policy plays in the response to humanitarian emergencies. It looks primarily at the behavior of donor states as driven by political considerations and as reflected in the deployment of military forces in response to international crisis.[2] It also examines the interface between humanitarian agencies and principles and the military. Chapter 7 examines the influence of domestic politics in donor countries, including the role of the media and advocacy in shaping international humanitarian action.

Each donor country has its own foreign policy interests, which are influenced by the behavior and actions of other countries and by domestic policies and politics. Although spoken of in reverential terms by aid organizations, the humanitarian imperative in and of itself is rarely a sufficient cause—and sometimes not even a necessary cause—to spark donor government action. Realistically speaking—and effective humanitarians must be realists as well as idealists—humanitarian considerations are always the bridesmaid, rarely the bride. In the words of political scientist Neil Macfarlane, "Humanitarian imperatives are only one—and not necessarily the most significant one—among a complex set of factors that impinge on the definition of interest and policy."[3] While those who set great store by the purity of humanitarian action might be reluctant to agree, the mélange of motivations that drive such behavior may not always be a bad thing.

Italy's engagement in Albania in the late 1990s offers a case in point. Economic problems and the 1997 collapse of the banking system in Albania provoked a massive social upheaval, leading the Italian government to fear a massive influx of people across the Adriatic. After failing to convince NATO and the Organization for Security and Cooperation in Europe (OSCE) to become engaged, Italy acted initially on its own, but eventually received a UN Security Council imprimatur for an Italian-led intervention. Operation Alba had the salutary effect, Macfarlane says, of "opening up access for international agencies to address humanitarian need in Albania."[4] In reality, the quality of the assistance provided by Italy, both then and in 1999 when Albania was itself inundated with refugees from Kosovo, has been sharply criticized. However, Italy's regional political concerns were an essential ingredient of the national and international aid efforts that were mounted.

When politics intrudes on humanitarian action, the higher the level of the policy maker, the higher the political quotient in the humanitarian equation. Human need looks more compelling on its own terms from the front lines than from donor capitals. Aid officials working at the local level, whether NGOs in the trenches or bilateral aid agency program officers in overseas hotspots reviewing project proposals, generally prioritize human needs over political calculations. Yet the diverging perspectives produced by different portfolios create debilitating tensions within a given organization. An illuminating example comes from Somalia in late 1992, when a group of agencies wrote to the U.S. president's national security adviser, urging the United States to support the deployment of "appropriately armed UN security forces tasked with protecting emergency supplies and staff." Two of the NGO headquarters that signed the letter did so against the recommendations of their field staff in Mogadishu, who, once the letter had been made public, were stuck with the backlash of recommendations they considered dangerous.[5]

But it would be wrong to conclude that politics always trumps human values, or that needs-based allocations of resources are invariably hostage to political ideology. When the Reagan administration in the mid-1980s was locked in proxy wars against the menace of the communism it perceived to be advancing in Africa, Asia, and Central America, Ethiopia experienced a devastating drought. Would its starving people be punished for the communist doctrine or agricultural policies of the regime of Mengistu Haile Mariam, whose strong-armed collectivization was implicated in the devastating food shortfalls? President Reagan's USAID administrator announced a policy based on the idea that "A hungry child knows no politics." It was greeted with relief (and surprise) by some of the NGO lobbyists credited by the administration as having been persuasive in achieving the outcome.[6]

A more recent parallel involves U.S. humanitarian policy toward North Korea during the closing years of the 1990s and, also under a conservative administration, during the early twenty-first century. U.S. strategic interests seemed inextricably interwoven with decisions about whether to assist in relieving the prevailing famine. Macfarlane asks, "Is it desirable to shore up a rogue state by helping to feed its own people, especially when its ability to do so is caused by overspending on defense and weapons development and the use of state funds to satiate an elite's thirst for luxury western goods? Or, conversely, might a vigorous humanitarian response advance other Western objectives, including promotion of peace talks on the peninsula, normalization of relations between North and South Korea, containment of the North Korean nuclear program development and weapons proliferation, and reduction in the danger of a North Korean implosion, bringing potential for regional destabilization?"[7]

Most Washington-watchers assumed that the United States would turn its back on chronic food shortages in this "axis of evil" country and lean on its friends in the UN and among NGOs to follow suit. To their surprise, U.S. aid policy was noteworthy for its relative depoliticization during this period. Yet politics are not immutable; perceptions of national interest change over time. Policies can be unmade in the light of new developments and by the evolving perceptions of national interest. Thus, with North Korea's withdrawal from its nuclear nonproliferation commitments in 2003, the continued provision of U.S. food aid through the UN World Food Program and collaborating NGOs edged closer to the bargaining table.

Historical ties can have an energizing influence on the military as well as the humanitarian side. Examples include the commitment of Belgian troops to UNAMIR in pre-1994 Rwanda, and the military intervention of France in Rwanda in 1994 and in Ivory Coast in late 2002. Britain's eventual activism in Sierra Leone reflects a combination of political and humanitarian factors: historic ties, Commonwealth links, large-scale humanitarian need, and possibly, lingering embarrassment over the Sandline weapons affair. The deep involvement of Britain in Rwanda and its relatively lesser interest in the grave problems of the DRC has been criticized by some British NGOs as reflecting the pet projects of senior officials—facilitated by the absence of any major articulated British foreign policy interest in the region. Just as Italy's high level of humanitarian and military involvement in the Balkans and Kosovo was partly a function of geographical proximity, so its aid to some countries in Africa has reflected historic ties. German links to Kosovo were so multifaceted and the scale of its military and economic assistance—bilateral and multilateral—so massive that some Kosovars viewed Bonn rather than Pristina as the country's capital.

Disproportionate spending is likely to flow to emergencies that are closer to donor countries than to those farther away. Examples include Australian funding to East Timor and the Solomons; U.S. and Canadian funding for victims of Hurricane Mitch in Central America; and European support to Bosnia and Kosovo. While geographical proximity can exert an understandably strong influence on donor behavior, humanitarian principles stress proportionality in the response to need and the protection of persons, regardless of where on the globe they, or donor nations, happen to be located.

Australia's significant expenditure on emergencies in Asia and the Pacific highlights the reality that funding from other donors for these regions is disproportionately low. By result if not by actual design, Australian aid thus exercises from a global perspective something of a shock-absorber function. To cite another example, the Swiss executive added Sfr 50 million to the government's aid budget in 2002 for flood relief in Eastern Europe, raising the total humanitarian budget of the Swiss Agency for Development Cooperation (SDC) by 20 percent and upstaging critical needs in southern Africa, for which staff had long been requesting additional funds.

Regional foreign policy interests may also elicit contributions from nontraditional donors to international efforts in a given region. Malaysia, China, and Singapore have contributed to East Timor. Nigeria, Guinea, and Ghana have provided troops to the UN peacekeeping force in Sierra Leone. China, Pakistan, India, South Korea, and Taiwan have been major donors to post-9/11 Afghanistan. Islamic solidarity appears to have widened the list of nontraditional donors to Afghan relief and reconstruction to include Saudi Arabia, Kuwait, Turkey, and the United Arab Emirates (some of which were donors to the Taliban regime as well).

In an innovative initiative reinforcing the perceived political interests of Japan and Asia as a whole, the Japanese government provided trust funds to the World Bank to facilitate the involvement of other countries such as Pakistan and Indonesia. Japan's contribution to Afghanistan in 2003 was its largest to any single nation. Japan is understood to have played a high-profile role not simply because of its desire to assume leadership in Asia but also as an investment in an eventual permanent seat in a reformed UN Security Council.

Regional peace and security interests can also ensure that a potentially catastrophic emergency is well handled. As noted earlier, the reasons for good donor coordination and generosity in East Timor in 1999 and 2000 had less to do with the humanitarian emergency itself than with a desire for stability in the region. If humanitarianism had been the primary concern, there would have been considerably more donor action during the previous twenty-five years, during which an estimated two hundred thousand Timorese died as a result of the brutal Indonesian occupation.

It was, in fact, political rather than humanitarian imperatives that rescued East Timor from its forgotten emergency status. Among these was a strong desire by Asian and Western powers to ensure political stability in Indonesia, one of the most important countries of Asia. When it became obvious that East Timor would become independent, it was important that the process not destabilize Indonesia and that it take place as peacefully as possible. Security of shipping lanes and oil in the Timor Gap were additional considerations. Concern about possible recriminations over previous donor apathy no doubt also played a role. In 1999, a positive confluence of political interests brought Australian, Japanese, American, and other concerns to bear on the humanitarian problems of this very small island. Not only was there unprecedented coordination between national donors, the UN, and the World Bank— there was, for the first time in a long chain of humanitarian disasters, adequate funding to meet the needs.

Consistent with geopolitical interests vis à vis East Timor—but at variance with humanitarian concerns—was the view in some donor capitals in 2003–2004 that Indonesia should not be pressed on human rights abuses or humanitarian access in Aceh and West Papua. The implicit humanitarian message was that human life is more valuable in one part of the Indonesian archipelago than another. The political subtext was that humanitarian concerns there, as elsewhere, can be trumped by geopolitics, oil, the political fragility of the Indonesian regime, and the perceived urgency of its cooperation in the wider war against terrorism.

The influence of Cold War–style superpower politics on humanitarian assistance has diminished with the demise of the former Soviet Union and the ascendancy of one remaining superpower. However, international geopolitics in one form or another continue to represent an important consideration, as demonstrated in Afghanistan and Iraq. It can still, for example, result in a disproportionately large scale of humanitarian activities in areas where the security and other interests of large countries are perceived to be at stake. Since bilateral aid is more concentrated in a selected number of countries than is multilateral aid, it is a more accurate barometer of the influence of antiterrorism strategies on aid allocations.[8]

The growing U.S.-led emphasis on—or perhaps obsession about— terrorism has multiple ripple effects on the humanitarian enterprise.

There can be no doubt that the post-9/11 emergencies in Afghanistan and Iraq drew humanitarian attention, expertise, and funding away from other crises. "Nearly half of all the funds given by donor governments in 2002 to the UN's twenty-five humanitarian appeals," notes Oxfam, "went to just one country, Afghanistan—a desperately poor place but one that was also top of the list of priorities in the 'war on terror.'"[9] In November of the following year, DFID announced a diversion of £100 million to Iraq that was expected to affect aid programs in some twenty-one countries, with British aid operations closing in six countries altogether. Desk officers in aid agencies point out that concerns about terrorism undercut the relative importance of objective assessments of need and increase the likelihood of "forgotten emergencies." The pressures that high-profile emergencies bring to the overall and the day-to-day management of humanitarian activities are so great that many veteran aid officials strongly prefer settings with lower geopolitical gravitas.

But antiterrorism is not an all-purpose explanation for country aid allocations. One analyst, writing in the medical journal *Lancet*, points out that there is little proportionality in allocations even among countries within the antiterrorist rubric. "If the threat of terrorist opportunism in Iraq is going to be cited as a reason for the urgency of donor aid to that country," asks Jerome Amir Singh, "why is the same reasoning not being used to rally massive aid for Somalia? That country is perhaps in a worse state of lawlessness than Iraq and is also a likely centre of terrorist activities."[10]

One of the signal developments of the post–Cold War era has been the higher priority accorded to humanitarian crises that fit into an international peace and security agenda. "For nearly twenty-two years, between its establishment and the Six Day War of 1967," notes analyst Ted van Baarda, "the [Security] Council passed no resolution on the humanitarian aspects of any armed conflict."[11] By the end of the century, it was regularly addressing humanitarian crises, including human rights abuses, as matters of international peace and security. Building on a recently established pattern, representatives of all fifteen Security Council member states themselves conducted a fact-finding trip to Afghanistan. Clearly "international peace and security" has in recent years been infused with a larger humanitarian component, although, as noted earlier, the higher level political profile of humanitarian issues can be a mixed blessing.

Some conflicts with major political import largely have been off limits to international humanitarian involvement. UN presence and Western humanitarian activities in Soviet-occupied Kabul during the Cold War were overshadowed by more generously funded programs for Afghans in neighboring countries, particularly Pakistan. But all crises behind the Iron Curtain did not become newly accessible with the winding down of the Cold War. International humanitarian access to Chechnya, and even forthright discussion of the situation of civilians there, has been limited by the political sensitivities and the importance of the Russian Federation. In fact, since September 11, the Russian portrayal of Chechen fighters as terrorists has complicated international access.[12] Or, in another example of humanitarian taboos, only in rare periods—during the *intifadas* and, more recently, with the erection of the concrete barrier on the West Bank—has there been wide-ranging international debate on the humanitarian dimensions of the Israeli-Palestinian conflict.

Donor government pressure on humanitarian actors can be a two-way street, as will be shown in the following chapter. The influence on Swedish policy of the Swedish Committee for Afghanistan is a case in point. It would be difficult to find traditional foreign policy reasons, such as promoting national security or enhancing trade, that would account for long-term Swedish largesse in Afghanistan. The engagement of Norway in peace processes in Sri Lanka, Guatemala, and Israel-Palestine reflects and reinforces the on-the-ground labors of Norwegian NGOs in those countries. The fact that countries referred to as middle powers lack self-serving foreign policy agendas in such places doubtless facilitates UN institutions and multilateral processes; conversely, multilateral involvement minimizes the need for high-profile bilateral aid initiatives.

Over the years such nations have cultivated more humancentric or humanitarian foreign policies than have the larger powers. This emphasis facilitates interactions with NGOs based in those countries, which have lighter political baggage and for which government funding becomes more compatible with their own agendas. By contrast, U.S. NGOs, even those without large-scale funding from Washington, carry a special burden by virtue of their nationality. The difference between the middle powers and others is not in the existence of political or foreign policy elements but rather in their nature and contents.

Foreign policy interests often exercise a major influence on the humanitarian behavior of UN agencies and NGOs. U.S. government officials with humanitarian portfolios make no secret of the way the policy process works and their own disenchantment with it. Humanitarian principles are a controlling consideration in USAID—at least in its democracy, conflict, and humanitarian assistance unit, says one senior official. There the staff is composed mainly of people with years of NGO service and with a time-tested commitment to humanitarian principles. But don't forget, he continues, "this is a government and not an

NGO. As a result, principles are 'smushed' through a sieve of requirements." The policy process is driven by the Office of Management and Budget, which adjudicates among competing priorities and where principles don't figure "at all." Elements in the state and defense departments, which have their own agendas as well, mete out additional punishment on what is left of humanitarian principles.

The wear-and-tear of policy and politics on principled humanitarian programs is not limited to the U.S. bureaucracy. Like their U.S. counterparts, officials in the U.K.'s Department for International Development (DFID) are committed to needs-based humanitarian programming. At the same time, in 2002 the United Kingdom was involved in only sixteen of thirty-five prominent international emergencies, suggesting the role of strong political factors in the priority-setting process.

Vulnerability to political pressure can have a direct impact on advocacy as well. In a major transatlantic face-off in 2003, Save the Children UK was pressed to end its criticism of U.S. military action in Iraq by its U.S. counterpart, Save the Children U.S., not least because the latter receives 60 percent of its income in the form of U.S. government grants and contracts.[13] The international director of another large transnational NGO speaks of being prevented from taking a position on the humanitarian crisis in the Middle East. The U.S. institutional member of his organization, he says, "won't allow it. This is partly because of the Jewish donor base and partly out of U.S. patriotism. They calculate that criticism of Israel could cost us [as an organization] $90 million. So we put out platitudes. And we have nothing to say about Afghanistan either." Despite an active constituency base, "seventy five percent of our funding comes from the U.S. government, so we are bound to reflect their policies, whether they are ours or not. The U.S. has been much more aggressive since 9/11 in making sure everyone falls into line behind their strategy. Play the tune, or they'll take you out of the band."

As terrorism has become an overriding preoccupation, its invocation by the United States has been used as an all-purpose explanation of political decisions, routinely shunting aside considerations of human rights and humanitarian concerns. Pressures on the selection of operational aid partners have escalated. The U.S. government now requires U.S. NGO grantees to certify that their operational partners overseas have no connections with terrorist groups. Washington has also pressured UN agencies to cut off funding for partner organizations alleged to have terrorist or other undesirable political connections. The U.S. and Canadian governments have also closed down a number of foundations and charities suspected of serving as conduits of funding for terrorist organizations. In 2003, however, a UN report concluded that despite international sanctions imposed against supporters of al Qaeda and former Taliban officials, "al Qaeda continues to receive funds it needs from charities, deep pocket donors, and business and criminal activities, including the drug trade."[14]

But there is also a more positive set of reasons for accepting resources from donor governments, even under such circumstances. Government funding, its recipients say, provides access to decision makers and an opportunity to influence policy. Moreover, they reason, government funds are appropriated for human needs activities: why should NGOs not use them accordingly? While both reasons may appear on occasion to be little more than a rationalization, many NGOs and members of the Red Cross movement reach decisions about whether to accept funding, not as a matter of global policy but rather on a case-by-case, crisis-by-crisis basis. In both Afghanistan and Iraq, a number of NGOs have concluded that the humanitarian space within which they can function with integrity has been significantly reduced by the geopolitical nature of donor involvement, and they have thus steered clear of government resources.

Following the failure of the United States to receive Security Council approval for military action against Iraq in 2003, a number of NGOs decided against accepting any funds whatsoever from members of the U.S.-led coalition, at least while hostilities were under way. Several expressed concern that collaboration with donor governments that are also belligerents could jeopardize their programs and personnel in other Islamic countries. Conversely, however, some American NGOs were under heavy pressure to accept U.S. government funds for work in Iraq—or face a reduction in such funds for work elsewhere. While arm-twisting of this sort is not an everyday occurrence, there is a strong correlation between donor foreign policy priorities and the risk to instrumental humanitarian agencies.

Foreign policy factors, positive and negative, result in a tiered response to emergencies. What might be called "first-class" emergencies constitute high-profile political crises such as Bosnia, Kosovo, Afghanistan, and Iraq. The characteristics are clear: a preeminent political or security interest by one or more major power; the lavishing of abundant military and economic assistance resources (in that order); the use of military forces to engage in hearts-and-minds activities, to the evident discomfort of traditional aid agencies; and, in a more general sense, a blurring of the borders between the humanitarian and the political. Hot-war scenarios also may make aid agencies need the security that international troops can provide, but may also make them more wary of accepting it.

The subtext of first-class crises is also clear. These are in the first instance humanitarian crises only by a stretch of the fertile political imagination, although they may become such in their own right over time. They command heavy media coverage that accentuates the involvement of Western actors and provides the close-ups of human suffering and rights abuses that both simplify and distort the broader picture. Such crises can also involve multiple clashes of culture—between international and indigenous actors and institutions, between civilian and military structures, and between fast-paced, externally driven change agents confronting slower moving, more traditional societies.

Second-class emergencies are the more traditional kinds of humanitarian crises, with serious and incontrovertible human need, substantial levels of displacement, gross violations of human rights, and perhaps demonstrable malnutrition or starvation. These crises generally attract an intermediate level of interest and involvement as reflected, for example, in the subscription of the UN's consolidated appeals. Two countries in this middle group during the five-year period beginning in 1997 are the Sudan and Mozambique, each of which received between $90 and $440 million each year.[15] While they fared considerably less well than first-class emergencies, both on a per capita basis and in the aggregate, they were not ignored altogether.

Third-class emergencies, with all of the pejorative implications in that expression, are otherwise referred to as "forgotten," "neglected," or "silent." Forgotten emergencies are the canary in the world's humanitarian coal mine. They demonstrate that the system is in routine violation of its core principles, particularly those of humanity, universality, and impartiality. Foreign policy interests or, rather, the perceived lack thereof, are to a large extent responsible for the phenomenon, although the Israeli-Palestine conflict and Chechnya—too hot to handle—are examples of the reverse. Lack of access to civilian populations is often given as the reason for weak donor response. Yet in reality response is low because they are of little interest to anyone and because there are no other compelling reasons for action beyond humanitarian need. Third-class crises are essentially ignored in the competitive world of higher profile emergencies even though most emergencies, in fact, are of the third-class variety. According to one authoritative study, "Between 1995 and 2001, just under half of the total humanitarian aid allocable by country was spent in the top ten recipient countries. . . . The rest of humanitarian aid is spread across more than 100."[16] Even high profile emergencies move from one class to another. Sierra Leone, East Timor, and Afghanistan were all variously first-, second- and third-class emergencies, depending on who was interested, when, and why.

A Danish analysis of the differing responses to international emergencies has identified three contributing factors: the degree of interest, particularly of a political or security nature, that donors have in the region; the comparative strength of international humanitarian actors, including aid agencies and leadership-providing individuals involved in the particular crisis; and the degree of media coverage. "Only occasionally" is media coverage the single key to rendering an emergency visible or invisible. "Rather, the security interests of Western donors are important, together with the presence and strength of humanitarian stakeholders, such as NGOs and international organisations lobbying donor governments. By and large, political interests outweigh media and humanitarian stakeholder involvement, although generalizations are difficult to sustain."[17]

The existence of a tiered approach to emergencies, based on considerations other than need, is accepted by donor governments and aid agencies as somehow inherent in the natural order. They concede that no invisible hand evens out the peaks and troughs of donor interest, reinfusing political calculations with a correcting element based on human need. In the words of Carolyn McAskie, a senior UN humanitarian official, "Most donor behavior is rational from a donor point of view. However, the sum total of all donor behaviors doesn't produce a rational whole."[18] Not only are there few synergies across the world's humanitarian apparatus; the impact of the whole is demonstrably *less* than the sum of its parts.

In any given year, the humanitarian apparatus holds an enormous number of meetings, usually at great expense in time and travel, wear and tear. Many such sessions have reviewed the dysfunctions of the aid system. In recent years, however, some of these routine discussions, largely on matters of coordination rather than effectiveness, have become animated by a sense of moral outrage over the patent inequities and iniquities of the system. Donors have begun to take steps to address the problems of politicization and disproportionality—and, in a broader sense, the uneven impacts—of humanitarian action. A modest beginning was made at a conference held in Stockholm in 2003 where governments agreed, in a very preliminary way, to a statement that a general principle of good humanitarian donorship required the allocation of "humanitarian funding in proportion to needs and on the basis of needs assessments."

This was a long way from the original draft, circulated in advance of the meeting, which talked about the "goal of meeting the entirety of global humanitarian needs."[19] But perhaps it was a necessary start to what might become a longer discussion about the fundamental injustice of a three-tiered approach to emergencies. Donor governments, who routinely respond to criticisms of disproportionality with the retort that there is simply not enough funding to go around, are beginning to acknowledge that the absence of adequate funding puts a higher premium than is normally understood on considerations of need. As that begins to happen, the uneasiness expressed by an increasingly concerned international public may be taken more seriously. "Admittedly, foreign aid is not usually recognised as a human right," notes one observer. "Some regard it as an altruistic act of rich donor states and thus, above critical scrutiny. Moreover, convention dictates that beggars cannot be choosers; however, even purported altruistic acts should be subject to critical appraisal and considerations of justice."[20]

On an individual level, some governments have taken promising steps. Some are increasing the percentage of their funding to multilateral organizations that are more focused on second- and third-class emergencies. On the bilateral side, the Swedish government has adopted explicit policies on longer-term transitional funding than would otherwise be possible for countries coming out of an emergency. The hope is that future emergencies can be prevented by taking a longer view.

Political interests are expressed not only through humanitarian activities but also through military instruments. Increasingly, military forces have become a fact of humanitarian life, not only offering overall security for civilian populations and humanitarian operations but also providing hands-on assistance and protection to people in dire straits. They have figured prominently in these various roles in the earlier analyses of Sierra Leone, East Timor, and Afghanistan—and of course in Bosnia, Kosovo, and Iraq as well. The political economy of the humanitarian enterprise reflects both the political dynamics of such activity and the competition that military contingents add to an already crowded aid marketplace.

There are three major reasons for this upsurge in activity by the military. First, with the passing of the Cold War, military and security forces are in less demand for their traditional roles and are searching for a new raison d'être. As a result, they have become more available during humanitarian emergencies for other duties. Many relief groups now employ security consultants or full-time staff with security expertise who assist in program strategy, decision-making on staff postings in volatile settings, and security training. While most agencies see such contributions as positive, some staff complain about the apparent opportunism involved and see the connection more as a liability than an asset. Some analysts view the presence of military personnel in the aid ranks as compromising the quintessentially civilian character of humanitarian work.

Second, there is more interaction between troops in their military roles and humanitarian agencies in their day-to-day work. The "protection of international peace and security," to use the gateway phrase for Security Council involvement, is increasingly seen to demand a more robust security presence than in earlier times. In the past, peacekeeping operations under Chapter VI of the UN Charter required the consent of warring parties. With a few exceptions, most peacekeeping operations up to 1988 were Chapter VI operations, lightly armed and dependent on the consent of all parties to lay down their arms. In such undertakings, there was limited interaction between international military forces and humanitarian organizations. The military might have provided air transportation for relief supplies, but its protection was seldom required by NGOs or UN agencies. Aid groups were usually far removed from the fighting, and in Chapter VI operations, the fighting had usually stopped by the time the humanitarian aid arrived. It was possible, therefore, for the military and humanitarians to exist in parallel solitudes.

In sharp contrast, some of the 1991–1995 operations (Iraq, Cambodia, Bosnia, and Haiti) and most post-1995 operations (including Bosnia, Kosovo, Sierra Leone, East Timor, the DRC, and Liberia) were authorized under Chapter VII of the UN Charter, which allows the use of force to restore peace and security. And no wonder. During the 1990s the concept of the nation-state came under greater challenge than at any time in the past two centuries—in Russia, Somalia, Yugoslavia, Haiti, Liberia, Sierra Leone, and elsewhere. Sometimes referred to as "expanded peacekeeping operations," Chapter VII undertakings are essentially coercive, dealing with threats to peace, acts of aggression, and cease-fire or human rights violations. Countermeasures can include political and economic pressure and the use of force. Such operations are not for peace*keeping* purposes, rather they are peace-*enforcement*, or possibly peace-*recovery*, operations. The various regional initiatives during the 1990s were virtually all peace-enforcement operations as well.

It is perhaps not surprising that today so many UN and regional "peace support operations"—PSOs, to use a more inclusive term—are more in the enforcement than the peacekeeping mode. The wars they deal with are increasingly led by interest groups and warlords more concerned with power, resources, and terror than with democracy, justice, or progress. Civilians—sometimes entire populations—are no longer accidental victims of war; they are often the primary target. The names of Pol Pot, Hun Sen, Saddam Hussein, Milosovič, Karadzič, Aideed, Sankoh, Cédras, Savimbi, Prabhakaran, Taylor, Mobutu, and others are written in the blood of millions of innocent civilians.

These "leaders" and their followers do not abide by standard rules of war. Most do not maintain conventional armies or observe Geneva conventions and protocols. They routinely attack civilians as part of campaigns of terror and do not exempt humanitarian agencies (or, for that matter, anyone else) from pillage and destruction. Where interlocutors have been identified and cease-fires arranged, factions may have no organized leadership or administrative structure for international actors to work with or to hold accountable. Although a more robust security presence is clearly needed, it is often unsuccessful in achieving its objectives. In such settings, military personnel naturally have a wider array of interaction with humanitarian actors, including convoy protection, security counsel, mine action, disarmament, demobilization, and community reconstruction.

A third reason for increased military-civilian interaction, and one not so well understood by NGOs transfixed by the threat of competition, is that the military recognizes the importance of civil society, humanitarians, and humanitarianism. Humanitarians were once ignored because they *could* be ignored: they either weren't present or their presence didn't matter. In today's complex humanitarian emergencies, however, civil society and humanitarian organizations may well be more important than governments. Consequently they must be understood and engaged if the military is to do its job right. As one ex-soldier puts it, "You can't empty the theater any more." And in the absence of a government or of NGO coordination, it should not be surprising that the military would take on new roles that they or their political masters believe they can implement faster or better than others. The problem with and for the military, however, is not so much in providing assistance better or faster, if this really is the case, but knowing when to hand over and withdraw.

This is the real operational issue framed by the stepped-up interaction: not that it is happening, but that there are, so far, few mutually agreed-upon boundaries and no mutually agreed-upon definitions of comparative advantage. Decisions whether a refugee camp will be constructed or a well dug are not made on the basis of whether the task will be done quicker, cheaper, or better by a civil-military unit or a humanitarian agency. There is no quartermaster in the sky who assigns this or that task to an institution according to a fixed and transparent set of criteria. Humanitarians may thus perhaps be forgiven for believing that, in an increasingly competitive marketplace, military forces are enjoying the inside track. "What is it about our field," asks one seasoned NGO official in exasperation, "that makes everybody think they can do it?"

NGOs and other aid agencies have traditionally shied away from working with the military, partly because they did not have to, but also because they did not want to—and vice versa. There were, and are, many reasons for this. One is *not* that most relief groups are pacifist. Humanitarian principles are perhaps the most fundamental reason the ICRC and many other agencies keep their distance. Military presence and action is first and foremost an expression of political objectives, an extension of the foreign policy of governments. By contrast, humanitarian organizations see themselves as functioning according to principles of neutrality, which involves a firm commitment to take no position on the causes of a given conflict, and impartiality, which makes need alone the controlling trigger of humanitarian action.

While the humanitarian organizations of the UN system and most NGOs have endorsed such principles, the commitment is not as firm for some as it is for others. A Chapter VII mandate may involve the United Nations in coercive operations where neutrality and access to civilians in rebel-held areas may be impossible. NGOs also differ among themselves on humanitarian principles and the relative importance they attach to them. The NGO community ranges from high-church priests of immutable dogma to ambulance-chasing opportunists, each charting its own relations with the military. Given the politicization of humanitarian action and the growing role of the military, what is the relative importance of principle? Do strict humanitarian principles offer a guide or a shield in today's complex emergencies? A guide of sorts, perhaps, but not a shield from criticism. For many organizations, the complexities of a fast-changing world seem not to be well served by unbending dogma.

Journalist David Rieff has argued that "to want to be neutral, and yet remain free to side with the victims is not realistic, especially in an age when aid workers can be murdered with impunity. Nor is it realistic to expect to benefit from funds from donor governments and still remain essentially independent." What is right for the ICRC and MSF may not be right for all organizations at all times, even for the ICRC and MSF. "Perhaps it is time to . . . acknowledge," Rieff says, "that independent humanitarianism is too divided and besieged to survive as before."[21] Besieged by the array of recent major crises and a confusing set of challenges and options, the humanitarian community has not benefited from a singularity of purpose, principle, and mandate.

But independence remains one of the first principles of most humanitarian agencies, and for good reason. NGOs must be versatile; they must be able to establish partnerships and move quickly, especially in the early days of an emergency. This is what makes them good at what they do. This is why they are funded by both individual and institutional donors. Indeed, the principle of independence—in a different sense for NGOs and for the UN's humanitarian organizations—is altogether fundamental, to an extent often underplayed by the agencies themselves.

The growing complexity of conflict, the changing role of peace-enforcement operations, and the evolving roles of humanitarian and military organizations have made the clear separation of the past virtually impossible. While some humanitarian organizations may set out to avoid all contact with the military, doing so may put the continuation of their programs, the health of their beneficiaries, and the security of their staff at risk. As Oxfam GB puts it, "Oxfam works in seventy countries around the world, including many in which we cooperate with UN humanitarian operations, and ten where we work alongside a UN peacekeeping mission. In many situations of conflict, the fulfillment of our mandate to alleviate poverty is increasingly dependent on UN protection."[22] But unlike MSF and the ICRC, Oxfam may regard this issue somewhat differently because it is both a relief and a development agency.

Conversely, however, association with the military can prove hazardous to the health of the humanitarian enterprise. Describing the experience of UNHCR in Bosnia, the agency's chief of operations, who struggled with the issue of whether to use military escorts for aid convoys, commented in June 1993, "Any attempt to use force has a whiplash effect throughout the entire operation."[23] Indeed, "protected" by military personnel, sometimes aid resources, clients, and workers become targets of one belligerent or another. The fact that UN peacekeeping forces provided convoy escorts, on occasion against the expressed wishes of UN humanitarian personnel, further complicated the issue.

Such are the dilemmas with which humanitarian organizations struggle. While the highest levels of professional judgment and behavior are essential, codes of conduct will not get humanitarians past roadblocks if soldiers say no. No great humanitarian advantage may result from discussion and coordination with the military. However, it will not result from isolation or withdrawal either. "If the humanitarian community does not accept any [military] protection," notes analyst Ted van Baarda, "it might, on occasion, find itself in a situation where it can deliver no assistance at all. If, on the other hand, the humanitarian community accepts military protection whole-heartedly and unreservedly, the warring parties will distrust humanitarian organizations and not allow them to pass. Somewhere along this line a *modus vivendi* may have to be found and a decision has to be made about the price, in political currency, humanitarian organizations are willing to pay."[24]

If the growing interaction of the military with humanitarians has led to a desire to maintain clear distinctions between the two, recent developments have called into question the utility of such distinctions. In an analysis of the deteriorating security situation in Iraq in November 2003, one NGO observed, "The Iraqi opposition to American occupation has erased the traditional lines between military and civilian aid personnel. All foreigners are targets in Iraq. Thus, the UN, the usually sacrosanct International Red Cross (ICRC), and most NGOs have departed the most fractious parts of Iraq. Those civilian aid personnel left in Iraq—primarily government employees and contractors—are so severely constricted by security concerns and so isolated from the world outside protective walls that their effectiveness is questionable."[25] It could be said, in fact, that some humanitarian agencies were remiss for failing to analyze the likely operational context in advance, and for exacerbating what was certain to be a contentious environment.

Also in November 2003 in Afghanistan, UNHCR announced that it would suspend resettlement activities in the eastern province of Ghazni following the murder by masked gunmen of a staff member traveling in a clearly marked UNHCR vehicle in broad daylight.[26] The killing was the latest in a six-month period during which aid agencies operating in the south saw their offices attacked and their national staff threatened, kidnapped, and even killed. At least twelve aid workers, including one ICRC expatriate, had been killed since March. In both Iraq and Afghanistan, aid personnel were struck by the apparent lack of discrimination in the choice of targets. The coordinator of the Afghan NGOs Security Office (ANSO) was quoted as saying that the incidents "not only indicated the breadth of attacks," which were escalating, on the UN, NGOs, government and the U.S.-led coalition forces but also the more precise and ruthless methods being employed."[27]

The absence of discrimination among the agencies that experienced violence raises the larger question of whether such discrimination existed largely in the minds of the agencies themselves, or also served a useful purpose in terms of local perceptions. One case study of popular attitudes toward aid in Afghanistan concluded, "The local population rarely differentiates between NGOs, donors, UN agencies and other foreign actors, who are all grouped together under the term NGO." The analysis connected the lack of differentiation with a broader indictment of the lack of local participation in aid programs generally. "In some respects, affected people appear to be spectators of aid, unsure how to engage proactively with the aid community."[28]

A still larger question concerns the relative importance of "agency" itself. Does it really matter whether a person in dire straits receives help from Handicap International, the Fifth Marine Expeditionary Force, or Bechtel? An MSF staffer in Sierra Leone, enraged at efforts by the UN peacekeeping force, UNAMSIL, to organize a "health day" in a remote town, conceded under prodding that it would be all right for the military to administer rabies vaccine to a child if it was bitten by a rabid dog and there was no other alternative. The rabid dog was hypothetical, but the proposed health day was not: if UNAMSIL didn't do it, nobody would, including MSF. The MSF aide, like many of his counterparts throughout the humanitarian enterprise, have difficulty establishing guiding principles that are both firm and flexible. Too dogmatic an espousal of humanitarian practice can undercut important individual and even collective acts of humanitarian urgency.

Other incidents over the years suggest that the carefully nuanced institutional distinctions maintained by individual agencies are more meaningful to themselves than to other actors, including beneficiaries, in conflict settings. Even organizations that made a public issue of distancing themselves from NATO in Bosnia failed to convince Serbs of their neutrality. MSF, which refused to accept direct funding from NATO member countries, was nevertheless repeatedly denied visas, even for staff with non-NATO nationalities.[29] In Iraq, an attack on the ICRC premises in 2003 led the ICRC to withdraw its staff at once. The ICRC believes that maintaining its distinctness is imperative—even to the extent of withdrawing from the theater—despite the fact that such distinctions may be lost on those on the ground.

Stepped up levels of activity by the military in the humanitarian sphere have led quite logically to increased competition across the resulting more-crowded playing field. As analyst Hugo Slim has said of NGOs, "Their pre-existing presence on the ground in many of the countries concerned, their self-mandating humanitarian missions, their willingness to take on often huge emergency grants from Western donors and their readiness to act as subcontractors to UNHCR, have seen them quickly (and voluntarily) inserted into the front lines of the international community's response to civil war."[30] UN organizations often serve similar functions for governments, although their mandates may be more codified in law or agency doctrine and their ability to resist political missions more limited than NGOs.

But numerous differences between military and humanitarian cultures heighten problems of communication and cooperation. These differences include terms of engagement, institutional cultures, the impacts of interventions on civilian populations, effectiveness, and the criteria used for determining it. One point of particular tension involves the "hearts and minds" activity of the military. A senior U.S. military official, interviewed in Kabul in November 2002, had no compunction in saying that the purpose of extensive civil-military activities by coalition forces was "to garner support for U.S. military objectives." Taking exception, one donor aid official viewed "the misuse of the term 'humanitarian' for hearts and minds operations with little attention or understanding for the principles of universality, impartiality, neutrality and proportionality [as] a troubling trend." Small wonder that aid agencies have expressed a clear preference for having the military provide security rather than engage in hands-on aid work. This preference reflects not only a wariness of competition but a judgment about the military's comparative advantage.

As analyst Hugo Slim also notes, many NGOs working in conflict situations were there with development programming before the particular conflict began. They may well differ from the military in their understanding of the situation and the appropriate response. Many intend to stay after the emergency ends and fear being compromised by working too closely with the military, especially in peace enforcement operations where charges of partiality against the military are common. Aid operations, particularly those managed by NGOs, tend to be no-frills, low-budget undertakings, contrasting sharply with more expensive, military-supported operations in which redundancy is a virtue and cost is no object.

Indeed, cost is a recurrent item of contention. In some countries such as the United Kingdom, Canada, Germany, and the Netherlands, a government's humanitarian budget has helped underwrite the costs of deploying military assets—sometimes over the strenuous objections of government aid officials. In others cases such as the United States, the cost has been borne primarily by defense ministries. For their part, military officials, seeking to reassure restive aid organizations—whether about the costs of the military or about the dunning by the military of government aid budgets—describe the funds available to troops for civic action as "pocket money" or "chump change." Reconstruction contracts in Iraq, however, were not exactly chump change, nor was the overcharging. At the end of 2003, a Pentagon investigation found evidence that a subsidiary of Halliburton had overcharged the U.S. government by as much as $61 million for fuel on no-bid reconstruction contracts.[31]

Then there is the cost of specific humanitarian activities. The Italian military spent $1,200 per refugee tent in Kosovo, a tenfold increase over UNHCR's costs. The British Royal Air Force quoted cargo rates six times higher than civilian airlines for shipping relief supplies to Rwanda. In sharp contrast with the transparency demanded of humanitarian procedures, NATO refused to disclose its humanitarian expenditures in Kosovo.[32] Moreover, simple cost comparisons, even if standard operating procedure, do not resolve more qualitative issues. During the Goma crisis, U.S. forces provided expensive and inadequate water purification systems designed for small numbers of U.S. soldiers, while the needs of sprawling refugee camps hung in the balance.

Many basic questions remain unanswered. Are aid agencies on target in questioning the military's understanding of humanitarian and refugee law, human rights, and the ability of soldiers to deal with displaced and traumatized people?[33] Do donor governments have an unexpressed favoritism for military over civilian agencies? On what basis are aid allocations made? Is it true that, as stated by a UN military liaison official, "With rare exceptions, humanitarian action by the military doesn't come at the expense of civilian agencies"?

Armed forces have standby capacities that most NGOs and UN agencies do not. Yet military standby capacity is not—nor should it be—designed for humanitarian purposes. First and foremost, it is and should be for military contingencies. Supplies, equipment, and personnel, therefore, may be inadequate or inappropriate to anything but the direst of humanitarian situations, and then only for a very limited period. Rather than transforming existing military standby capacities into something more humanitarian, it makes much more sense for governments to support the development of civilian humanitarian standby capacities. Ironically, however, when the Red Cross, Oxfam, MSF, CARE, UN agencies and others *have* developed standby capacities, these are often limited by funding constraints and by donor suspicions that they are trying to expand their empires. The lack of transparency among donor governments about the rationale for making allocations to certain countries and aid agencies is mirrored by a similar opaqueness on the military side. In short, if anything is more difficult than ensuring the effectiveness of one set of agencies, it is doing so for two sets.

Indicative of a growing give-and-take with the military, however, aid agencies, the UN system, and governments have spent considerable time reviewing the issues and clarifying positions. InterAction, the professional association of U.S. NGOs, has participated in numerous discussions with the U.S. military, both generic and specific to individual conflicts and in a variety of training exercises at military installations. The UN system's Military and Civil Defense Unit has approved guidelines that permit use of, or collaboration with, international military forces, but only in exceptional circumstances. The Oslo II Guidelines, finalized in March 2003 after lengthy consultations among governments and international organizations, affirm the "UN identity and civilian nature of humanitarian assistance," distinguishing clearly between the functions and roles of military and UN humanitarian actors. "A humanitarian operation using military assets must retain its civilian nature and character," the guidelines state. "While military assets will remain under military control, the operation as a whole must remain under the overall authorization and control of the responsible humanitarian organization. This does not infer any civilian command and control status over military assets." In an attempt to defuse competitiveness, the guidelines specify that UN military and civil defense assets, "like all humanitarian assistance, are to be provided at no cost to the affected State and receiving agency."[34]

The war in Iraq led the UN secretariat to issue guidance regarding interaction between UN personnel and military forces. Building on the

Oslo Guidelines, the guidance reaffirmed basic humanitarian principles such as independence, neutrality, and impartiality that were then translated into detailed, practical "do's and don'ts" for aid personnel in the field. The guidance also reaffirmed the indispensability of civilian authority and responsibility for humanitarian activities. "When in doubt, the civilian and independent nature of United Nations humanitarian assistance must be emphasized." The fact that these ground rules were issued during the first week of the Iraq conflict in March 2003 and were framed in operationally specific terms was helpful as the UN and associated humanitarian actors worked to establish appropriate relationships with the U.S.-led military coalition.[35] Although the Oslo Guidelines reflect a hard-won consensus among governments, it remains to be seen whether they will influence the behavior of donors themselves in using their own bilateral military resources in the humanitarian sphere in Iraq and beyond.

Several countries have developed new, comprehensive military doctrines on peace support operations that are explicit about the importance of civil-military cooperation and coordination. The Swedish military has the following to say on the subject:

> Civil-military operations are concerned with the harmonization of civilian and military interests within a theatre of operations. These could range from dealings with local government or authorities, UN, GOs [government organizations] and NGOs, and local civilians, refugees and displaced persons. . . . [I]t is vital that the civil-military programme is fully integrated into the overall campaign plan, and the day-to-day conduct of operations. . . . Priorities should therefore be coordinated at formation level and integrated into any theatre-wide plan.[36]

Although the Swedish army has acknowledged that humanitarian activities should be undertaken by civilian actors, the idea of being "fully integrated into the overall campaign plan" alarms many humanitarians, concerned as they are about neutrality, impartiality, and independence. The issue was taken several steps forward in 2002 and 2003 when humanitarian agencies were clearly designated by the U.S. and U.K. governments as part of their campaign to win the hearts and minds of Iraqis. U.S. Secretary of State Powell's reference to NGOs as "force multipliers" of U.S. military strength and "an important part of our combat team" was particularly inflammatory.[37] His later appeal for NGOs to remain in Baghdad so that the adversary would not win by forcing their exit was also unnerving. MSF quickly clarified that it was not part of the war effort. Decisions to deploy, remain, or withdraw were not driven by considerations of military strategy. Humanitarians are not in the business of picking winners or sending political messages to belligerents.

Source: By Ricardo Martinez. ©CartoonArts International/CWS.
El Mundo, Madrid, Spain (April 3, 2003). Reprinted with permission.

Today, many humanitarian organizations are increasingly persuaded that the insecurity that frequently prevails in humanitarian crises makes military forces an essential ingredient in their own ability to function effectively as aid agencies. At the same time, however, experience with the military in places such as Kosovo, Afghanistan, and Iraq reinforces the inclination of aid agencies to keep their distance. Because humanitarian efforts and those who manage them enjoy greater freedom in lower profile conflicts, military-humanitarian cooperation is less highly charged in such settings as well. Many aid groups express a preference for multilateral rather than bilateral or regional peacekeeping initiatives. Thus the UN imprimatur on the work of the ISAF in Kabul made the aid community more comfortable in collaborating with it than with the U.S.-led coalition, which was present on its own authority.

For its part, the military seems much more aware of the need for cooperation and joint activities. In Chapter VII situations, this may reflect a recognition that soldiers will be unable to leave until there is a solid basis for peace and that peace-building is something that generally lies beyond the purview of soldiers. Should they relegate this strictly to others? Is there room for greater cooperation? Will independence, impartiality, or neutrality be compromised by greater civilian-military cooperation? Is it enough for an NGO to say, for example, that "CARE staff, equipment and operations will remain clearly independent of and distinct from any military force"?[38] The answer to such questions is: "It all depends." It depends on the nature of the conflict and the accompanying insecurity, on the perception that combatants have of the international military force (which will undoubtedly change with time, sometimes virulently), on the mandate that the force has been given and its implementation of that mandate, and on the capacities of the humanitarian organizations on the ground.

If military forces are extensions of national foreign policy objectives, specific military contingents reflect national agendas and cultures. A clear illustration of this was provided by the international response to the 1994 Rwanda crisis. The French and many other nations eventually sent troops into the theater under one pretext or another, but all of them were too late to halt the genocide. U.S. military contingents in Kigali and Goma functioned under political constraints that reflected U.S. policy objectives: Downplay the genocide, mop up the casualties, ensure minimum military exposure to risk. Hence the anomaly of U.S. troops all decked out but with no permission to leave the relative security of the Kigali airport. A Japanese contingent treated the medical needs of refugees in Goma in late 1994, flying the flag but confined initially to the relative security of the airport, well away from the throngs of refugees needing attention.

The contributions and profile of smaller countries to the Rwanda response were also remarkably consistent with their cultures. Ireland, for example, sent two separate contingents. Sixty military personnel were seconded to UNHCR and to two Irish NGOs. Wearing civilian clothes and without weapons, they were indistinguishable from ordinary civilian aid staff. A second group, also provided at no expense to recipient aid agencies, was made up of a dozen government civil servants, again to assist in the operations of the three aid groups. The government's decision followed extensive public debate, and its impacts were followed with interest. The Irish NGO GOAL had lobbied the authorities to send Irish troops to Rwanda to protect Irish NGOs; Concern and Trocaire had opposed such a move while supporting an Irish commitment to a multilateral force. "The secondment arrangement gave the Irish government the best of several worlds," concluded one review. "It responded to public entreaties from those who were horrified by the suffering in Rwanda and wanted Irish troops to intervene. Yet it also reflected the concerns of the Irish military that dispatching troops to Rwanda would overextend financial and personnel resources and might involve them in an internal armed conflict, possibly in a peace-enforcement mode."[39]

A decade later, a similar sense of national identities was evident in the PRTs established by the United States in Afghanistan. As noted earlier, in selected provinces U.S. humanitarian, political, military, special forces, and intelligence personnel were all located under a common roof. As other national members of the coalition assumed responsibility for individual PRTs, divergent national foreign policy goals and military styles emerged. "[T]he British-led PRT in Mazar [was] very much focused on seeking to reduce tensions between the major power holders in the North." Meanwhile, the Germans, taking over the PRT in Kunduz, were caught in a tug of war between the German defense minister, whose emphasis was on civil-military activities, and the minister of economic cooperation, who sought to insulate aid from association with political-military objectives. "Different external states," concluded one observer, "have sought to create their own models in the various regions of Afghanistan, based on local conditions and, in the case of the USA, clear military objectives based on the war on terror."[40]

A common theme in many of these deployments, however diverse their particulars, was that involvement by national military forces was an exercise in global citizenship. Japan in Rwanda and Germany in Kosovo were exercising their first out-of-area missions since World War II and laying the groundwork for their eventual (hoped for) permanent membership on a reformed UN Security Council. Global citizenship also figured in the decisions of smaller powers such as Ireland. Commitment of troops provided a point of entry and sense of involvement for the countries with smaller populations and fewer resources to contribute.

All that said, there is a bottom line. Military forces are not created or intended for providing humanitarian succor. Their intervention into the humanitarian arena is problematic in principle and practice, and the blurring of lines is good for neither. The use of military assets to protect and deliver humanitarian assistance should be avoided, except when there is no other option or where not doing so would result in the loss of life. Humanitarian action remains a quintessentially civilian action that, adequately resourced and with prearranged standby capacity, could meet the needs of most emergency situations that arise.

"The new humanitarianism," a term coined by British analyst Mark Duffield, positions humanitarian action as part and parcel of a broader effort to promote Western values (e.g., the market, democracy, human rights) and a "liberal peace," whose aim is to transform dysfunctional and war-affected societies on Western borderlands into cooperative, representative, and stable entities.[41] In this thesis, aid workers are the advance guard, staking out a Western presence and agenda and, when they come under duress, providing the rationale for a military-led "humanitarian intervention." An intriguing thesis, the notion may nevertheless read too much into the patchy, inadequate efforts that mark so much of the humanitarian enterprise.

Much has been written in recent years about humanitarianism as a substitute for other forms of action. Until the Rwandan genocide had ended and the need for international peacekeepers had largely passed, that emergency was treated by most UN Security Council members as a humanitarian problem, rather than as a political or security issue. The domination of the Rwandan refugee camps in the Congo by *genocidaires* was portrayed as an indictment of UNHCR and its partner NGOs rather than of the governments that turned down an urgent appeal for troops from the UN High Commissioner for Refugees and the UN Secretary-General. For several years the Bosnian crisis was treated as a humanitarian problem rather than a political and military issue, with the failure to halt ethnic cleansing laid at the humanitarian doorstep. Thus, humanitarian action often becomes a fig leaf for political and military inaction. Political leaders reluctant to take more decisive and appropriate measures thrust aid workers into the breach. In such instances, funding for humanitarianism functions in effect as a smoke and mirrors operation, concerned more with being seen as doing something—anything—rather than with mounting serious assistance and protection efforts.

In recent years, some believe, the humanitarian enterprise has sought to become more clear about its areas of competence. Others argue that the opposite has happened, with the intrusion of development, recovery, governance, justice, and other issues into the humanitarian arena. While effective relief delivery and human rights protection can contribute to the easing of civil tensions and strife, in most situations there is no substitute for the conflict resolution skills of professional mediators.

Similarly, while day-to-day humanitarian activities in volatile settings require more security than aid personnel themselves can provide, often there is no substitute for international muscle and monitoring. Even humanitarian agencies that prefer consent to a more muscular approach acknowledge that they cannot provide the needed force element themselves. Greater clarity about what the ICRC calls the "specificities" of humanitarian action is an investment in protecting the humanitarian sector from the all-too-easy scapegoating and fig-leafing it routinely receives. Humanitarian action has enough problems being effective on its own terms without having to cover the nakedness of a wider set of international actors.

As noted in Chapter 1, even the term "humanitarian" is itself routinely abused for political purposes and because of the lateral movement of humanitarian action into what might be called noncopyright areas:

development, aid-induced pacification, justice, and good governance.[42] Policy makers have at one point or another referred to the objectives of the wars in Kosovo, Afghanistan, and Iraq as humanitarian. The next step, describing *the wars themselves* as humanitarian, then becomes a small one, which seems to follow as day follows night. Applying the same logic late in 2003 amid the escalating violence in Iraq, the purported voice of Saddam Hussein called upon Iraqis to wage a holy war against the occupying troops. "Fighting them is a legitimate, patriotic, and *humanitarian* duty," the voice said.[43]

In sum, politics is a familiar driver of humanitarian action. Creative tension between humanitarianism and politics is not necessarily a bad thing. But politics has a perennially bad driving record, pointing to the need for corrective action to limit the damages. Likewise military forces, as extensions of national foreign policy, increasingly interact with humanitarian institutions. While they have indisputable comparative advantages to contribute, they have emerged in recent years more as competitors in humanitarian action than as facilitators. Moreover, they are not a substitute for effective policies geared to conflict prevention and resolution, development, and peace. In that respect military assets are, like humanitarian action itself, an indispensable but at best partial contribution to a more just and secure world.

7

Domestic Considerations:
Me First

We should be careful to get out of an experience all the wisdom that is in it—not like the cat that sits on a hot stove lid. She will never sit down on a hot lid again—and that is well; but also she will never sit down on a cold one any more.
—Mark Twain, "Fenimore Cooper's Literary Offenses," 1895

Although this book is about the international dimensions of humanitarian action, some of the key drivers can be found within the domestic politics and constituencies of donor countries. This chapter examines the place of stated humanitarian policies among the many possible influences, which include diaspora groups, historical connections, and the power of individuals—not only individual policy makers and managers but individuals with consciences pricked by human suffering. The chapter will also draw together some of the lessons of earlier chapters in examining the power of the media as one of the most complex drivers of humanitarian action.

A logical hierarchy of starting points for a discussion about humanitarianism might begin with humanitarian principles—neutrality, impartiality, proportionality, and so on, as discussed in earlier chapters. The discussion might then logically move to policies: the framework within which a particular agency or government acts, individually or in concert with others. The structures and delivery mechanisms that give substance to these principles and policies would be next, and the actual timing and form of assistance would be determined by need. Earlier chapters have made the point that while such hierarchies do exist within each donor government and within most front-line UN agencies and NGOs, they do not come together in actual emergencies to form a coherent whole. The total is often considerably and embarrassingly less than the sum of the parts.

One reason is that, where humanitarian spending is concerned, the behavior of donor governments can be influenced or completely overshadowed by domestic factors that have little or nothing to do with humanitarianism or need. Regional, historical, and personal connections can play a part. Individual politicians and civil servants, diaspora communities and NGOs may work to override stated national policies. Rock stars, actors, and even bus drivers can put a crisis on any given country's map. And media, especially television, can be a powerful motivator, as well as a source of distorted perceptions and disproportionate response. It is appropriate, however, to begin a discussion of domestic influences with a consideration of governmental policies, because these are the ostensible bedrock on which budgets are approved and spending decisions made.

No government's humanitarian policies are freestanding; instead, they flow from a country's foreign and domestic policies and politics. Often framed in terms of humanitarian principles, donor policies range widely from those that are clearly articulated (as is the case in Switzerland, Sweden, Britain, and Australia) to those that are not (for example, Canada and the United States). Parliaments in some countries legislate binding ground rules governing the objectives and allocations of emergency assistance. Swiss law not only provides clear objectives for the activities of the SDC, it specifies that resources will be equally divided among the ICRC, United Nations agencies, and NGOs. In other countries, there is an absence of clear policy and officials consequently enjoy broad latitude in its application.

Recent years have seen a tendency toward wider definitions and more inclusive humanitarian policies. France has created an interministerial committee, linking the ministries of development, defense, health, and the interior to coordinate planning, crisis response, and longer-term recovery. Britain has created two conflict prevention funds, bringing together the Foreign Office, the Ministry of Defense, and DFID with funding for expanded operations into security sector reform, disarmament and demobilization, and other areas hitherto off limits for official development assistance and humanitarian consideration. Similar committees and coherence mechanisms are being developed elsewhere.

American legislation is framed in more general terms, leaving most country allocations and delivery choices up to U.S. officials. This opens the way for fierce institutional combat across the executive branch in Washington, where the State Department's Bureau for Population, Refugees, and Migration (BPRM) sees its primary funding clients as UNHCR and the ICRC, while USAID's Office of Foreign Disaster Assistance (OFDA) channels most of its assistance to NGOs and the UN's WFP. As noted in the previous chapter, the Office of Management and Budget, which orchestrates the overall U.S. national budget—slicing the pie into different size pieces for various federal entities—concerns itself little with humanitarian policies.

U.S. officials sometimes express impatience with outsiders who do not take time to understand essential distinctions between USAID and the State Department, between OFDA and BPRM, and between their respective enabling statutes and accountabilities. Outsiders bewildered by the U.S. labyrinth would undoubtedly find European Commission structures equally opaque and arcane. But even where policies are clearly articulated, as in Britain or Australia, front-line agencies say of the former that there is no effective overall U.K. humanitarian policy. And Australian NGOs criticize the Australian Agency for International Development (AusAID) for "policy on the run."

Policy may derive deliberately or accidentally from architectural issues. In some countries, all official development assistance—developmental and humanitarian combined—is managed by one agency, sometimes an integral part of the foreign ministry as in Ireland and Italy, sometimes with an arm's length relationship as in Canada and Britain. In other countries there are real dichotomies. In Japan (and in the United States), food aid is provided by the ministry of agriculture, but decisions about its allocation are made in the foreign ministry, resulting in high levels of ambiguity about who is actually in charge. In Germany, the foreign ministry has primary responsibility for humanitarian delivery, while BMZ, the development ministry, has responsibility for bridging the gap between relief and development. BMZ therefore programs a lot of its funding through WFP, while the foreign ministry deals largely with UNHCR. Adding further potential for confusion, the cabinet position for the foreign ministry (based in Berlin) is usually held by one party in a coalition government, while BMZ (based in Bonn) is held by another.

Humanitarian policy confusion and obscurantism is often the source of misunderstanding and antagonism among donors, and between donors and the field agencies that deliver humanitarian assistance. Rather than exhibiting policy coherence, donors can behave as though they are in a bazaar, funding favored agencies for reasons known only to themselves, sometimes encouraging individualistic and erratic "cowboy" behavior by grantees. There are also varying degrees of consistency between articulated donor policy and actual implementation. And some policies, while not written, are well understood. Flag-flying, for example, is not stated by any government as a principle, a policy, or even a minor goal, but it is near the top of the agenda for many. Badging and national identification are, in fact, among a plethora of often unstated domestic policy considerations affecting the delivery of humanitarian assistance.

There are refreshing exceptions. Articulated in The Hague, the Dutch government's commitment to the multilateral system and its impatience with the flag-flying proclivities of other donors are reflected with remarkable precision in the field. In Afghanistan, for example, the Netherlands channelled its contributions to NGOs entirely through the United Nations and did not require the display of its logos by its operating partners. NGOs from outside the Netherlands received some of the grants, to the evident discomfort of Dutch-based agencies.

Inconsistencies within and among donor agencies abound, not just in practice but also in nomenclature. Donors interpret the words humanitarian, reconstruction, recovery, and peace-building in very different ways. Linking relief and development (LRD) is broadly recognized as essential to building sustainable peace, but many donors have no particular mechanism for funding recovery and reconstruction work. Those without ongoing bilateral programs will leave a country as soon as the emergency is deemed to be over. While they have clear authority to respond to emergencies, many have difficulty in funding reconstruction activities. As a result, some define emergencies expansively, to allow for continuing involvement. Policy in this area is a source of particular frustration to NGOs, which often find themselves forced to apply for a series of short-term grants, often for durations of only three or six months. The resulting discontinuity is reflected in patchwork approaches on the ground and an absence of transparency in donor-partner relationships. This area urgently needs change if humanitarian action is to be more than what one writer calls "global poor relief and riot control."[1]

Aid officials caution against bald comparisons between donors, as if the policy formation and implementation processes of the United States, United Kingdom, Japan, or the European Union should be expected to have the clarity that prevails in Switzerland, Sweden, Australia, or the Netherlands. And it is not surprising that donor policies and programs—and the national foreign policy contexts in which they are formulated—would differ significantly. But while it makes good sense for individual donors to carve out a particular niche within the humanitarian financing economy, greater thought must be given to the composite puzzle into which the separate pieces ostensibly fit. In any case, it is not unreasonable to scrutinize policy processes, regardless of their justification, if they have negative effects on civilians in distress.

Major donors in particular can have a larger impact on the international humanitarian enterprise and thus bear disproportionate responsibility for the current widespread disarray in humanitarian financing. In fact, one senior U.S. aid official expressed that the single most important global improvement in humanitarian donor behavior would be for the United States to achieve greater coherence in its own policies. That coherence would have a more salutary influence on the system, he believed, than would the more standard remedy of harmonizing the policies of all donors.

A government's other policy interests and constituencies are often reflected in its approach to humanitarian financing. Norway gives greater humanitarian assistance to countries such as Guatemala, Sudan, and Sri Lanka where it supports efforts for peace and reconciliation. Twenty-five years of activism by the Swedish Committee for Afghanistan is reflected in the twenty-year stretch of Swedish International Development Agency (SIDA) involvement in Afghanistan before 2001 and in the significant levels of SIDA funding for humanitarian and reconstruction work afterward. Such interest was particularly welcome and significant at a time when other donors were only just becoming engaged.

Policies can protect. They can be valuable in helping aid officials fend off importuning politicians on the home front, inappropriate funding applicants, and other scavenging elements from across the government bureaucracy. Aid officials in various governments also use policy as an anchor in rapid onset emergencies. At the same time, policy may prove less useful in major crises than emergencies with lower political profile. But even clearly stated policies can be broken or ignored, as will be seen from the following examples.

First, *history* can have a major influence on a government's humanitarian spending. Examples abound of countries whose financial support for humanitarian activities reflects their historical relationships with a given area. Chapter 3 demonstrated that for East Timor, Japanese aid had strong World War II connections. Similarly, Australia, the United States, Canada, and others could be regarded as using their aid programs to compensate for their lack of interest in East Timor's humanitarian crises between 1975 and 1999.[2] The considerable Portuguese support recalls Timorese history as a Portuguese colony for almost five centuries. East Timor chose Portuguese as one of its official languages, attracting language-teaching expertise and technical assistance from Portugal as well as Brazil, which quickly opened an embassy in the country. However, some in East Timor see this choice as a possible cause of future conflict: Because the language was spoken only by returning exiles, they had the first pick of senior government positions, at the expense of those who stayed and fought inside the country for twenty-five years. The ensuing resentment is real—and understandable.

Second, *conditionality* regularly raises its ugly head in humanitarian spending. Some donors insist on the use of their nationals in humanitarian programs, or they will be more generous if their nationals are placed in key positions. Others tie humanitarian funding for UN agencies to the use of their national NGOs, consultants, and companies. Some countries give preference to their own NGOs because of the visibility such work commands on the home front. National NGOs, in their advocacy as well as their delivery modes, are often more attractive to donors than more remote, bureaucratic, and sometimes unpopular

UN organizations. Japanese construction companies were major beneficiaries of Japanese funds for reconstruction in East Timor, even
though they were often commercially uncompetitive. Some 70 percent
of U.S. foreign aid appropriations is spent in the United States. This
fact is a selling point for Congress, but it is seen as a liability by those
who believe that economic assistance should first and foremost stimu-
late growth and improve lives in poorer nations. Such are the downsides
of tied procurement.

Private business has long benefited from humanitarian and reconstruction contracts, but in recent years, big business has become much
bigger and more obvious. When U.S. Vice President Dick Cheney was
secretary of defense in the early 1990s, the Pentagon paid a company
named Kellogg, Brown & Root $3.9 million to produce a feasibility
study on how private sector contracting could be used to save money
for the military. Kellogg, Brown & Root subsequently received another
contract to implement their proposal, and when Cheney retired, he
became president of Halliburton, an energy holding company, of which
Kellogg, Brown & Root is a subsidiary. There is more than a little irony
in the fact that Halliburton, under Cheney's management, took in some
$23.8 million to rebuild Iraqi oil fields damaged by the U.S. military
during the first Gulf War.

But in this me-first world there is more, much more. In 2002, Kellogg, Brown & Root received a contract worth up to $7 billion from the
U.S. Army Corps of Engineers to provide the U.S. Air Force with logistical and maintenance support. And Bechtel, the largest construction contractor in the United States—once headed by George Shultz, Ronald
Reagan's secretary of state—received contracts in Iraq that were expected
to total $680 million over eighteen months. Writing about "squeezing a
profit from the wreckage of Iraq," Chalmers Johnson says, "These
open-ended contracts did not come about through competitive bidding
but through backdoor deals guided by the Bush Administration. Oversight is virtually non-existent."[3] Small wonder that NGO advocates of
increased funding for foreign aid make sure to include representatives
of the U.S. Chamber of Commerce and other corporate interests in
their lobbying delegations to Capitol Hill.

The political economy of Iraqi reconstruction was on display in living color in late 2003. Pentagon guidelines limited eligibility to bid on
$18.6 billion in U.S.-funded reconstruction contracts to firms based in
the sixty-three nations of the U.S.-led Coalition Provisional Authority.
This stipulation eliminated companies from France, Germany, Canada,
and Russia—countries that in the UN Security Council had led the opposition to the war. Although commercial considerations played a major
role in the Pentagon's decision, the punitive message was clear. The cries
of outrage from Paris, Berlin, Ottawa, and Moscow also demonstrated

ANOTHER CHAOTIC SCENE AS THE TRULY DESPERATE
FIGHT FOR MORSELS OF AID.

IRAQI AID DISTRIBUTION

RECONSTRUCTION CONTRACTS IRAQ

RECONSTRUCTION CONTRACTS

Source: By De Adder. ©Artizans. Halifax Daily News, Halifax, Canada.
(April 9, 2003). Reprinted with permission.

strong resentment at their exclusion from the gravy train. Even though
the decision was presented as being based on "essential security interests of the United States," it came at a time when the United States was
seeking to expand the political ownership and burden-sharing of Iraq's
reconstruction.[4]

Almost touchingly naive by comparison, British humanitarian aid is
now completely freed of tied procurement. DFID can fund NGOs of any
nationality, for example, removing the issue of national identification and
focusing more on geographic, sectoral, and performance-based criteria.
For several donors, food aid is often available because of, and is tied to,
domestic procurement. Nevertheless, some countries provide cash rather
than commodities to the WFP. Ninety percent of Canadian food aid must
be sourced in Canada. The idea, however, of triangular transactions,
involving purchase of commodities with donor funding in a third country
near a given crisis (or even in the country itself), has now taken root. Benefits include both greater burden sharing and lower cost, even though
direct stimulus to the donor's own economy may be reduced.

Third, *diaspora and activist groups* often play a major role in influencing the financing decisions of donor governments. Gujaratis in Britain
were major contributors to NGO fundraising campaigns at the time of
the 2001 Turkish earthquake. Turkish-born Australians encouraged the

Australian government to respond to the earthquake, even though Turkey was a distant priority. Italian support for an Argentinean disaster was influenced by the presence of a sizeable Italian community in Argentina. Canada's Minister for Asia-Pacific Affairs, Raymond Chan, insisted that CIDA contribute to a relief effort in Taiwan after the 1999 earthquake, even though Taiwan was not eligible for official development assistance (ODA) and even though it hardly needed the pittance that was eventually extracted from an overstretched CIDA budget. A pro-Massoud lobby in France resulted in pre-2001 French aid being skewed mainly to the north of Afghanistan. Fretilin political activists such as José Ramos-Horta and the East Timor Action Network (ETAN) built a base of quiet political support that was finally activated for East Timor in 1999, influencing funding decisions in Portugal, Brazil, Ireland, and the United States. The U.S..administration requested $10 million from Congress for East Timor in 2000 and received $25 million.

Finally, *other domestic agendas* regularly intrude on humanitarian principles and policies. U.S. funding for family planning activities has reflected the attitudes of successive administrations and their constituent bases among "right to life" and "pro-choice" groups. Funding to UN Fund for Population Activities (UNFPA) was cut during the administration of Ronald Reagan, reinstated during the Clinton years, and then slashed again during the George W. Bush administration. During the mid-1990s, Germany funded housing projects in Bosnia, not because of housing needs per se, but to encourage Bosnian refugees in Germany to go home.

It would be a mistake to assume that the influence of domestic politics is always negative and distorting, or to limit the existence of such influence to the major donors. The political economy of humanitarian financing is characterized not only by discontinuities and parochialism but also by the creative efforts of some donor governments at gap-filling. The United States and the European Union debated the issue of GM food aid, with domestic interests in recipient countries seeing GM food as a cover-up for donor efforts to expand or preserve commercial market share. Sizing up the standoff, the Swiss and Canadian governments agreed to absorb the cost of milling GM food to enhance its acceptability to wary, drought-affected countries in southern African. The disinterested observer could be forgiven for wondering, however, whether the core issue was international trade and market development, the human health risks of GM food, or the relief of starvation.

Keeping ODA at or above the OECD target of 0.7 percent of a nation's GNP has become a point of pride for many smaller countries, with scores of civic, religious, and solidarity groups firmly committed to sustaining or improving contribution levels. There are indeed a number of humanitarian superpowers that have distinguished themselves by the level and the steadiness of their contributions, as well as by the quality and responsiveness of the funding they provide. Officials from governments with superior track records in humanitarian financing—the Netherlands and Sweden are examples—note that the support among their citizenry for responding to emergency and reconstruction situations provides them with "a fairly free hand" in their use of resources. In contrast, officials from countries in which the public is less well informed and less engaged believe that their hands are tied when it comes to responding creatively and in less self-serving ways to particular challenges.

There is one dismal sleight of hand in humanitarian spending statistics that is worth mentioning. Since 1982, donor governments have included in their ODA calculations costs associated with the travel of refugees to and domestic support in their own (i.e., the donor) countries, for twelve months. At something between $5,000 and $14,000 per capita a year, these costs are significantly higher than the average expenditure per beneficiary overseas, which in 2001 ranged between $20 and $177. Australia has even counted in its ODA total the costs of interning boat people who sought refuge in Australia. One quarter of all reported humanitarian spending in 2001—and as much as half in the cases of Austria, Canada, Denmark, and France—never left the country of origin.[5] As in the case of tied procurement, some truth in packaging would be a healthy antidote to overestimating the generosity of wealthier nations.

Since humanitarian policy is neither self-starting nor self-correcting, concerned individuals can sometimes dramatically influence public awareness and donor policies. Irish rock musician Bob Geldoff played such a role in the Ethiopian famine of the 1980s, and more recently U2's Bono was key to raising awareness about humanitarian and debt issues. Tom Hyland, an activist bus driver in Ireland, helped put the East Timor crisis on the map of Irish policy makers during the 1990s. A strong development or foreign minister can influence the volume and the quality of allocations by country, by sector, and by delivery mechanism. Foreign Minister Lloyd Axworthy is credited with having raised Sierra Leone among Canada's humanitarian priorities, in part as a test case for his own human security agenda. Development Minister Jan Pronk made it his personal business to visit humanitarian crises, returning to report in person to the Dutch parliament, mobilizing his ministry and colleagues throughout the government and galvanizing Dutch public opinion. His influence on Dutch financial and military engagement in several major crises was palpable. Aid and human rights workers also recall with appreciation Ireland's President Mary Robinson's visit to Rwanda in September 1994, Irish Foreign Minister David Andrews' visit to East Timor in April

1999, and British International Development Minister Clare Short's leadership on Rwanda and Sierra Leone.

Such factors as government visibility and a politician's ego may affect the timing of a decision. A Canadian humanitarian aid package for southern Africa was approved within two weeks because the minister wanted something to announce at the 2002 G8 meeting that took place in Canada. For exactly the same reason, a package of Canadian project approvals for Afghanistan was delayed for months until the minister could visit personally and make the announcement in Kabul.

Strong-willed drivers of policy can overplay their hands. The visit of ECHO head Emma Bonino to Kabul in September 1997 is credited with helping mobilize European sentiment in support of the human rights of Afghan women. But it led overnight to harassment and increased difficulties for aid personnel and Afghan women in the country itself. A visit by U.K. Minister Clare Short to Kabul in mid-2002 was welcomed by many UN agency personnel, then under what they considered unreasonable pressure from the Afghan authorities to be more responsive to the government's relief and reconstruction agenda. The Kabul authorities, however, made no secret of their view that her message and approach were high-handed and patronizing. And while Short developed a reputation for integrity, compassion, and good understanding of her brief, she was far from consistent, often overriding stated government policies, developing pet projects and pet countries, and— until her final showdown with Prime Minister Blair over Iraq—staying well away from larger geopolitical questions.

Although Short was regarded as part of the British "old left," she reflected views about humanitarian and development spending shared by an increasingly vocal right-wing establishment, particularly in the United States. "Who represents the people of the world?" she asked in a 2001 BBC interview. "It's the governments. . . . Having lots of NGOs squawking all over the place won't help. They don't speak for the poor, the governments do."[6] Compare her sentiments about NGOs with those of American conservatives. The American Enterprise Institute— where, according to President George W. Bush, "some of the finest minds in our nation are at work on some of the greatest challenges to our nation"—has set up an NGOWatch Web site to track the growing influence of nongovernmental organizations.[7] At a 2003 conference "NGOs: The Growing Power of the Unelected Few," one speaker cited NGO opposition to the delivery of GM maize to southern Africa and use of DDT to fight malaria as examples of eco-imperialism and a "callous disregard for life. . . . NGOs definitely provide benefits in the short run," he said, "but in the long run, their influence is almost always malign."[8]

One might conclude that humanitarian NGOs had been lobbying governments in favor of murderers or child molesters. In fact, NGOs do lobby governments on humanitarian issues, but many have such a symbiotic relationship with governmental funding agencies that overt criticism and major public schisms are rare. Clare Short objected to mild NGO requests for reconsideration of British funding for pipelines and dams that promised to cause dislocation and hardship for people in Cameroon, China, and elsewhere. The American Enterprise Institute was reflecting Bush Administration outrage at the reluctance of some American NGOs to fall in line behind government political and military policies in Iraq, as well as its own conservative political agenda.

Referring to NGOs as government contractors, Andrew Natsios, the head of USAID (and himself a former NGO executive), said, "If you even mention your own organization once when you're in the villages, I will tear up your contract and fire you. . . . You are an arm of the U.S. government right now, because we need to show the people of Iraq an improvement in their standard of living in the next year or two. And I have to have it clearly associated with the U.S. government."[9] Natsios was speaking about Iraq at a time when U.S. policies and presence were in danger of unravelling. But the tensions for NGOs—between receiving government resources and dancing to tunes demanded by the piper—are real and perennial.

Fits of domestic pique are not unique to the great powers. Australian government core grants to UNHCR were dramatically reduced in 2002 after the refugee agency made critical comments about Australia's ominously named Pacific solution for illegal refugees, including women and children: putting them in detention camps or shipping them off to Pacific islands such as Nauru. "No connection at all," said government officials. "Cause and effect" said observers who could add and subtract. UNHCR has proceeded with caution, but it has proceeded nevertheless, in raising concerns about proposed EU legislation that might impinge on international refugee law. Like NGOs, UN agencies must be wary of biting the hands that feed them.

The American Enterprise Institute takes aim squarely at NGO advocacy. NGOs are wolves in sheep's clothing according to AEI adjunct fellow, John Entine. "Anti-free market NGOs under the guise of corporate reform are extending their reach into the boardrooms of corporations."[10] Failing to see the irony, perhaps, in the AEI's own NGO status and its own high-profile advocacy, Entine and other AEI stalwarts ignore the fact that NGOs, or civil society organizations, or charities, or whatever else one might call them, have always been about two things: helping people and promoting change. The Anti Slavery Society helped runaway slaves. But it was, more importantly, an unabashedly political organization that advocated an end to slavery. NGOs working with handicapped children provide services, but they are also fierce protectors of the children's rights.

Similarly, international human rights organizations such as Amnesty International and Human Rights Watch have had much to say over the years about conflict—not just about conflict's impact on the lives of ordinary people, but about its causes as well. One extraordinary NGO campaign in recent years that had every intention of extending its reach into the boardrooms of corporations, and did so successfully, was the campaign to halt the flow of "conflict diamonds," used to fuel some of the most devastating wars in Africa during the 1990s and beyond. More than three million people in Angola, the DRC, Sierra Leone, and Liberia died directly or indirectly in wars financed by rebels who occupied diamond fields and sold their booty into a completely opaque and unregulated diamond trade. Lest the number of dead pass by too quickly, let us repeat: *three million.*

At the height of the conflict diamond phenomenon, a billion dollars' worth of the rough diamonds—which eventually found their way into the showrooms of Tiffany, Cartier, and other jewelers—were being used each year to buy AK-47s, rocket launchers, and bullets. Mining firms thought nothing of using mercenaries, more politely known as private military contractors, to protect their interests, import weapons, and even to fight wars. One of the most concentrated forms of wealth, diamonds were subject to no questions, either inside or outside the industry. A campaign started in 1998 by British NGO Global Witness and Canadian NGO Partnership Africa Canada led eventually to the creation of a broad NGO coalition. In January 2003, an international diamond certification system was inaugurated, endorsed by more than fifty governments and the diamond industry itself.

Today, any rough diamonds shipped across borders must be accompanied by a government certificate attesting to their origin and their freedom from taint. The scheme is backed by an industry chain of custody, a set of internationally agreed-upon standards for monitoring and control, and a global data base of all international diamond production and trade. Among several factors contributing to the end of diamond wars in Africa, one was undoubtedly the Kimberley Process Diamond Certification Scheme, an example—like the 1997 Treaty to Ban Land Mines—of important and effective advocacy, and NGO-government collaboration on a major humanitarian issue.[11]

When he was president of MSF, James Orbinski said, "We affirm the independence of the humanitarian from the political." Where advocacy is concerned, the distinction must necessarily be somewhat nuanced, and MSF itself has certainly not shied from taking strong political positions where humanitarian principles are at stake. Neil Macfarlane observes, "The humanitarian imperative is best served not by avoiding the political process but by consciously engaging it. Creating and sustaining space for humanitarian action may—and there is an element of irony here—be facilitated by the political engagement of aid agencies, particularly by effective advocacy. This engagement is not a sacrifice of humanitarian principle but a defence of it."[12]

Advocacy is aimed at changing policies. Policies may also simply be overridden. In Sweden, the minister responsible for SIDA is explicitly forbidden from adding personal agenda items to policies adopted by parliament (in fact it is unconstitutional for any minister to micromanage independent government agencies), but this is far from universally true. Occasionally, even in Sweden, a minister tries to take direct action. CIDA minister Maria Minna was in El Salvador in 2001 when an earthquake struck and took a personal interest in ensuring that Canadian aid was quick off the mark—not a bad thing. But personal attention from high levels can be amateurish and can deflect agencies from larger humanitarian needs. When Cyclone Zoë struck the Solomon Islands on December 28, 2002—the height of the Christmas season when giving is at its peak in the West—the German development minister demanded action. Officials had a difficult time persuading her to back off. Meanwhile, in Australia, AusAID "went live," bypassing NGOs and the Red Cross, dispatching aircraft and boats, and only later discovering that in fact there were no deaths or serious injuries. Humanitarian theater often plays to negative reviews.

High-profile politicians and celebrities are not the only ones with influence over where and how humanitarian assistance is delivered. Officials within government aid agencies have tremendous influence, and in the absence of political pressures and undue media attention, they are, in a sense, the guardians of the agency's humanitarian policies and vision. This can work in various ways and to various ends. A single official in CIDA was largely responsible for changing Canadian food aid policy, significantly reducing food aid deliveries in favor of additionalities—what was billed as a bigger bang for the food aid buck. Vitamin A, for example, can be provided for less than a dollar per child per year, with a much greater impact than straight food aid delivery. Good idea? Not as far as WFP and food pipeline agencies were concerned. Vitamin A is not much good to a starving baby in a refugee camp.

A different kind of individual—the wealthy philanthropist—is emerging with ideas about policy and its implementation. The Bill and Melinda Gates Foundation in 2000 was endowed with $25 billion to improve equity in global health and learning. In 1997, businessman and philanthropist Ted Turner announced a historic gift of $1 billion to support the United Nations, with specific reference to children's health; the environment; women and population; and peace, security, and human rights. Turner's gift was especially innovative in that it sought to redress and influence the payment of back dues owed by the United States to the United Nations. And businessman George Soros, through his Open Society Institute and the Soros foundations network, spends half a billion dollars annually promoting the rule of law, respect for human rights, democratically elected governments, and market economies. Among the Soros grants: support to Global Witness for its work on the diamond campaign. This grant and undoubtedly many others must give the American Enterprise Institute—watching NGOs from its frosty aerie—many a sleepless night.

Individual philanthropy, however, is not without its problems. Like governments, individuals have their interests and priorities and can be as prone to micromanagement as the bureaucrats they seek to energize—or outflank. And while Ted Turner's support for the United Nations may have helped embarrass the United States into paying back dues, many felt that it actually helped let the United States off the hook for the full bill. Philanthropists and foundations are thus vulnerable to the dangers that humanitarian organizations themselves face: of undermining the acceptance of responsibility by the actors whom they seek to energize.

Other mechanisms can be used to influence domestic public opinion and provide helpful recognition of humanitarian efforts. One of the best known is the Nobel Peace Prize, which has often been awarded to "works in progress" to provide encouragement, or to individuals and organizations that are unabashedly political in their pursuit of peacemaking and the humanitarian ideal: Bishop Belo and José Ramos-Horta, MSF, the Land Mine Campaign, Amnesty International, the United Nations itself.

"Political considerations in aid are a given," laments a mid-level government official, before continuing on a more upbeat note. "Yet many people in the aid business would like to bridge the tension between politics and human need." That bridging often takes place successfully on a day-to-day basis by committed people working quietly behind the scenes, but it is not easy. "We sometimes feel like a horse, galloping across a frozen lake," said a German official. "We never know when we're on dry ground. Usually it's ice." He was referring to the somewhat thankless and unpredictable job of trying to improve or implement policies in the ways that civil servants must, by attending endless coordination meetings, trying to explain the often unexplainable—upward to supervisors and sideways to implementers, reporters, domestic interest groups, and politicians—all in the cause of less "me too" and more responsible results.

◄

A major factor in domestic decision-making and in the political economy of humanitarian action is the news media. Humanitarian agencies and donor governments have relationships with the media that at times can be highly supportive of and beneficial to the humanitarian enterprise, and at other times, deeply antagonistic and even damaging. In 1995, UN Secretary-General Boutros-Ghali told the editors of *Time* magazine, with a certain bitterness, "We have 16 members in the Security Council: the 15 members plus CNN. Long-term work doesn't interest you because the span of attention of the public is limited. Out of 20 peacekeeping operations, you are interested in one or two. Two years ago, it was Mogadishu. Now it is Sarajevo. Tomorrow it will be Haiti. And because of the limelight on one or two, I am not able to obtain the soldiers or the money or the attention for the 17 other operations. Nobody was taking care of what was going on in Rwanda. It was one of my personal greatest failures."[13] Years later, Roméo Dallaire, the Canadian general who headed the abortive UN peacekeeping effort in Rwanda, said something similar. Recalling a scandal involving two figure-skating champions, he observed, "There was more coverage of Tonya Harding during the three and a half months of the Rwandan genocide than there was of the genocide."[14]

Aid critic Michael Maren describes a five-step cycle of famine reporting.[15] Step one is the early predictor story—a news release from Rome or from an NGO about an impending disaster and the need for action to avert it. Step two occurs when a few organizations manage to attract one or more reporters to the area. The story then becomes more than the famine; it is about how the famine is being ignored. Step three begins when more news organizations arrive, to "expose" the famine. The suffering of people then becomes "a morality play starring the news media." Step four occurs when the numbers grow. "How many people have to die before the famine fires its booster rockets and becomes a major media event?" Maren asks. A lot, with numbers often bearing no relationship to reality. Most front-line agencies know they will never receive enough to deal adequately with the problem, so exaggeration becomes the humanitarian's stock in trade. Step five occurs when the media arrive in full force. "Now the crisis has become a cause. An international public has been mobilized. Donations flow."

In truth, many parts of Africa are in chronic step one mode, and few move beyond it, regardless of need, and regardless of newsworthiness.

It has become fashionable to argue, in fact, that the CNN effect is *not* a major factor in the provision of emergency assistance and that political interests and proximity are more powerful stimulants of humanitarian action. Angola and Sudan, for example, with no media attention to speak of, have received several hundred million dollars worth of humanitarian assistance in recent years. And North Korea, with virtually no media coverage, received significantly more than Sudan or Angola between 1997 and 2001. This reflects in part the need, and in part the strategic interest of the donors involved. The media played no appreciable role.

Where strategic interests are not a major determinant, however, the media may play a key role in the initiation of mass public support. Consistent with Maren's step two, this was the case in Biafra in 1967 (initiated by one determined reporter, Frederick Forsythe) and in Ethiopia in 1984 (by another determined reporter, Michael Buerk). The media may also make the difference between a generous response and one that is less so: Its coverage of, and the humanitarian response to, the Mozambique floods of February 2000 were considerably more generous than the much worse Orissa cyclone, only a few months earlier in October 1999.[16] This was in part because the Indian government made it difficult for international reporters to get to Orissa. It was also because the Mozambique floods were framed by dramatic shots taken from helicopters—and by one incredible visual: a woman who had given birth in a tree.

The media can play a role in holding both donor governments and humanitarian agencies accountable for their efforts, but this function is uneven and unreliable. Many emergencies receive no international media attention and virtually no humanitarian response. That said, the media can be very important in drawing public attention to a humanitarian emergency. One reason for the success of the conflict diamond campaign was the NGO media strategy. NGOs targeted business editors and specialist newspapers like the *Financial Times*. They also worked on stories in magazines like *Vanity Fair, Esquire,* and *National Geographic*—magazines with an affluent readership and the heartland of diamond advertising.

The media also can play a positive and sometimes necessary role in shaping public impressions of need. Sustained media attention, however, is important to creating political movement. One reason for the lack of international public interest in Sierra Leone during much of the crisis there was the episodic and brief media coverage. In addition, there are problems with complexity. The public, politicians, and decision-makers cannot understand complex issues if they are presented mainly in thirty-second sound bites. International NGOs thus had great difficulty in raising funds for Sierra Leone, with one Canadian NGO unable to cover even its fundraising costs.

Unlike NGOs, governmental donors sometimes ignore the media, or try to. Some fear the media and are annoyed by it; the media can pressure governments to do things they would otherwise be inclined to avoid. When Britain hired South African helicopters for its relief effort during the Mozambique floods in 2000, the British press howled that too little was being done. As a result, the government felt obliged to send British helicopters despite the enormous distance and cost, delivering them too late to be of any great use and giving the media a second stick with which to beat the government. An interesting study has been done of the relationship between the Australian media and government over the issue of East Timor between 1975 and 2000. Here the media played a key role in keeping human rights and humanitarian issues in the public eye, creating real friction in Australian-Indonesian relations.[17] In other instances, governments *need* media attention before they can allocate or reallocate funding to a new emergency. They may actually work to generate media coverage to justify disproportionate spending in major political-humanitarian emergencies such as Kosovo, Afghanistan, and Iraq.

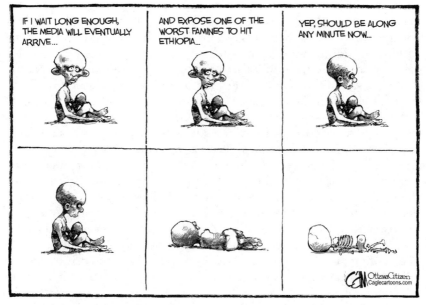

Source: "Ethiopia" by Cam Cardow. © Cagle Caroons, Inc. The Ottawa Citizen, Ottawa, Canada (May 16, 2003). Reprinted with permission.

Regardless of pressure from the media, humanitarians, and celebrities, however, no amount of publicity will force a government to do something it is determined to avoid. In July 2003, President Bush took a week-long goodwill tour of Africa. The timing could not have been worse because both the Liberian government and Liberian rebels were appealing for the United States to send peacekeeping troops to end a war that had been waxing and waning for fifteen years. With U.S. media attention focused firmly on Africa and this particular issue, the pressure for U.S. action was great. After days of inaction, the president ordered a naval task force to head for Liberian waters. A week later, the humanitarian situation in Monrovia had become grim. Food and water had all but disappeared, and most relief agencies had fled. "Everybody is trapped, it doesn't really matter which direction you go in," one foreign visitor to Monrovia told the UN news service, as forces loyal to President Charles Taylor traded automatic arms fire with rebels in the background. "This is a people being slowly starved to death," he added. "There are no food supplies coming in and there is no rice left. There is very little food and there is rain coming down. There are appalling sanitary conditions. People are very sick. . . ."

Here was a stove lid that would not have burned the U.S. cat. The government and the two rebel factions all asked for U.S. peacekeeping troops. The Congressional Black Caucus and American public opinion supported an intervention. The United States has a long history in Liberia and could have earned tremendous goodwill through a deeper engagement in African peacekeeping. And while the job of pacifying Liberia would not have been quick or easy, Liberia was not Somalia, and it was not Vietnam or, for that matter, Afghanistan or Iraq. Nevertheless, it was not until August 11 that the first international peacekeepers finally arrived, none of them from the United States. With a U.S. naval flotilla now lying offshore, Nigerian and other West Africans finally stepped ashore. In fact when a handful of U.S. marines did land, their job was only to beef up security at the U.S. embassy, where civilians had been laying out the bodies of dead children for media effect. Liberia had reached step four, but step five—booster rockets and donations—never happened. In due course, the U.S. and European reporters decamped, the flotilla sailed away, and Liberia faded from the world's television screens. The humanitarian emergency, however, continued.

Some humanitarian events are more newsworthy than others. NGOs had funding pushed at them in 2002 by governments and private donors alike after the highly photogenic Goma volcano eruption, but they could not get adequate funding for the much larger ongoing emergency elsewhere in the Democratic Republic of the Congo, despite reports of as many as 2.5 million deaths in thirty-two months. "You know instinctively what will sell and what won't," says an NGO director, speaking from years of experience. "You can't raise private donor money for Angola; you need sustained media attention." He might have added Sierra Leone, Liberia, the DRC, and a dozen other places to the list.

There is of course concern that the media can be used politically. By their own admission, journalists were part of the wishful thinking on Afghanistan at the beginning of the 2001 crisis. Years earlier, they had joined a misleading genocide refrain on Biafra.[18] In 2002 they reported widely on a story about the sexual abuse of children under the care of humanitarian agencies in West Africa without ever investigating it directly, and without following up to see what action, if any, had been taken. The embedding of journalists within military units in the 2003 Iraq war also raised questions about media objectivity and coverage of civilian casualties.

It should be recognized, however, that the media are not a humanitarian instrument as such, and journalists are not part of a humanitarian cheering squad. They have their own needs, missions, and institutional politics and ethics. Even very sympathetic journalists must winnow real news from the avalanche of turgid press releases and exaggerated statistics they receive from governments, UN agencies, and NGOs. On any given day, between thirty and forty news releases and press items about humanitarian emergencies are posted on the UN's

Source: © Chappatte-www.globecartoon.com/war (November 5, 2001). Reprinted with permission.

OCHA Relief Web. Exaggeration aside, there are very real needs, but there is only so much disaster news that the media can and will handle at one time.

⇒

In the winter of 1974–1975 a terrible famine struck Bangladesh. Hundreds of thousands of people faced starvation. Outraged by the television images, a Canadian living in Kingston, Ontario, began a fundraising campaign. In a few days he raised about C$60,000, and he promised his donors that every penny of it would go to feed the hungry. There would be no bureaucracy, and no administrative costs. Understanding that any shipments had to comprise food that was both nutritious and appropriate, he had a Canadian milling company produce almost forty tons of a corn-soya-milk blend. He then went to CIDA and asked for an aircraft to fly the food to Bangladesh. Aghast at the potential cost—the flight would have cost more than the food—CIDA refused. In a self-righteous, me-first dudgeon, the man then went to reporters—who took his side, wondering why CIDA would let money stand in the way of saving lives. In the end, Air Canada donated cargo space on a flight going empty to London, and CIDA—unable to withstand the withering media attack—paid for the onward shipment. It was probably the most administratively costly food shipment of all time.

Humanitarianism, perhaps one of the most noble, urgent, and desperate of all causes, has been much usurped by the needs of the giver. The cause has become confused by image and ego—personal, national, and institutional—and by factors that have virtually nothing to do with saving lives and protecting livelihoods. As a result, it is amazing that anything is accomplished by the end of the long, winding road between good intentions and those who survive on the edge of life in war zones and refugee camps. That good people step in to help and press and advocate is not a substitute for a proper systemic response to human need. Sharpened policies, clearer mandates, and better definitions may help, but tinkering at the margins of a system that is so anarchic and so prone to manipulation by vested interests is not enough. The humanitarian enterprise, if it is to deal more effectively with the causes and the results of human calamity, requires a housecleaning of enormous proportions.

8

Scenes of Riot:
The Humanitarian Free-For-All

A degree of constructive competition could be a tonic. The mandates of different agencies must not be a cover for inefficient monopolies.
—Mukesh Kapila[1]

Constructive competition might well be a useful tonic. However, in today's humanitarian world, the shortage of money, combined with donor earmarking, has created a dog-eat-dog competition that is as relentless as it is unconstructive. This chapter examines the scramble among international NGOs for attention and funds, the instrumentalization and crowding out of Southern NGOs, and the convoluted and not very successful efforts within the UN system to reduce competition in favor of better priority-setting.

When thinking about the money spent by Western countries on humanitarian action, it is important to remember that all of it is derived from individuals. Not just some of it; *all* of it. Ninety percent of the money is filtered through governments that obtain it in the form of taxes. About 10 percent of it is given to NGOs and a handful of other organizations as direct donations by individuals responding to appeals.[2] (A pittance is provided in some countries by the private sector and foundations, but the amount is so small it is barely noticeable.) Of the 90 percent controlled by governments, some is spent directly on emergency relief or is channeled through the government of a recipient country. This amount—known as bilateral assistance—is small and usually restricted to natural disasters where local governments retain some delivery capacity.

In complex, man-made emergencies—that is to say war in its various manifestations—most governments make an approximate three-way split in their allocations. About one-third of governmental humanitarian spending is channeled through Red Cross movement affiliates. This also falls under the bilateral rubric, not because another government is involved but because decisions about what to fund and at what levels are made by the donor government alone. (Obviously "unilateral" would be more appropriate than "bilateral," but in the world of international assistance, technically there is no such thing.) Sometimes these funds will be directly channeled through the national Red Cross or Red Crescent society. Sometimes they will go to the International Federation of the Red Cross (IFRC) or the International Committee of the Red Cross (ICRC).

Another third of what donor governments allocate is channeled through NGOs—mainly Northern NGOs and those with headquarters or some management presence in the donor country. Although European NGOs can apply across European borders, the Danish government tends to give to Danish NGOs and the Belgian government tends to give to Belgian NGOs. Like funding for the Red Cross, this form of spending also falls under the heading of bilateral assistance. Some of the support for NGOs will be in the form of cash, and some in commodities—mainly food. Some of what Northern NGOs receive will in turn be given to local NGOs, but Northern NGOs will program a large part of the money directly themselves.

The final third, roughly, goes to UN agencies in the form of cash and commodities. This is known as multilateral assistance. UN agencies will spend some of the money directly, some of it through national and local government agencies, and some through NGOs. The major UN relief agencies—UNHCR, WFP, and UNICEF—spend between one-third and half of what they receive through a combination of international and local NGOs, which act as partner organizations or contractors for the sponsoring agency. Because NGOs receive something like a third of governmental humanitarian spending directly, plus one-third to one-half of what the major UN agencies spend, and because they raise about 10 percent of total humanitarian funding from private donors, they program half or more of the relief assistance in any given emergency. NGOs are the workhorses of the international humanitarian sector.

The split described here is approximate. It varies from donor country to donor country, from one emergency to the next, and from one stage of an emergency to another. NGOs and the Red Cross typically receive more in the early stages of a sudden emergency than UN agencies, in part because they often can move faster. As time passes, and as the coordinating and leavening role of UN agencies comes more to the fore, they are more likely to receive a larger proportion. And as Chapter 1 indicated—and as demonstrated in Iraq, Afghanistan, and East Timor—private sector firms also receive contracts from governments (and occasionally from UN agencies) for emergency and reconstruction efforts. As well, there are claims from the military for both humanitarian funding and a greater humanitarian role.

Because very few emergencies are adequately funded, the demands on governments from each set of actors always outstrip available funding. There is another way of saying this: Competition among implementing agencies is stiff. In theory, this should not be a bad thing. As in business, sellers of services—UN agencies, NGOs, etc.—compete with sellers. And buyers of services—government donor agencies—compete with buyers. Governments, since they hold most of the money, should be able to get the best and most appropriate service for the needs at hand. Competition thus could help reduce costs and sharpen quality.

But humanitarian funding operates in an imperfect market, one where financial and humanitarian decisions are made for very political reasons, where quality is often given the most cursory consideration, and where advertising and national identification (i.e., flag waving) often substitute for substance. And while there is certainly much competition among sellers, there is, in fact, little among the buyers. Paris may want to keep up with the Washington and London Joneses in terms of the latest fashions, but actual spending will be determined very much by foreign policy considerations and domestic political concerns. Buyers may compete in matters of image, but in matters of substance the free market analogy does not apply. For example, when the Afghan government looks for an agency to rebuild the country's crumbled irrigation infrastructure with donor funding, it has no way of setting the supply options side by side and making a judgment purely on cost effectiveness and quality.

The sellers of services—NGOs; the Red Cross movement, UN agencies—also scramble for attention and money, both within and among the sectors. Private sector firms and the military may also become involved. Competition is fierce, and there will inevitably be a howl of protest, for example, if a Japanese firm gets a contract that might have gone to a more traditional humanitarian agency, or if a platoon of soldiers puts a roof on a hospital and asks for reimbursement from a government's humanitarian budget. UN agencies watched the evolution of the European Union's ECHO with dismay, their calculators at the ready. ECHO, a multilateral expression of the combined EU member states, gave 40 percent of its budget to NGOs between 1991 and 1997, and about 30 percent to UN agencies. Between 1998 and 2001, however, two-thirds went to NGOs and the Red Cross, and one-fifth to UN agencies.[3] While direct contributions from European governments to UN agencies did not decline during these years, the UN share of total European humanitarian spending did decline as a result of ECHO priorities, and everyone in the funding queue knew it. Was this an accident? Policy? A statement of dissatisfaction with the United Nations? A reflection of personal preferences of ECHO management? A harbinger of things to come? Nobody quite knew how to read the humanitarian tea leaves.[4]

With the exception of some public fundraising done by UNICEF and one or two other UN agencies, all of the money spent by the United Nations is derived from governments.[5] Money for UN peacekeeping operations is drawn from assessed contributions. This means that if a peacekeeping force is mandated for East Timor by the Security Council, UN members will make a compulsory financial contribution, according to a preset formula. Bangladesh may send more peacekeepers than Thailand, and Zambia may send none, but each will contribute financially in accordance with the agreed formula, and Bangladesh and Thailand will be reimbursed by the United Nations from the general pool for their direct on-the-ground costs. In the case of East Timor, the inclusion of humanitarian activities within the overall UN peacekeeping budget helped ensure adequate funds for the UN's aid agencies.

Where humanitarian action is concerned, however, almost all contributions to the United Nations are voluntary. UNHCR, UNICEF, WHO, and the rest start each year with a nominal budget and no cash beyond unexpended funds carried over from previous years, sometimes large, sometimes negligible. They have no idea whether they will meet the target, or when. Personnel departments, required by the vagaries of donor funding to expand and contract from one year to the next and to practice every possible economy, find themselves criticized when—as was the case with UNHCR in the early days of the sudden Kosovar outflow into Macedonia—they are overwhelmed by events. National governments make contributions according to their interest in the plans put forward by each of the UN agencies, their appraisal of a particular agency's capacity, and the priority they give the emergency in question. In the underfunded and highly competitive world of programming agencies, this led to problems during the 1970s and 1980s.

Just like NGOs, UN agencies would put their best foot forward, inevitably exaggerating their particular competencies if not the need. Like actors upstaging one another, they would gravitate to the spotlight and play to what they thought the audience wanted. If a donor wanted children, or protection, or gender, one agency after another would step forward with a proposal. The better an agency's donor antenna and the better its public relations, the more likely it was to receive the attention and the money it needed. The bigger the agency, the larger and more specialized the staff in the donor relations unit was likely to be. "Mission creep" became the order of the day, and coordination among UN agencies was doomed in most circumstances before the first syllable of the word could be uttered.

The problem of runaway competition was addressed in the early 1990s through the creation of something called the Consolidated Appeal Process—the CAP. While known to few outside the humanitarian sector, the CAP deserves review in some detail, as it illuminates the sector's political economy. Each year, the family of UN agencies in a given humanitarian crisis gets together to discuss among themselves and with other humanitarian actors the various needs for assistance and their capacities to respond. They compile a joint appeal, which details what each agency proposes to do in the year ahead. Each November, the CAPs from the major emergencies are grouped and forwarded to donor governments for review and funding. The CAP includes proposals by and for NGOs as well and is supposed to be a coordination exercise as well as a priority-setting mechanism. And, of course, because it is prepared for donor governments, it is the primary UN fundraising tool for specific emergencies. With this new tool, unseemly competition and posturing could be dispensed with, and decisions—at least those involving UN agencies—could be made on the basis of need. The CAP was to herald a new approach to the multilateral ideal, better donor response, and an end to donor cherry-picking of their favorite projects.[6]

It never happened. Despite some improvements, very high levels of donor earmarking—cherry-picking by another name—continued: as much as 85 percent in the case of resources received by UNHCR and WFP. Donors earmarked—and continue to earmark—their contributions by country, by agency, and by project. And they continued to drag their feet into each funding cycle. Dislodging funds from governments is as tricky and as theatrical as it ever was. As noted in an earlier chapter, Afghanistan provides a case in point. An effort to create a strategic framework that would project the broad outlines of policies and programs, avoiding project-level micromanagement, proved problematic. The fact that neither donors nor agencies were willing to limit their freedom of action, however modestly, undermined the general availability and effective use of aid resources.

Earmarking is partly about continued government dissatisfaction with the perceived ineffectiveness of individual multilateral agencies and related concerns about accountability. But the pressures of geopolitics, domestic political interests, and bureaucracy (described in Chapters 6 and 7), continue to loom large. Earmarking is fundamentally about control. One result is that the intended role of multilateral agencies in leveling out the peaks and troughs in humanitarian financing—among regions, countries, and emergencies—has diminished. The so-called forgotten emergencies, which reflect a lack of bilateral donor interest, result from the absence of unearmarked funds with which UN agencies can respond to otherwise unmet needs. As a halfway house between the bilateral and multilateral concepts, ECHO can (and says it intends to) address this issue. ECHO can obviously depoliticize funding from its constituent members, but it also introduces its own priorities and earmarking into the system. Since its inception, ECHO has behaved very much like a bilateral agency in its choice of emergencies, delivery channels, and contracting procedures.

The CAP, in fact, has only contributed to the earmarking phenomenon.[7] By asking UN agencies to lay out their wares on a smorgasbord each year, donors have helped create a system that gives cherry-picking new emphasis. Even donors who would prefer not to earmark have become part of a system that encourages it, allocating their own contributions against specific countries, sectors, and projects.

Many donors complain, in explaining their decisions, that a given CAP is simply an interagency wish list without the tough-minded vetting of priorities needed to bring individual projects into line with available funding. Nonetheless, even those CAPs that are more rigorous—in mid 2003, Angola was described by UN officials and donors as such an appeal—fail to generate the necessary resources. By the end of the year Angola had achieved only 53 percent of its target. "It's a mad world," observes one OCHA official, "in which agencies appeal for what they can get and donors provide what they think their actions will support." Even granted the unevenness in the quality of CAP appeals, donors who do not take the CAP process seriously undermine the possibility of an effective global and country-specific response to need. And while some do take the CAP process seriously—among them Sweden, the Netherlands, and Ireland—others barely give the CAP a serious nod. In the late 1990s, some ECHO field staff were openly derisive of the CAP, treating it as a waste of their time and energy.

Donors require accurate and comprehensive assessments of need as well as realistic programming requests. In the absence of the former, which may completely dwarf the latter, there is no foundation for an effective humanitarian response. It is critical to understand the extent and severity of need, regardless of what donors can or will provide, just as a doctor needs to know all of the injuries in an accident victim, not just the ones he will treat himself. But when presented with needs they cannot meet, donors accuse UN agencies of being unrealistic. "The 2002 CAP for Indonesia was only funded 31 percent. It is totally unrealistic for them to request so much. Why don't they prioritize?" asks a frustrated AusAID official.

Beneath the frustration lies confusion about the CAP. Is it an assessment and priority-setting exercise, a fundraising tool, or a coordination effort? Or is it all three? Different donors answer the question differently. In truth, each function is critical, but the CAP cannot perform them all. Assessment will identify need; coordination will contribute to the efficient use of resources; and fundraising will mobilize them. Fundraising is always likely to be more supply-based than needs-based, pitching its message at perceived donor interests, priorities, and resources. Despite immense needs, a professional fundraising document would never request funds, as in the Indonesian CAP, that are out of all proportion to the resources available. In the confusion, therefore, large CAPs on the one hand are never adequately funded and seem only to frustrate donors, and smaller CAPs, on the other hand, reflect lower expectations and deflated needs.

Several important items are lost in the mix. The first is a sense of priority. Donors repeatedly ask for priorities in the CAP because, in the absence of adequate funding, they want to know what they can say "no" to. But priorities are rarely identified clearly for precisely this reason—because each UN agency knows that the question really means, "Which foot would you prefer to have amputated?" For FAO, an agriculture program may be the number-one priority. And the FAO director may never agree that her programs should be made secondary to those of WFP or UNICEF. Who then will decide that therapeutic feeding is more or less important than seed distribution? In the absence of priority-setting within the CAP, the decision—in the form of earmarking—will be made—and is made—on a daily basis by desk officers in Stockholm, Ottawa, Canberra, and Brussels. The lack of authority given to the humanitarian coordinator at the country level limits the system's ability to make difficult choices.

Multilateral agencies have the ostensible advantage of encouraging burden-sharing. In fact, the prime rationale for multilateral assistance is that it ensures more equitable coverage of need. Whether that objective is borne out in practice, however, is difficult to determine. Certainly the desideratum is undercut by the pattern of donor government earmarking. Australia earmarks for Asia and the Pacific because other donors do not. USAID is concerned that falling levels of Canadian and EU food aid place an undue burden on the United States. Other donors deprecate what they consider undue U.S. influence in WFP. The unevenness of the CAP from country to country also undercuts the goal of proportionality in resource deployment.

As if to underscore the absence of needs-based allocations, improvements in the CAP process have not been matched by an increase in donor subscriptions. Indeed, because it is regularly undersubscribed, the CAP remains a forum for competition and exaggeration except when the process is controlled by an effective, tough-minded, and objective humanitarian coordinator. Even with good in-country coordination, donors still make decisions about UN agencies based on their assessment of program-specific capacities and individual country program managers. Agencies that develop a bad reputation may take years to rehabilitate themselves in a donor's estimation.

Donor priorities often, if not always, trump UN agency priorities. The WHO director in one crisis country laments that all the donors want to support HIV/AIDS, despite his best efforts to raise funds for a more prevalent and more treatable disease. A UN electoral support project in another country became an implementer's nightmare. None of the fourteen donors wanted to pay for vehicles and gasoline; ECHO wanted all staff contracts denominated in euros and used a different exchange rate; and Japan wanted Japanese stickers on everything bought with Japanese funds, a requirement that took the time of three individuals for two days.

Food is perhaps the most obvious example of donor priorities outbidding those of front-line agencies. The choice for those in need and for those on the front lines is seldom between food and something else, it is between food and nothing. And when food aid is your only tool, like the proverbial hammer in search of a nail, hunger is always perceived to be the most serious problem. While food aid may well be needed, in most emergencies bread alone is seldom adequate. In addition, food is a clumsy tool. It is more dependent upon supply than demand; it takes time to mobilize, funds to transport, and elaborate systems to track; it is much less flexible than cash. It should, but often cannot, be sensitive to local market conditions, culture, and protein requirements. It should be, but as in Southern Africa in 2002 was not, sensitive to political considerations about genetically-modified food and long-term market implications.

Some UN agencies are underrecognized as contributors to humanitarian action. In the twenty-eight months following the East Timor crisis, the United Nations Volunteers (UNV) supplied thirty personnel to UNHCR, seventy-nine to UNDP, eleven to WFP, seven to UNICEF, and nineteen to other UN agencies. In addition, it provided more than five hundred individuals to support and manage the electoral process before the crisis erupted. The fact that it is funded only indirectly through the CAP process and does not have an independent funding base contributes to its relative anonymity. Similarly, some NGOs that implement huge proportions of the UN humanitarian effort resent that they are usually (in their view) underfunded and are rarely recognized publicly for their work.

A review of the 2002 donor response to six CAPs can be found in Appendix 1. Several conclusions can be drawn from looking at how donor governments funded these appeals for Angola, Sudan, Tajikistan, the DRC, Sierra Leone, and Afghanistan.[8] First, whether or not UN agencies are setting priorities in the CAP, donors clearly set their own priorities. With the exceptions of WFP, UNHCR, UNICEF, and OCHA, most UN agencies receive little or none of what is requested through the CAP. Food is a higher priority for donors (at least for the United States) than it is for UN agencies: Although food represents only half of what was requested in most CAPs, it usually received about 75 percent of donor resources. Other sectors (agriculture, water and sanitation, health, and education) received less priority attention from donors and significantly less than was requested. The response to these six CAPs in 2002 suggests that UN requests do not reflect donor priorities very well. Another way of saying this is that UN priorities are best met when they pertain to food (WFP), refugees (UNHCR), and women and children (UNICEF).

Something else emerges. The CAP usually includes requests for NGOs. Red Cross and ICRC requests are separate, but with that exception, the CAP is ostensibly a reflection of the combined estimate of need in a given country for all of the operational agencies. While NGO requests are included in the appeal, little or nothing of what they actually receive is recorded in the UN tally at the end of the year. This is not because they received no funding; it is because the UN does not take the NGO component seriously enough to find out what they received. Or it is because the NGOs do not bother to report to the UN on what they received. NGOs believe, in any case, that they are included in appeals only as window dressing. Without additional and aggressive fundraising, they will receive little donor attention and not much active UN support when the CAP is being marketed in those donor capitals that get the most attention.

In fact, in most of the six countries in question, NGOs received at least as much as they requested through the CAP, but it was almost entirely allocated, delivered, and recorded outside the CAP. In Sudan NGOs received nine times what was requested on their behalf in the CAP. There as elsewhere, donors also funded a wide variety of projects submitted by NGOs, projects not even mentioned in the CAP. It is not rocket science, therefore, to conclude that the CAP does not fully reflect need as perceived by donors, because significant funding goes to projects and delivery agents not included in it. Nor is it difficult to conclude that while NGOs may be willing to play a kind of coordination game through the CAP, both they and their donors work to a very large extent outside it. If most NGOs waited for funding to arrive via the CAP, they would starve to death.

All of today's major international assistance-providing NGOs grew out of emergencies, war, and the humanitarian impulse. Save the Children was founded in 1919 in Britain, after the First World War. Foster Parents Plan was a product of the Spanish civil war of the 1930s. Oxfam emerged from the efforts of a group of Quakers—the Oxford Committee for Famine Relief—to send assistance to those suffering in the Greek famine of 1942. CARE emerged from World War II, World Vision from Korea, and MSF from the 1967–1970 Nigerian civil war.

Many typologies have been developed in an effort to describe NGOs. Where humanitarian action is concerned, the categories usually relate to their philosophical origins. Thomas G. Weiss posits a range between "classicists" and "solidarists."[9] Classicists—notably the Red Cross family—avoid political engagement, seek consent for their work, and espouse neutrality and impartiality as a working creed. Solidarists take sides, are willing to override sovereignty, and are not worried about taking a public position. A variation on this spread puts the ICRC at one end of a spectrum beginning with impartiality and independence, and public service contractors at the other, willing if not eager to follow the money. Abby Stoddard has devised a four-part typology: religious NGOs committed to address injustice and express solidarity; "Dunantist" organizations that have their roots in Red Cross humanitarian principles; and "Wilsonian" NGOs, mostly in the United States, that espouse economic improvement and liberal politics and see humanitarianism as broadly compatible with U.S. foreign policy goals.[10]

With the notable exception of MSF, most NGOs today complement their emergency work with development efforts, and historically these came to outweigh the former, often by a factor of ten to one. Ironically, however, all have been forced by the events of recent years to devote an increasing proportion of their attention and income to humanitarian activities. Even though development had become the primary focus of NGO attention, thirty years ago—and even as recently as 15—NGOs led on humanitarian programming. They were almost always first off the mark, and they were the most vocal advocates in emergencies such as Biafra, Bangladesh, and Cambodia.

Today the tables have turned, with NGOs no longer able to set the pace. First, large NGOs cannot afford to "sit out" an emergency for fear of losing market share. CARE US did stay out of Turkey, Chechnya, the Balkans, and the terrible Mozambique flood of 2000, but others such as the International Rescue Committee and Mercy Corps simply moved into their territory. In its own assessment, Oxfam suffered by staying out of Somalia. If an NGO chooses not to be involved, individual donors have difficulty understanding why it wouldn't be there—especially if it's a name-brand NGO—and institutional donors begin to wonder whether the NGO can be counted on elsewhere. Even agencies that have invested heavily in nurturing informed constituencies—the Mennonite Central Committees in the United States and Canada are examples—report inquiries from stakeholders about what they are doing in the latest emergency.

Many international NGOs have leveraged the resources they receive from donor governments and UN agencies to such an extent that they have lost the initiative both programmatically and geographically. As NGO critic Alex de Waal puts it, many are "inherently opportunistic."[11] Where money is concerned, this opportunism manifests itself in two ways, one with regard to the donor public, and the other with regard to official donor agencies. Where the public is concerned, de Waal sees a humanitarian Gresham's Law at work:

> The agency most determined to get the highest media profile obtains the most funds. . . . In doing so it prioritizes the requirements of fund-raising: it follows the TV cameras, employs pretty young women to appear in front of the cameras, engages in picturesque and emotive programmes (food and medicine, best of all for children), it abandons scruples about when to go in and when to leave, and it forsakes coop-eration with its peers for advertising its brand name. Agencies that are more thoughtful. . . . fail to obtain the same level of public attention.[12]

Agencies that according to this definition are more thoughtful, of course, tend to receive less money and are less able to assist in the field. In fact, thoughtful agencies may appear to take the humanitarian imperative less seriously than some of their hyperactive counterparts. In the end, the issue is as much about the media and those taxpayers who are moved by news accounts to make donations as it is about the NGO's thoughtfulness. In 2001, the Irish NGO, Concern, did an experiment in fundraising for Sierra Leone. It had two public relations firms undertake direct mail appeals, one with a development theme and one with an emergency theme. The alarmist message raised ten times more money.

One "more thoughtful" effort, at least where coordination is concerned, is the Disasters Emergency Committee (DEC) in Britain. When an emergency of a certain magnitude arises, twelve participating agencies pool their fundraising efforts in a joint campaign. The BBC and other media run special public service announcements, and receipts are divided according to a formula, which considers an organization's size, its track record, and its on-the-ground capacities. The DEC raised £16 million for the 2002–2003 southern African drought, and in two weeks during August 2003 it raised £2.5 million for Liberia. The DEC grew out of a time when British agencies were not permitted, and could not afford, to advertise on British television; it was an arrangement between NGOs and the only two television companies of the day to get a non-competitive public service message across. Necessity, the mother of this invention, proved to be both useful and constructive.

But even this exemplary NGO fundraising coordination—which has something to teach NGOs in the United States, Europe, and elsewhere—

is fraught with internal competition and calculation. MSF decided to stay out of the DEC, believing it could do better on its own. (As some NGOs say, MSF "hates collaborating.") The twelve participating organizations want the DEC to be the "Best of British," and if one large NGO remains outside, it will be operating in direct competition with all the others. In competition with the DEC, MSF might do considerably better than if it was in competition with all twelve members fundraising on their own. The dynamic works the other way as well. Many agencies that want to be part of the DEC have been refused. The Irish NGO, GOAL, and Islamic Relief have been turned down, ostensibly because they do not meet DEC's size criterion. UNICEF, which would certainly meet the size criterion, has been turned down because it is a multilateral UN organization, and British NGOs—like NGOs in other countries—feel that UN agencies should not be poaching on NGO fundraising territory.

In the view of some donor agencies, many NGOs have become service providers rather than programming agencies in their own right. In fact, some international NGOs have become little more than ambulance chasers, parachuting into an emergency situation with certain skills and undoubted commitment but little or no funding and often no geographic expertise. This was certainly the case in East Timor. When institutional donor money was locked into a World Bank trust fund, many international NGOs soon left for greener pastures. CARE Australia's biggest program in 2003 was actually in faraway Serbia—unusual, to say the least, for an Australian NGO concerned about poverty. But Serbia (and Canberra) is where it found a donor. Even an NGO's unrestricted money will follow donor priorities, because inevitably they will need it for the front end of program operations and to subsidize and smooth out the dry periods between donor contracts. These are the institutional realities of the situation.

Iraq represented a new scale in the instrumentalization of humanitarian agencies by donors, with a level of politicization not seen before. The bombing of the UN's Baghdad headquarters in 2003 could perhaps be explained by the UN's ambivalent historical role with regard to economic sanctions, weapons inspection, and even the war itself. But bombs aimed at the ICRC and threats against other humanitarian agencies was something new, at least in scale. The perception that NGOs based in Europe and North America might be part of a Western crusade was reinforced by the presence of so many of them, even though the humanitarian need itself was not great. One humanitarian mapping exercise explains it this way: Although there was no major food or displacement crisis in Iraq and only pockets of vulnerability among civilians, "Aid agencies whose services were not essential at the time found it important to continue to be engaged in Iraq. The stark choice was between cooption and irrelevance: for fear of losing funds and contracts, many agencies found reasons to stay on, regardless of their particular mandate."[13]

Although many donors have little apparent hesitation about co-opting NGOs when it serves their interests, many governments seem increasingly wary, even critical, of NGOs. Issues of legitimacy, transparency, cost, capacity, programming rigor, discipline and, in a broad sense, professionalism, are frequently raised. Increased donor wariness may result from a recognition that dependency is a two-way street. NGOs may have become more dependent on governments for their funding. But most donors are at the same time heavily dependent on NGOs as operational partners. In Ireland, 46 percent of the government's emergency funding is channeled through NGOs, 57 percent if ICRC is included in the calculation. Between 1997 and 2001, ECHO spent more than 60 percent of its budget through NGOs. In an unusual twist, the U.S. government encouraged the formation of an NGO food aid consortium at the time of the 2002 southern African drought described in Chapter 8, in an apparent attempt to inject some competition into its relationship with WFP.

NGOs are often lumped into a single category, when in fact they come in a wide variety of sizes and shapes, histories and competencies, interests, and attitudes. Donors can pick and choose among NGOs to suit their own purposes and needs. NGOs are favored in some cases because they can be held more accountable than multilateral agencies and also because they generally provide more national visibility. Thus funding an array of NGOs is likely to make coordination somewhat more elusive. Donors want and encourage the rainbow, but at the same time decry the effects on coordination.

Despite the plethora of agencies, however, most NGO emergency assistance in reality is delivered by six or seven major NGOs, or families of NGOs. Using 2001 figures and looking at only eighteen of the largest Northern NGOs, Development Initiatives had calculated that the mega-NGOs managed between $2.5 and $3 billion or something between 45 and 55 percent of global humanitarian assistance, derived from both public and private sources.[14] Conversely, the remaining resources are divided in far smaller portions among countless other agencies.

For some donors, NGOs are a key part of "badging" humanitarian assistance, serving as exemplars of national identity—although, few donors will admit to using NGOs for flag-waving. Germany uses German NGOs because "they understand German thinking" as well as German accountability requirements. While logical from a donor point of view, the impact of this approach can be problematic at the delivery end. Kosovo provides a telling example. "To policymakers and parliamentarians in

Bonn (later Berlin), it seemed eminently reasonable that German government food aid should be channeled to the [Area of Operation] under German [military] command for use in bakeries operated by German troops, to make bread for Kosovar civilians who would also be served by German NGOs."[15] Micromanagement of this sort understandably drives multilateral program managers crazy.

Runaway bilateralism is also reflected in other donors' insistence on NGO badging, requiring that their symbols be prominently displayed on commodities programmed by NGOs. ECHO, for example, has a line item in all agreements that its name and logo must be prominently displayed on all vehicles purchased with ECHO money. Britain and Australia have new pro forma agreements with larger NGOs, pre-approving them for emergency support. Oxfam Australia scored badly on its submission in Canberra because it failed to discuss how it would promote Australian identity. One Oxfam staffer said that putting the usual Aussie kangaroo stickers on wells in Afghanistan made no sense: "People there think the kangaroo is a big rat."

For all NGOs, the scramble has a lot to do with the *quality of money*. Funds can be raised in a variety of ways: advertising, public service announcements, bake sales, bequests, and direct mail campaigns. All are used to raise general, untied income for a charitable organization. This income can be used for any purpose, within the context of whatever regulations guide charitable organizations in a given country. NGOs also organize special appeals during emergencies. These appeals enjoy varying degrees of success, usually in relation to the amount of news coverage an emergency receives and how it is framed. De Waal is right about emotive and sometimes questionable NGO fundraising, but there is a reason for it: It works. And in the heat of a killer famine or in a refugee camp where people have been on half rations for a year, most front-line workers and certainly the beneficiaries themselves do not care how the money is raised. As one Canadian fundraiser put it, "The only tainted money is money that t'ain't mine."[16]

There are several reasons NGOs work so hard to raise emergency dollars. The most obvious is so they can respond to needs independently of institutional donors. Independence allows a British NGO to go to Afghanistan even when there is no DFID money (as was the case through much of the 1990s) or an U.S. NGO to go to certain parts of Central America when there is no USAID money (as was the case through much of the 1980s). Privately contributed funding allows an agency with food expertise to go beyond what WFP and USAID might pay for. It also allows NGOs to act quickly, before institutional funding is available, or to pay for bridging operations while they wait for donor decisions, final payments, and new phases.

Other reasons for emergency fundraising are less obvious, however. One is the hope that an individual who contributes fifty euros to an emergency may be converted next year into a development donor, and possibly one who will provide donations over several years, perhaps even making a bequest to the agency. Another—and this is a key element in the political economy of humanitarian assistance—is that private donor money is essential to leveraging funds from institutional donors. Certainly, contracting with governments and UN agencies has become the norm for many NGOs, but governments and UN agencies are often chary with their money, even when interests and locales coincide. Contracts are tight, specific, and often inadequate for the needs at hand. As a result, NGOs may have inadequate funding to program food aid, for example, for maximum long-term effect. Or they may be unable to pay for the staff or follow-up and recovery programs that are necessary to achieve real results and to link relief and development. A dollar in untied funds raised from private donor constituencies is worth at least twice that to most NGOs, compared to a dollar raised from donor governments that is earmarked for a specific emergency. In fact, NGOs view untied funds as priceless—they cannot function effectively or creatively without them.

To maintain a core humanitarian team, NGOs need a basic level of programming activity. What may seem like opportunistic behavior to donor governments, therefore, may be nothing more than efforts to keep the NGO engine fueled and running, with pit crews at the ready— good management. UN field operations are no different. They, too, need a certain level of programming activity to justify and sustain a core team of professionals and support staff. Project funding may be the preferred operating mode of donor governments, but emergencies do not usually coincide with project funding cycles. Hungry people cannot wait for a go-ahead from Rome or Paris to eat; refugees cannot wait for permission from Washington or Ottawa to flee when soldiers start shooting; monsoons do not await the decisions of desk officers in Tokyo and Brussels. And even if NGOs are sometimes forced to wait, it is exceedingly difficult to run a professional organization on a patchwork of projects and short-term funding.

Twenty years ago, most donor governments started giving their major NGOs multiyear program funding for development work, recognizing that they could be trusted with the funds (and evaluated later), and that this approach would significantly reduce transaction costs and timeframes. But the old-fashioned project approach continues in the humanitarian sphere, where it is even more dysfunctional. The project approach to funding humanitarian activities, in fact, makes no sense. Combined with the voluntary—some might say whimsical—nature of

governmental humanitarian spending, it almost guarantees that humanitarian assistance will be slow if not late, patchy if not wildly dispropor-
tional to need, and confused if not completely uncoordinated.

These problems, so well known to UN agencies, are passed on with
embellishments by UN agencies to their NGO partners. Like donor
governments, they generally expect NGOs to "bring something to the
table," a euphemism usually meaning that NGOs should pay for their
own administration and capacity-building costs. One major donor, for
example, comments that "the premise of our grant making . . . is that
the NGO wants to do and believes in a program, but we consider that
it is the NGO's program and that they are responsible for its continuity.
Perhaps part of the problem," the aid official continues, "is that NGOs
do not make the necessary commitments to specific sectors or parts of
the world and don't forego being in every spotlight situation." WFP
argues along similar lines that its own costs are higher than those of
NGOs, in part because NGOs have "access to private funds to defray
some support costs."[17]

Behind such statements lie layers of complexity and misunderstanding that without doubt contribute to a climate of mistrust and thinly
veiled animosity. NGOs have only two sources of funding: institutional
donors such as governments and UN agencies, on the one hand, and
private individual donors, on the other. Individuals give money to save
lives, not to "defray some support costs" of WFP and other large
organizations. NGOs are caught in the middle. Institutional donors,
which should be the first to understand the need for institutional support, are often the most miserly in providing it.

And the competition between NGOs and multilaterals shows. Many
NGOs cannot understand why their governments give money to WFP
or UNHCR, when it will just come back to them in the end—minus the
13 percent (or more) administration charge that will be removed in
Rome or Geneva. Multilaterals are equally critical of NGOs with small
egocentric agendas that simply get in the way of state-building and
national responsibilities. "NGOs criticize us," says a senior WFP official, "but they have the freedom to walk away whenever they want. We
cannot." The flip side of this comment comes from a senior European
NGO official, complaining about the arrogance of UNHCR in Rwanda
and Kosovo. "'It's my way, or no way' they told us, and we hoped they
would eventually get a good dose of humility. In Kosovo they did when
NATO took over, and they have not recovered yet."

Not surprisingly, given the inadequacy of money for humanitarian
emergencies, the competition for market share occurs not only between

NGOs and UN agencies. Among NGOs it is perhaps even more fierce and is becoming sharper as the larger NGOs streamline and consolidate their transnationalism. Competition has an up side, which includes economies of scale, the ability to specialize and globalize, greater attention to results, the possibility of linking relief and development, geographic spread, and experience. Its down side involves the old problems of exaggerated claims, demeaning advertising, and poor coordination.

In fact one credible school of thought posits that competition among NGOs for humanitarian contracts does not cut waste or curb corruption—it does precisely the opposite. In a climate in which short-term contracts are the norm but startup costs are high and an NGO must maintain a sizeable staff and infrastructure to compete successfully, the scramble for funding becomes paramount. Coordination problems may not be as much a product of poor communication as a direct result of competition in a crowded aid market. Analysts Alexander Cooley and James Ron argue that competitive tenders and renewable contracting generate incentives that can produce dysfunctional outcomes. "Some [NGO] headquarters order their country offices to become financially self sufficient, exacerbating the competitive dynamic. Securing new funding is an ever-expanding part of the [NGO's] function, pushing other concerns—such as ethics, project efficacy, or self-criticism—to the margins."[18]

As noted earlier, NGOs are often the favored delivery channel for donor governments at the beginning of fast-onset emergencies, but as the emergency evolves, funding will become more dispersed among UN and other agencies. This can create a ballooning problem for NGOs at the outset of an emergency and a subsequent need to downsize even though the needs they are addressing remain. In 2000, World Vision had fifteen institutional donors in East Timor, but two years later there were only three. CARE Canada normally has two emergency programmers based in Ottawa, but on occasion the number has risen to more than fifty. And donor appreciation of NGOs as a delivery channel is vulnerable to major mood swings. NGOs may be seen as fast, courageous, and efficient in one situation, and unrealistic, mercenary, and grasping in another. Doubts are expressed by some donors about NGO cost-effectiveness, but in the absence of real data and good comparative evaluations, this sentiment is only a stick to beat them with. When WFP tried to compare its delivery costs to those of NGOs in 2002, it inevitably found that it was comparing apples and oranges and could reach no substantive conclusion, except that NGOs and WFP are different, and therefore have different costs.[19]

NGOs that stand on principle and refuse what they consider to be unreasonable donor requests, or NGOs that turn down underfunded contracts, are likely to be undercut by "NGO defectors." For example,

MSF could walk out of the Goma refugee camps in a righteous dudgeon over support to Hutu extremists, knowing that it would not make any difference in human lives, because other NGOs would quickly fill the void.[20] The lack of coordination and coherence across the NGO community always makes it possible for governments to play some agencies off against others. NGOs can play the same game, limiting the extent of their coordination so as not to divulge information to potential NGO competitors.

Many NGOs are also ethically exposed to charges that they are not neutral, impartial, or independent of their government's foreign and domestic policies. U.S. NGOs have been criticized for their willingness to follow the U.S. State Department's lead into areas of questionable programming (Central America in the 1980s; Afghanistan in 2002; Iraq in 2003). German NGOs were keen to sponsor programs for returning refugees to Bosnia in 1997 and 1998, not because it was safe for the refugees but because speeding them home from Germany was a priority for the German government. Many European NGOs still have bad memories about their behavior in Kosovo. Others have been criticized for political advocacy that goes beyond strict humanitarian norms (e.g., the call for U.S. troops in Somalia) or for lack thereof (e.g., no position whatsoever on the Israel/Palestine dispute). This mélange of economic and ethical, ideological and institutional factors further complicates an extremely complex funding relationship between institutional funders and NGOs. Maintaining capacities from one emergency to the next, reinforcing an agency's identity, remaining in good standing as a member of the NGO family, covering overheads, and meeting an NGO's own priorities represent a multifaceted and difficult management problem.

Apart from occasional training grants, donors generally do not support functions that would increase NGO capacities or contextual awareness. Building the capacities of Southern civil society, however, has become an essential element in the mantra of donor agencies and Northern NGOs—not to say an essential ingredient in operational programming. Yet it is the exceptional Northern NGO or international donor that will work seriously to help create an emergency capacity with a Southern face. Mostly, capacity-building means training for service delivery.[21] It is rarely responsive to the local organization's need for institutional enhancement or its own priorities. Typical six-month funding cycles also work against longer-term capacity-building.

Competition between Northern and Southern NGOs for the same resources also works against the goal of one advancing the capacities of the other. In addition, international NGOs and UN agencies all need local staff, and because they pay good salaries, they can very often depopulate local organizations, including government, of the best talent. Afghanistan represented a noteworthy but cynical laboratory: The initial year of international engagement after 9/11 led to a net loss of capacity in almost all local institutions, governmental and nongovernmental. It remains to be seen whether and if the Afghan government's insistence on exercising authority and control will swing the balance to the positive side of the ledger.[22]

When Sierra Leonean NGO leader Thomas Turay returned to Sierra Leone at the end of the 1990s after a four-year absence, he found that some new efforts at capacity-building had been made. But he spoke of a trip to Bo, where earlier there had been only a few international NGOs.

> Now there was Oxfam, Action Contre la Faim, Médecins sans Frontières and Africare, to name a few. There were several church organizations as well. I saw NGO vehicles everywhere. World Vision had a fleet of vehicles and bikes. It was difficult not to notice them all. If you went to the Black and White Restaurant, you could see dozens of vehicles parked outside at lunch time. The presence of so many international NGOs and so few local NGOs was in my opinion a sign of weakness in the local capacity building processes that so many international organizations claimed to be enhancing.[23]

Worse, he found serious mistrust and unhappiness between the international food pipeline agencies and local NGOs. "The local organizations in my opinion were basically 'errand boys'—their main role being to distribute food and take insults from hungry and angry internally displaced persons who frequently accused them of misappropriation. When food supplies dried up, the local NGOs that had been engaged in such food distribution became redundant, and simply became targets for accusations of fraud." Turay continued,

> My general observation was that suspicion and mistrust between international and local organizations increased during the 1999 rebel attack on Freetown. There was more competition than co-operation regarding who was doing the most as a humanitarian actor, and who was *seen* to be doing the most. There were more short-term projects than long-term strategies. Some international NGOs behaved like tourists. They flooded the country when times were sweet and they disappeared during rough times. In addition to January 1999, most had disappeared between May 1997 and February 1998 when the Armed Forces Revolutionary Council took power, and they disappeared again in May 2000 when there were rumors of an imminent RUF attack on Freetown.

The growing vulnerability of humanitarian activities makes it that much more difficult to address Turay's criticisms. The possibility of building greater mutuality into the humanitarian apparatus, an undertaking

that would require a fundamental rethinking of expatriate-local relationships, is discussed in Chapter 10.

Where the UN CAP is concerned, it is generally understood that this
should be a reflection of priority needs in a given emergency. Most
CAPs are significantly underfunded, while at the same time, activities
not described in the CAP receive a considerable proportion of donor
funding. It could, *but should not*, be assumed that underfunding in one
area is made up by funding for the other. It could, *but should not*, be
assumed that CAP plans and priorities are worthy, on average, of only
60–70 percent donor funding, and that the CAP process is incapable of
identifying the other priorities to which donors commit at least one-
third of their humanitarian funds.

   If donors are serious about achieving a more needs-based approach
to programming, they should work with the United Nations, NGOs
and the Red Cross movement to make the CAP more inclusive. This
can be achieved by ensuring (and insisting) that all humanitarian actors
are part of the consolidated humanitarian assistance process. The UN
system will have to be more accommodating of non-UN actors, and
donors will have to refrain from rewarding free-lance behavior, working
to ensure that non-UN actors behave more like team players. NGOs
will stop behaving like cowboys if donors refuse to fund cowboy behavior and if the UN system gives NGOs the respect they deserve. The
same holds true for UN agencies: There should be no freelancing with
donors unless significant new developments during a given year require
additional funding. A strengthened CAP would represent an investment
in a more multilateral approach to humanitarian crises, even if certain
funds continue to be channeled bilaterally.

   A small incident that took place many years ago serves as a kind of
metaphor for the humanitarian free-for-all. At the end of the Biafran war
in January 1970, dozens of journalists flooded into the former secession-
ist territory, anticipating scenes of starvation and genocide. The genocide was absent, but hunger was rampant. Veteran Canadian journalist
Peter Worthington said, however, that cameramen were having a hard
time getting good action shots. "To their shame," he later wrote, "several
foreign television cameramen helped create scenes of riot by throwing
Nigerian money in the air and letting the hungry masses scramble for
it."[24] Donor governments do not exactly toss their money in the air—
quite the opposite, in fact—and the aim is certainly not to create scenes
of riot among competing multilateral agencies and NGOs. But given the
inadequacy of donor financial support and the scramble of competing
agencies and priorities, too often this is the effect.

9

Trust and Mistrust:
Assessing Needs, Judging Performance

At the center of the problem was this: The million and a half refugees who were allegedly in Somalia didn't exist. The Somali government liked to say 1.5 million. Journalists liked to say 1.5 million. It sounded good and added weightiness to their stories.
—Michael Maren, *The Road to Hell*[1]

Mukesh Kapila, head of DFID's humanitarian operations in the 1990s and subsequently UN Resident and Humanitarian Coordinator for the Sudan, says, "Of all the major worldwide public endeavours, the financing of the global humanitarian system is the most primitive, based on little rationality and even less accountability."[2] He and many others argue that there is little trust in the humanitarian system—little trust *of* the humanitarian system by many donors (and vice versa), and little trust *within* the system among the front-line agencies. This chapter argues that the problem is not so much a lack of accountability, but too much accountability to the wrong people, for the wrong things.

There are two basic problems in the assessment of need. The first is that there is no commonly agreed-upon way of measuring humanitarian need. When an agency says that 400,000 people "face starvation," what does it mean? Does it mean that disaster is imminent? Does it mean that relief food must be mobilized for that number (or perhaps more to allow for margins of error)? Seed? Camps? Water and sanitation? Is the number accurate? Is it what the agency thinks will be funded? What it can manage? Whatever the number means, will it remain accurate for a month? Three months?

The second problem—even more profound—is that those with money (governments) do not much trust those who spend it (UN agencies and NGOs). The lack of trust derives from two factors. First, a food delivery agency looking at a humanitarian problem is likely to think of food as the solution. A health agency is more likely to think of

203

health inputs. Establishing priorities between this input or that may become a mutual back-scratching exercise in the absence of a more objective tool for establishing what the needs actually are. The most urgent inputs may have nothing to do with food or health. Or the answer to hungry people's need for food may not be food aid, or only food aid.[3] And on top of what outsiders can provide, people do have their own ways of dealing with crises. These can be strengthened or weakened by the way outsiders interact with them.[4]

But there is a larger issue. Many of those assessing needs are the ones who submit project proposals and spend the money, and this is thought to constitute a conflict of interest. NGOs, it is said, might exaggerate the number of people in need because their institutional survival depends on donations and grants: the more the merrier. The same is suspected of UN agencies. An ODI study explains the problem this way:

> It is a feature of the current system that, for the most part, assessments are conducted by implementing agencies. . . . such assessments are often carried out in order to substantiate funding proposals. This clearly raises a question: how can we expect such an analysis to be objective, when the agency itself has an apparent vested interest in the result? Why, more specifically, would a donor—assuming it is concerned with objectivity—trust the analysis of an agency that is asking it for funds?[5]

Kapila argues that "to regain trust in the humanitarian system there would have to be changes—through separating needs assessments by impartial experts from the financing of agencies."[6] Most theories of business management would doubtless concur.

The lack of a commonly agreed-upon approach to measuring humanitarian need, however, does not mean that NGOs and UN agencies make up numbers on the back of envelopes and then multiply them by ten. Nor does it mean that there are no measurement tools at all.[7] There are, in fact, many such tools, and that may be part of the problem. OCHA has established Humanitarian Information Centers and published a Field Information Management Handbook. The United States has its own conveniently pocket-sized *OFDA Handbook* and has sponsored a SMART initiative—Standardized Monitoring and Assessment of Relief and Transitions—based on crude mortality rates and under-five nutrition as key indicators. Country or region-specific initiatives have also been developed: a Program Management Information System (ProMIS) in Afghanistan and a Southern Africa Humanitarian Information System (SAHIMS). ECHO has developed a vulnerability index, rating countries against eight measures, including levels of mortality and malnutrition, exposure to natural disasters and conflict, number of refugees, and others. The Centre for Research of the Epidemiology of Disasters (CRED) at the Université Catholique de Louvain maintains an international disasters database, and the Heidelberg Institute for International Conflict Research produces an annual conflict barometer. The USAID-funded Famine Early Warning Systems Network (FEWS NET) aims to strengthen the abilities of African countries and regional organizations to manage the risk of food insecurity by providing timely and analytical early warning and vulnerability information. Most UN agencies and the larger NGOs have developed early warning and assessment systems of their own, and those organizations with ongoing development programs in vulnerable countries can also rely on the independent observation of their field staff, local government, and partner organizations.

The tools fail, or succeed only partially, not because they are inadequate—although some clearly are. They fail because donors ignore or mistrust them, or are so mesmerized by their own particular systems that they cannot see the wider humanitarian implications of unilateralist behavior. In fact where early warning is concerned, there are so many tools and systems that the repeated lack of early action is little short of disgraceful. With the exception of Cambodia after 1974, there is not a single human-made humanitarian disaster and few food-related disasters that have not received early warning aplenty. The specter of famine loomed in southern Africa from late 2001, but donors were slow off the mark for reasons that had little to do with early warning, objective need, or adequate predictive data. They were paralyzed by political considerations, and when they did move, even more political squabbling ensued. A chronic humanitarian crisis in the Democratic Republic of the Congo has been underfunded for years, not because of poor warning or poor needs assessment, but because donors simply do not regard the DRC as a priority. Early warnings and late warnings, along with dozens—if not hundreds—of studies on humanitarian needs in Sierra Leone, Liberia, Burundi, Nepal, Palestine, Ethiopia, Chechnya, Indonesia, and elsewhere have consistently been ignored.

There is no doubt that a universally accepted tool for assessing humanitarian need would be useful, even invaluable. And it should be independent of all competing and vested interests—perceived or real. But before the lucky university or think tank that wins the contract begins designing such a tool, commitment in principle should be sought from the largest seven or eight donor agencies to accept and use what eventually emerges. One more tool in the already cluttered toolbox will not solve the problem unless there is a genuine commitment by donors to use it together.

For donors, an additional problem with existing tools is that they fail to set priorities, as noted above and in Chapter 7. The UN consolidated appeal process (CAP) brings together the priorities of each UN agency into a single document. But it tends not to prioritize very well among and between agencies. WFP puts forward its food priorities and UNHCR puts forward its priorities for refugees. Reflecting the institutional sensitivities involved, however, there is rarely a paragraph in the document saying that food is more important than refugees, or vice versa. Donors are left to their own devices in deciding how to respond. This is a further argument for an independent needs assessment mechanism, although independent should not be understood as something independent of the current multilateral system. OCHA is mandated with precisely this function, and in many cases carries it out well.

It is worth adding that the problem is not so much that priorities are never presented to donors as that donors have their own priorities. These are—as earlier chapters have shown—geographic, sectoral, political, time-bound, financial, and sometimes personality-driven. That is why, even if the CAP could set forth more clearly defined and vetted priorities, WFP, UNHCR, and UNICEF would still receive most of the funding, while WHO, UNFPA, FAO, and others would continue to lag behind. That is why food shipments outclass agriculture, and children are favored over adults. It is why an Afghanistan will always do better than a Sri Lanka (even though the Afghan government asked for less food and more of other things). That is why Kosovo will always do better than Sierra Leone, and Iraq than the DRC. At its root, the issue is not really about needs or needs assessment.

What about the question of conflicts of interests, and the suggestion that UN agencies and NGOs deliberately exaggerate numbers and needs in order to advance their financial and institutional priorities? Certainly there is a problem about truth in advertising, or at least selectivity in advertising. NGOs have long been criticized for undignified "starving baby" fundraising, which stresses helplessness and dwells on symptoms rather than causes and longer-term solutions. This approach to fundraising has always been successful, however. In 1969 a British fundraising consultant provided a simple formula for dealing with the public: babies. "Show babies," he said, "all the time show babies and more babies."[8]

That advice, by and large, has been adopted and retained, although some agencies are committed to stressing human dignity and self-reliance rather than the pornography of suffering. Bernard Kouchner, MSF's founder and later Minister for Development Cooperation and Humanitarian Action in the Government of France, endorsed *la loi du tapage* (the law of hype) in his 1986 book, *Charité Business*. He argued that it is "necessary to popularize misfortunes and make use of feelings of remorse."[9] This is the political economy of fundraising. It works—but it works because there has been so little effort by NGOs, by the

UN system, and especially by donor governments to educate taxpayers with more comprehensive stories about cause and effect, need and response.

It is also common practice in the world of international development and humanitarianism, and in most areas of grant-making more generally, for those seeking funds to exaggerate need and to promise more than they can deliver. Typically, in order to get five, nine must be requested. In a highly competitive environment—made competitive by great needs and inadequate funding—exaggeration not only pays, it is sometimes the only thing that will dislodge funding from donors who themselves have too few resources and too many supplicants. In 2002, all UN agencies combined requested $5.1 billion in humanitarian assistance from donors. They received $3.3 billion. Over the previous decade, the average was about 60 percent of what was requested. William Paton, UN humanitarian coordinator in Tajikistan, explained the problem in relation to the UN appeal for 2004. It is impossible, he said, to plan activities "based on the fictitious belief that we were going to get 100 percent of a purely needs-based appeal. We have to adapt our description of the amount needed, based on how much we think the market will bear."[10]

To suggest that NGOs and UN agencies are inherently untrustworthy in their funding requests is to suggest a level of cynicism, even corruption, that is not just grossly unfair. It reverses the logical order of trustworthiness, blaming the front-line agencies for bad arithmetic when it is donor governments that cannot or will not provide adequate and predictable resources. Imagine a hospital with a number of departments, specializations, and wards, each funded by several independent donors, each with its own priorities. Imagine that each ward and each department has its own board of management made up exclusively of these donors. Imagine that the obstetrics ward is overfunded, the oncology department is underfunded, and there is no money at all for research or building maintenance (the hospital is expected to raise this from the public). The funding comes mostly in three- and six-month tranches completely at the discretion of donors. Money sometimes arrives after the period to be covered has ended, and many of the staff are on six-month contracts. Imagine the electricity bill not being paid for six months and the power disappearing entirely for weeks.

Imagine the visit of a major donor to the children's ward. The donor has already funded the first ten beds out of a hundred. Imagine the scramble for attention by the nurses and doctors responsible for the next nine blocks of beds: all wearing T-shirts and baseball caps with the names of their ten beds on them, repeated whenever reporters come through. Imagine what conclusion each donor would come to about how well the hospital is managed. Imagine that their solution is to criticize the hospital managers and ward supervisors and research departments for not coordinating their efforts better; for not setting proper priorities; for wasteful spending. Imagine the donors sitting down together to discuss the problem and debating "What actually *is* sickness?" "What is health?" "Can we reach a common definition of cancer?" "Do we trust the diagnoses of the doctors?" "What about the coping strategies of the patients?" Imagine the feeling of vulnerability of the hospital staff, no matter how well or badly they are managing things, in talking back, in telling their "lady bountiful" donors that their egos, their demands for greater effectiveness and efficiency, their underfunding and cherry-picking, have created a hospital that is incapable of meeting their demands, or the needs of the patients. Imagine the feeling of the patients, waiting with no certainty for beds, doctors, and medicine.

The humanitarian enterprise, in fact, is run very much like this sort of hospital, with distant financiers paying for those parts they favor, but only on a selective basis, often late, and rarely with enough resources to solve a problem, much less to prevent future problems. Too often, the patients receive only a passing glance. Then, rather than accepting responsibility for refusing to create a unified, professional, adequately funded hospital, the financiers accuse the doctors and nurses of greed, vested interests, even corruption, and tighten up the funding criteria further still.

Time and timing play critical roles in determining the effectiveness of humanitarian action. Obviously, timing is more critical where food is concerned than in any other kind of assistance; people cannot survive more than a few days without sustenance. But timing is important in all humanitarian action. Timing is an element in the choice of delivery channel. NGOs sometimes have a timing advantage over UN agencies. They may be able to move faster and so may receive more funding in the early stages of an emergency. This is not universally true, however; UN agencies were present in the Balkans before most NGOs.

Recognizing the difficulties, donors are likely to be less selective in their partners and less demanding of results early in a fast-onset emergency than they will be as it evolves. The situation in Kosovo and East Timor in 1999 contrasts with that at the same time in Sierra Leone, which was as needy but where the emergency had built up over eight years. The political imperatives, objective needs, and media pressures will all have more weight at the outset of an emergency; considerations about coordination, results, and professionalism will develop later. Conversely, money is harder to get as an emergency ages; this is sometimes because of declining needs, but donor attention and money may also be diverted to newer, more high profile emergencies.

Donor financial years differ, ending variously on March 31, June 30, September 30, and December 31. This affects responses to time-bound appeals and can create cash flow and programming problems for implementing agencies. Unfulfilled donor pledges cause problems for everyone, including intended beneficiaries and other donors. And political disagreements can slow payment schedules to a snail's pace. By 1997, the United States had disbursed only $207 million out of the $500 million pledged in 1993 to the Palestinian Authority. Similar problems have bedeviled donor pledges for Cambodia, Rwanda and, more recently, Afghanistan.

Some donors can act quickly, while others are extremely slow. Rapid British and Swedish support for vehicles, generators, and other hardware was much appreciated in East Timor. Donor alacrity changes with time, however; as the weeks and months pass, donors tend to become more paper- and results-oriented. Results-based management, however desirable in principle, may have severe limitations where time-frames are short and distances are long. Some donors have delegated humanitarian decision-making to the field, while others require most decision-making to be done at headquarters. Such choices have time implications. Despite their own timing problems, donors often have unrealistic timing expectations of front-line agencies. For example, AusAID put out a call for submissions from NGOs for the longstanding southern Africa drought on the Friday before Christmas 2002, with a closing date of January 3, 2003.[11]

Donors may stay involved in an extended humanitarian crisis for years, but most funding cycles are short, which makes strategic planning for implementing agencies very difficult. While there are reasons for this, it makes even medium-term planning very difficult for UN agencies and NGOs. That, of course, is not news to donors, many of whom treat short timeframes and funding cycles as a given. In fact, one government aid official would like to shift the onus to NGOs. "Why have NGOs continued to rely so heavily on donor funding for long-term crises?" she asks. "Perhaps there should be some longer-term sustainability of programming efforts by NGOs so that they actually plan on the funding having to come from someplace else." The comment revives the old debate. NGOs have only two sources of funding—institutional donors and private donations. There is no "someplace else." If all NGOs were to cut back on government donors for long-term crisis funding, the NGO presence would simply decline by the amount of the cutback. Private donor funding is limited: It is frequently tied to a particular emergency; and it is usually given only when the emergency is "hot" and well publicized. While many NGOs talk earnestly of developing a larger funding base among private contributors, few have succeeded in doing so.

The fact remains that chronic emergencies do not fit the standard donor project cycle. Another way of saying this is that donor project cycles are not adequate to the needs they aim to address. Some donors want an exit strategy before they even become involved in an emergency. This is especially true of departments with limited mandates and timeframes such as USAID's Office of Transition Initiatives. By contrast, many of today's emergencies are more open-ended. They do not fit donors' traditional funding cycles, timeframes, and exit strategies.

The tendency in examining the donor response to a crisis is to isolate it from other events. Figure 1 shows some of the major emergencies of 1999. Three simmering crises flared into major humanitarian emergencies that year—Sierra Leone, Kosovo, and East Timor—while others in Afghanistan, Orissa, and Turkey demanded attention as well. Each one competed for donor staff time and funding, helped or hindered by media attention, geopolitical and domestic concerns, and other factors. The competition for time, attention, and resources can be enormous, even without complicating political factors.

When should spending move from relief to recovery and reconstruction? Each donor has its own gauge. As a timing issue, this creates uncertainty for implementing agencies in planning and unevenness in linking relief and development. Such decisions are often made without consensus among donor agencies. Some move too quickly, creating a vacuum. This was the case in Haiti during the mid-1990s, and there was general agreement in East Timor early in 2003 that the pace of transition there had been too fast. It happened again in 2004 when donors pledged $520 million for the reconstruction and long-term development of Liberia, $32 million more than the target set by the United Nations. At the same time, a separate UN appeal for emergency relief and disarmament, set at $137 million, had actually received only $5 million.[12] In other cases, the shift comes too late, creating dependencies. For example, as early as mid-2002, the Afghanistan government was calling for an end to humanitarian funding, cash, and traditional food aid distribution, and a start to reconstruction. Despite a debate in recent years about the continuum between relief, reconstruction, and development, few donors provide resources that can be used with the flexibility needed in protracted complex humanitarian emergencies.[13]

Antagonism frequently develops between host governments and NGOs as a given emergency moves toward the recovery phase. Host governments resent the resources bestowed by donors on NGOs and find NGOs difficult, if not impossible, to coordinate. They become increasingly anxious about demonstrating their own credibility and

Table 1 Humanitarian Emergencies 1999

	Sierra Leone	East Timor	Afghanistan	Kosovo	Orissa	Turkey
Jan	RUF invasion of Freetown; massive destruction and loss of life	Talks lead to agreement on ballot reindependence	—	Crisis continues from 1998: 863,000 refugees; over 500,000 displaced, 10,000 killed; Yugoslav offensive in Kosovo; March 24 NATO bombing campaign against Yugoslavia begins	—	—
Feb	—	—	Earthquake; 70 dead, 18,000 affected		—	—
March	—	—	—		—	—
April	Peace talks begin in Lomé	Liquica massacre	—	78 days of bombing; 600 civilian dead, massive destruction	—	—
May	Cease-fire agreed-upon	Violence escalates	—			
June	RUF attacks Guinea	SC establishes UNAMET; violence continues	2.6 million Afghan refugees in Iran and Pakistan; fighting in last half of the year leaves 250,000 displaced; serious food deficits regionally; UN sanctions imposed because of Taliban support for al Qaeda	Bombing ends June 10		

(continues)

Table 1 Continued

	Sierra Leone	East Timor	Afghanistan	Kosovo	Orissa	Turkey
July	Peace agreement signed	—	—	—	—	—
August	—	Voter registration & campaigning; violence continues	—	—	—	Earthquake; 18,000 dead, 100,000 affected
September	—	Vote; massive violence; INTERFET troops arrive	—	—	—	—
October	SC authorizes creation of UNAMSIL	Indonesians leave, UNTAET established; first troops arrive	—	—	Orissa cyclone; 10,000 dead, 12 million affected	—
November	Serious cease-fire violations; first UNAMSIL troops arrive	—	—	—	—	—
December	—	—	—	—	—	—

authenticity to their citizens. This was the case in Mozambique during the 1990s, when donors parceled out various districts among themselves and NGOs. Some observers referred unkindly, but not without some accuracy, to the "Donors' Republic of Mozambique." For their part, NGOs are often reluctant to cede initiative to governments they regard as weak or corrupt, and they are often encouraged in their position by donors who want the greater accountability NGOs can provide. This dynamic was problematic in Sierra Leone in October 2002 where NGOs were concerned, and even more problematic in Afghanistan in 2002–2003 with regard to UN and bilateral agencies. Some humanitarian actors, however, are as comfortable in assuming sovereignty as are host politi-cal authorities in delegating it.

Definitions and mandates aside, donor investments in the transition from relief to development and in postemergency development efforts are very much an ad hoc affair. Too often the donor's exit from a country in crisis takes precedence over the exit of the country itself from crisis. Each humanitarian agency winds down according to its own institutional imperatives, making whatever arrangements for follow-up activities it deems best, which in many cases are none at all. In fact most emergencies, including those described in earlier chapters, are the product of both short- and longer-term factors. Even sudden natural disasters can be considerably more severe if governments have not stocked food or have mismanaged agricultural policies. If the current huge investments in humanitarian assistance globally are to be sustained, longer-term development issues must be addressed comprehensively *during* the emergency phase. Donors must develop common strategies to address relief and development issues concurrently and to plan for the longer term. This may be beyond the mandate of humanitarian departments in donor agencies, but it is not beyond the mandate of the donor agency itself, whether or not it intends to stay on after the emergency is over. To excuse the absence of such planning on the basis of institutional priorities and architecture is tantamount to donor delinquency.

Predictable funding is a key element in all successful planning and implementation, not least humanitarianism. Short donor timeframes lead to unpredictability and therefore poor planning. This is exacerbated by the compartmentalization of funds and departments in donor agencies, which reduces the possibility of funding for recovery and reconstruction and for linking relief and development. There are, however, a number of innovations worthy of wider consideration.

Australia's peace, conflict, and development policy "aims to reduce the traditional distinction between development and humanitarian assistance." Australia argues that the CAP needs a separation of "wider humanitarian needs from narrower institutional ones"—not a bad idea if it leads to more holistic funding approaches. In East Timor, USAID's

OFDA used "pre-grant authorization letters" assuring selected NGOs of eventual funding so they could advance other funds and move quickly. A Tufts University team is credited with demonstrating to USAID in 2002 that the Afghan emergency was ongoing, with endemic drought continuing, rural assets depleted, and life not expected to return to normal in the short-term future. This required a more sophisticated, longer-term approach to recovery than the U.S. government and many agencies that it funded had been willing to consider. World Bank reconstruction funds have a one-year time frame, which is an improvement on six-month tranches. Norway made a four-year grant to the IFRC for reconstruction in Bosnia.

None of this is very complicated or radical, except within the context of traditional compartmentalized humanitarian thinking, which has seen emergencies as short-term affairs, with clear beginnings, middles, and ends. Apart from natural disasters, this type of old-fashioned emergency barely exists any more, and a different approach to timing and budgets is long overdue. In protracted emergencies, donors must find ways to make longer-term allocations, even if they are notional and provisional. This would help implementing agencies plan better, find and retain good staff, develop greater synergies between relief and development, and become more professional in other ways.

There is another side to the trust issue. The humanitarian world is made up of people—real individuals with history and experience. At senior levels in the field and at headquarters, many of these people are known to one another. Regardless of nationality, their paths have crossed many times over the years, whether in the heat of an emergency situation or at meetings and pledging conferences. Many have worked closely together in one context or another—in the Red Cross, the United Nations, or an NGO. In the Kosovo crisis, for example, many of those deployed to the field by this agency or that knew each other from having worked together in other major emergencies. Chapter 3 described the important work of two senior UN officials in East Timor—Brazilian Sergio de Mello and New Zealander Ross Mountain. Chapter 5 describes them again in key roles in Iraq. Tracking their careers back through the three previous decades, it would not be difficult to find connections and crossing paths in Sudan, Lebanon, Cambodia, or Kosovo.

These are two examples of many and suggest another aspect of trust: the positive aspect that grows out of collaboration, friendship, and time. In fact there is doubtless a personal economy of humanitarian assistance, which often allows actions to happen in emergency situations where there has been no formal needs assessment because there has been no time, and where the contract has not yet been written or the funds provided, but where the situation demands that something must be done. Management literature often ignores or deprecates personal relationships and networks as a poor basis for doing business, particularly where government funds are concerned. But without the personal connections and the trust that goes with them, critical deals often would not be made in time (or ever), and humanitarian action would languish. The personal economy of humanitarian assistance can act as a buffer against rules and an intransigent official line, on the understanding that informal agreements can later be written in the appropriate language.

"Trust" is both a verb and a noun. As a verb, it means to be confident; to place confidence; to do something without fear or misgiving; to rely on the truth or accuracy of someone or something. As a noun, it can refer to the character, ability, strength, or truthfulness of someone or something: one in whom confidence is placed. Often it refers to an interest or a property held for the benefit of another, or others—often in the form of a legal agreement. Virtually all of the front-line humanitarian delivery agencies are trusts in both the informal and the formal sense of the word. The Red Cross and Red Cross national societies and NGOs are formally established as trusts—legally incorporated as non-profit organizations, with tax-exempt status in many countries. And UN agencies receive money from governments in trust, against a promise to deliver goods and services according to agreed-upon contractual obligations.

It has become fashionable in some quarters to say that NGOs are not accountable, that they are unelected, self-selecting do-gooders, meddlers and critics. The truth is that while NGOs operate with a degree of latitude, they are certainly accountable. Formally, they are accountable to their boards of directors and to the government authority or authorities under which they are legally incorporated—a non-profit corporations branch, a charities office, a government department of revenue. They are accountable to their private donors, who may stop giving if there is even a whiff of scandal. They are accountable to their institutional funders, who insist on, and pay for, third-party evaluations of projects, programs, and institutional capacities. They are watched by the media, which can make or break an NGO fundraising effort overnight. They are answerable, whether they like it or not, to the governments of the countries in which they work. Perhaps the most weakly exercised NGO responsibility is the one they owe to their beneficiaries. As noted earlier, even well-considered acts of altruism should be subject to critical appraisal and considerations of justice. In this particular weakness, however, NGOs are not alone. Most giving in life focuses too much on the needs and motivations of the giver, and too little on the receiver.

On the institutional giving side of the equation, this book has made the point that there is no model humanitarian architecture for all governments, and that in fact, no two donor systems are exactly alike. This stands in fairly sharp contrast to other forms of official development assistance and ensures that the mix of pressures and players makes coordination more complicated than might otherwise be the case. It can become especially problematic when there is a fast-onset, high-profile emergency such as Kosovo or Afghanistan. In Canada before 9/11 there were six people, all of them within CIDA, with portfolios related to Afghanistan. Once the larger crisis began, however, as many as twenty-four government departments became involved. In March 2003, USAID's Disaster Assistance Relief Team (DART), which usually functions with a dozen members, had more than four times that number, from a wide variety of agencies.

Responsibility for relationships between donors and UN agencies is thus lodged in different ministries and bureaus, or it is shared among various government officials. Individual UN agencies may well receive conflicting guidance from different government stakeholders. The problem has been described as the "humanitarian triangle": different people speaking for the same donor in discussions at a UN agency headquarters, in the field, and in the donor's headquarters. The problem is not just the inconsistency in the guidance provided; it is also the directive nature of their participation, acting almost like leaders of sovereign states. A complicating factor is the perception among UN officials that they are sometimes expected to take their cues on major policy and programming issues from very junior officials, many of them without field experience and many of whom soon move on to other assignments.

An absence of consistency in a given government can lead to contradictory positions from the same donor as well as among donors. For example, there is no agreement among major supporters of WFP as to whether food aid activities should be limited to emergencies or should also include development. There are diverse donor opinions about whether an agency such as UNHCR should emphasize protection rather than assistance, and whether its caseload should receive a comprehensive package of services from UNHCR. The issue of where in the UN system to place responsibility for internally displaced persons (IDPs) has also proven divisive. For some, UNHCR is seen as shirking responsibility if it simply "drops refugees off" at their village; for others, anything more is mission creep. In the face of conflicting guidance, a given agency has difficulty maintaining the attention and confidence, and sometimes the trust, of all its diverse and opinionated contributors.

Perhaps the most debated issue of humanitarian architecture today concerns the links within donor governments between emergency assistance and political objectives. There is a growing consensus among donor agencies about the need for a more comprehensive approach to humanitarian emergencies, taking into account prevention and mitigation and combining military, political, and humanitarian instruments in remedial efforts. For some donor governments, the "new humanitarianism" reflects "a willingness to include the actions and presence of aid agencies within an analytical framework of causal and consequential relations"[14] and to make direct links between humanitarian action and a range of other interventions, from conflict prevention to peace enforcement. An example is the Common Foreign and Security Policy of the EU, which plans to bring together humanitarian, trade, technical assistance, foreign affairs, and crisis management under a single framework, creating a more efficient EU foreign policy. There is valid concern, however, that a more comprehensive approach to conflict prevention and resolution could compromise basic humanitarian principles, especially if they are incorporated within a tight political framework or a military command and control structure. All of this can make for much confusion in the decision-making chambers of a UN agency or an NGO, often reflecting similar confusion in a donor agency's capital city.

Standardizing a particular approach across the donor community may be politically unrealistic. It is not impossible, however, for donors to mitigate the negative impacts of their structural and political diversity on UN agencies. There is something to be learned from governing boards in the private sector, the nonprofit world, and within government, which bear a common accountability for organizational behavior and achievement. Board members are *trustees*, with allegiance to a range of stakeholders. They are responsible for setting policy and standards of ethics and prudence, and they are expected to defend, protect, and advance the organization's aims and objectives.

This is not, however, a good description of the governing boards of most UN agencies. These boards are made up almost exclusively of government representatives of varying seniority and from varying ministries and departments. The individuals change frequently, they may or may not articulate a well-defined headquarters position on an issue, but they very much represent the interests of their employer first and foremost. If executive board meetings are at all like other donor meetings, participants are likely to talk at cross purposes, agreeing to disagree politely but expecting the agency in question to meet all demands, no matter how contradictory. This ultimately relegates real governance of the agency to the best devices and sleights of hand of its managers, who given the political economy of the situation, must treat their donors with kid gloves. Depending on the severity of a given problem and the divergence of viewpoints, an agency could find itself without a functional governance mechanism at all. Political and institutional compromise is at best a shaky basis for creative and assertive field operations.

To expect all governments, especially donor governments, to give up their role on governing boards or to welcome executives with strong backbones would be unrealistic. However, consideration could be given to reducing the size of governing boards, to having a system of fewer government representatives, to bringing in knowledgeable but disinterested professionals, and to creating mechanisms by which boards or their executive committees (including nongovernment professionals) could discuss substantive issues in greater detail and more frequently than is currently possible.

If the architecture of giving is variable, so too is the architecture of receiving. The question of trust cannot be disassociated from the central issue of coordination among the agencies that convert donor resources into humanitarian action. Every observation made of donors in this book could be matched by a companion comment about those who receive donations. Governments are chided for a lack of firm commitment to financing multilateral institutions, yet the UN agencies are an uneven lot. Some governments are criticized for favoring the military or the private sector over nonprofit civilian actors, but the can-do spirit of the military and the bottom-line calculations of business have some advantages over the might-have-done hand-wringing of NGOs. Donors are faulted for inattention to capacity building among Southern civil society institutions, but the UN also has a patchy record here, and Northern NGOs are not much better. Donors are criticized for putting too little reliance in the consolidated appeals process. Yet the CAP, despite its improvements, is rife with its own evident compromises.

In the absence of a firmer multilateral anchor, it is inconceivable that the international humanitarian enterprise can provide greater proportionality in the response to human need, wherever it exists. The points of accountability of UN agencies are boards made up of member states. But it is unlikely that negative political inroads into the global functioning of humanitarian work can be minimized without more strenuous efforts by the UN and its political stakeholders to honor the cardinal humanitarian principles of neutrality, impartiality, and independence.

At the heart of the architecture of receiving is the UN Office for the Coordination of Humanitarian Affairs (OCHA), headed by an undersecretary-general who also serves as the UN's emergency relief coordinator. In the checkered evolution of coordination, OCHA is an improvement over its predecessor Department of Humanitarian Affairs (DHA), as DHA was an improvement over the UN Disaster Relief Organization (UNDRO). Notwithstanding the progression, however, the centrifugal forces of implementation routinely overmatch the centripetal efforts of OCHA, whether at headquarters or in the field. That donor policies complicate the coordination conundrum does not relieve OCHA of its responsibilities to orchestrate effective humanitarian action. There is no substitute for a more assertive UN coordinating nexus, which will require not only more discipline and team-play by UN agencies but also a more restrained and supportive approach from donors and NGOs.

An analysis of the architectures of giving and receiving cannot conclude without acknowledging the artificiality of the construct itself. There is no gainsaying the widespread gaps that exist between donors with resources and implementing agencies needing such resources (not to mention beneficiary populations, who often have ways of marshalling and managing resources of their own). Such imbalances in power relations are a fact of life, but they do not need to be antagonistic or destructive. The challenge of the future will be to move beyond mutual recrimination and finger-pointing and to embrace more creative approaches that can alter the entrenched, divisive, and dysfunctional political economy of the humanitarian enterprise.

In recent years there has been shrinking commitment to the multilateral ideal reflected in the creation of the United Nations and the Bretton Woods institutions. This is especially true in the humanitarian field where donor earmarking has increased to as much as 80 percent or more of UN agency budgets, and cherry-picking has become the norm rather than the exception. Earlier chapters have discussed encroaching domestic and international priorities of government donor agencies, but other, less cynical reasons have been proffered for such micromanagement. In some cases, poor humanitarian sector performance in the 1990s reinforced violence, and government donors as a result were obliged to step in and take a larger role. Second, the "results revolution" has obliged donors to be more demanding of contractors. As an ODI report puts it, "Donors have a democratic duty to their constituencies to ensure the effective use of public funds."[15] And finally, "Humanitarian organizations do not have a monopoly of responsibility for humanitarian action. Indeed, discourse on humanitarian policy over the past decade has emphasized that the *absence* of political engagement, not inadequate assistance, is the primary threat to populations suffering the consequences of war and other forms of strife."[16]

Weakness in political engagement and funding adequacy are not mutually exclusive concepts. Greater political engagement might well be a good thing, but it can certainly be demonstrated that much greater funding is also needed for the humanitarian sector. And where political engagement is concerned, there are many shades, ranging from the irresponsibility of the Security Council members who made decisions about Rwanda in 1994 to the highly nuanced approach to security sector reform, good governance, humanitarian assistance, and longer-term development used by Britain in Sierra Leone after 2001.

Regarding the democratic duty that donors have to their constituencies to ensure the effective use of public funds, nothing much has changed in recent years. What did actually change is the role of civil servants after two decades of government downsizing and outsourcing and another decade of chatter about "results." The anxieties and neuroses these trends have created within governments have worked their way through to front-line agencies, which can conveniently be held accountable by civil servants for everything, while at the same time receiving from governments less and less leeway to do what they believe to be professionally correct.

As further justification for erosion of the multilateral ideal, it is argued that multilateral institutions have been inadequate in delivering and coordinating assistance and are "weakly accountable to their individual funders."[17] Greater effectiveness in humanitarian spending is a prominently stated aim for most donors. No donor appears satisfied with the overall effectiveness produced by the current system. Effectiveness is, of course, no less important an issue for donors' partners, who are judged on the quality of their delivery. The desire for effectiveness and the way it is measured, however, can lead to dysfunctional behavior.

Weak accountability to funders can almost certainly be remedied by simply withholding funds. The problem is not really weak accountability, however. It is that governments everywhere are earmarking more, they are developing their own unilateral framework agreements with UN agencies, and they are evaluating implementors six ways to Sunday, because they themselves are being pressed to demonstrate results (more about this below). But through all of this, the donor-imposed conditions under which the implementors must work are rarely, if ever, examined. The growth of conditions and demands are described as "legitimate and appropriate," and as "greater policy input into decision-making," when in fact it is mostly just common garden-variety micromanagement. Even when input is more substantive, six or twelve governments insisting on greater policy input into decision-making in one UN agency is not just unmanageable—it is a recipe for programmatic disaster.

Donors are observably not always concerned about longer-term impact, especially when the intervention's prime motivation is more political than humanitarian. Attempting to hold humanitarian actors accountable, therefore, without considering the extraneous factors that impinge on their effectiveness (geopolitics, donor behavior, other humanitarian actors, peacekeeping forces, warring parties, local government, the media) will inevitably be unsuccessful and is pointless. There is no evidence of a positive correlation between donor conditionalities and effective programs. In fact there is probably a negative correlation. Furthermore, risk aversion (rather than risk management) may direct greater resources to "safer" emergencies (e.g., East Timor rather than the DRC). While this tendency may contribute to greater effectiveness in a well-resourced crisis, it may also weaken the effort and exacerbate suffering in a neglected emergency. Demands for overly detailed risk assessments in fluid situations can also be time consuming and diversionary, particularly when there is urgency in launching humanitarian activities.

Useful cross-cutting evaluations of emergency assistance remain infrequent, although interest in postmortems has grown during the past decade.[18] One cross-cutting review of support to internally displaced people provides an example, as well as an exception to the general rule. Supported by several donors (Denmark, Sweden, ECHO, the Netherlands, the United States and others), the review examines agency performance as well as donor behavior in several countries of Asia and Africa. Most reviews, however, do not extend beyond the parameters of a specific agency or a specific emergency. Often the focus is even more narrow. Referring to the southern Africa drought described in Chapter 5, the head of a large international NGO in Zambia said, "I programmed $18 million in cash and kind, including food, from twelve major donors during 2002 and 2003, and not one asked me what the overall impact of that was. They were only interested in their own little piece of it."[19]

The outcome of the uneven attention to results is very little documented memory and even less interagency learning. Any cross-fertilization between emergencies is ad hoc. No methodology exists to compare who does what most effectively in terms of results or investments, or to assess the damages caused by lack of adequate funding. There is no measure, for example, of the value of NGO empowerment or rights-based approaches as contrasted with the bottom-line style of private contractors. In addition, almost all evaluations are *by* donors *of* those who deliver emergency assistance: UN agencies and NGOs. There are few examples of evaluations of donor agencies themselves. And there is also very little independent academic research on humanitarian effectiveness. Research commissioned by the agencies, not related to funding and institutional considerations, is the exception rather than the rule. The imbalance contributes to a prevailing attitude of mistrust and cynicism, upward as well as down: "I profoundly resent the fact that donors consider themselves immune from empirical analysis," says a senior UN official.

Despite a growing results orientation, most donor funding, as noted in Chapter 7, does not appear to be merit-based. Consequently, incentives for greater effectiveness are unrelated to an agency's desire for future grants. And when donors talk about a greater emphasis on results, it is by no means clear what they mean. The concept of results is clear enough in long-term development programming, but it is not evident what more might be squeezed out of an already underfunded feeding program in a refugee camp. If you want to measure better-nourished children, you need a baseline. When would this be done? When the refugees arrive? When the project is submitted? When the project is funded? When the food arrives? There could be months between the first and the last. There are few commonly agreed-upon objectives, indicators, targets, or measurement tools in the humanitarian field. Even such standards and indicators (for example, those of the Sphere Project) may be completely unachievable if funding is inadequate or if events (such as continuing conflict) or other actors (such as warring parties or local government) intervene.

"The incessant demand from donors for greater transparency is part of a controlling mechanism; it isn't about accountability," says a senior NGO official. Thus monitoring and evaluation for accountability often work at cross-purposes to monitoring and evaluation for learning. If accountability is the objective, failures will be downplayed or hidden by recipient agencies in order to preserve funding. "There is a real fear of being held accountable among NGOs," says an NGO evaluator. "The fear is not a concern about embarrassment or even failure; it is about money, and a general donor (and media) intolerance for failure." Thus a system ostensibly committed to accountability actually discourages it.

In confidence and to each other, donors express concerns about individual managers and the leadership in some UN agencies and NGOs. Weak donor confidence in turn has a negative impact on volumes and types of funding, a problem that goes largely untreated. Yet most donors at one time or another have foisted questionable senior people onto the UN system. For example, a former development minister from a donor country was accepted by UNDP as a resident representative because the donor was an important contributor. A one-time schoolteacher, the ex-minister was not a success in the posting. Is this kind of negative pressure offset by donors' confidence in having their nationals in key positions within UN agencies? A commitment to excellence should in fact call such donor behavior into question, but the issue is rarely discussed.

A number of codes of conduct have been developed over the past decade, often at the initiative of practitioners themselves. Some governments now insist that the NGOs they fund subscribe to Sphere Project standards, for example. However, codes are often limited to specific programming sectors, NGO compliance remains voluntary, and when funding is inadequate, no code or exemplary performance can make adequate supplies of food and medicine appear. In the field, the Sphere code is widely under-used. "Sphere has made me old fast," says one of its developers, exasperated with its limited uptake by the humanitarian sector.[20] Lip service is also paid to the do no harm concept, which is embraced very lightly by many NGOs. "Our agency's Do No Harm Manual is embarrassing," says an NGO field worker, frustrated by the lack of progress in the manual's implementation.

Problems aside, a number of specific new evaluation and quality improvement initiatives bear watching, and, where appropriate, replicating. One is the independent Afghanistan Research and Evaluation Unit (AREU), supported by the Netherlands, Switzerland, and Sweden, which injects a more reflective approach into program operations as they are being carried out, rather than after the fact. AREU was actually set up as an NGO, with a tripartite board composed of donors, UN agencies, and NGOs. The UN Development Group has instituted a competency assessment system for all seeking to become resident coordinators, even if they have already served in that capacity. An independent firm in Toronto administers the test, which is building confidence in the competencies of incoming coordinators.

One feature during the 1990s was a growing variety of initiatives that aimed to enhance the quality of humanitarian assistance: the Active Learning Network for Accountability and Performance in Humanitarian Action (ALNAP), the Humanitarianism & War Project, the Humanitarian Policy Group at the Overseas Development Institute (HPG/ODI), Sphere, the Red Cross/Red Crescent Code of Conduct, the Humanitarian Accountability Project, and People in Aid.[21] If a quality problem exists in humanitarian action, it is not because nobody is thinking about the issue. Many of the initiatives, however, have been fraught with lengthy debate in their development, followed by indifferent application. This is not so much because humanitarian agencies don't want to do better or to be held accountable, but because there is almost no way that higher standards can actually be met in fluid, politicized, underfunded emergency situations. The fear that failure will result in reduced funding is itself a powerful disincentive. The vexed political economy of standards and evaluation almost guarantees that learning will be constrained and, as a result, that program quality will suffer. It is a vicious circle.

A recurrent theme in this chapter is that the issue of accountability has often been taken to the point of dysfunctionality. The demand for accountability ostensibly aims to satisfy taxpayers that money channeled through UN agencies, NGOs, and others is being well spent. But in its standard application, it contains a large element of control—and threat. Because of low donor tolerance for failure (in a business that deals by definition with collapsed or malfunctioning governance and human insecurity), accountability processes as currently applied can actually drive real lessons underground, especially the important lessons that might be derived from failure. The upshot is high levels of mistrust and an approach to evaluation that is limited in scope, imagination, and learning potential. The pathologies inherent in the political economy of humanitarianism are reflected in, and reinforced by, the prevailing approach to accountability. Useful lessons can be learned from evaluating difficult and risk-prone enterprises, if punishment is not a likely outcome. This is not to suggest that willful or repeated mistakes should be ignored, but that mistakes are much more likely to be repeated if they are hidden.

A more holistic approach to needs assessment and evaluation is badly needed, one that puts learning at center stage. If this is done well, donors' accountability requirements will probably be satisfied in the process—as a byproduct rather than as the only product. Evaluations should transcend one organization, one emergency, and one donor. And the focus should be broadened from the delivery end of the chain to encompass the entire system, from design and supply to result. There should be much greater emphasis on multidonor evaluations that take a variety of approaches—geographic, sectoral, comparative—assessing the role of donor organizations, comparing delivery mechanisms, and examining results. Joint evaluations should be widely posted on the Web sites of donors, agencies, and evaluators. While there may be more than enough blame to go around, the humanitarian enterprise is too important to continue to be marked by the levels of mistrust that currently prevail.

10

The Way Ahead

Lay then the axe to the root, and teach governments humanity. It is their sanguinary punishments which corrupt mankind.
—Thomas Paine, *The Rights of Man,* 1791

The humanitarian world can be divided into three broad sets of people and organizations. The first is composed of those in need—refugees, displaced people, victims of war and famine, people trying to put their lives back together after a cataclysm. The second set is made up of the front-line organizations that minister to them: UN agencies, international and local NGOs, the Red Cross movement, private sector firms, and sometimes the military. The third set is made up of those who pay the bills: mainly the governments of industrialized countries and the individual donors who make contributions to NGOs. This book has demonstrated that the political economy of humanitarianism is based to a great extent on the needs and demands of those with the resources—donor governments—and to a decreasing extent on the professional assessments and capacities of front-line delivery agencies. The actual needs of those in trouble as framed by the people in extremis themselves are given fairly short shrift in the overall scheme of things.

The most prominent characteristic of global humanitarianism as it is practiced today is its voluntary nature. Governments, like individuals, provide assistance across borders—if they feel like it. There are no obligations beyond the moral, no consequences (for the givers) of doing less than enough, or of doing nothing. There is often more calculation than compassion, and the calculation itself is too often narrow, inward, and myopic. For the victims of calamity, it is a casino economy operated like a giant charity: the charity of nations.

At the center of the humanitarian enterprise lies the United Nations, created to save and protect the world from the scourge of war. Despite

225

the United Nations and its agencies, despite the Red Cross which can sometimes act as an alternative or a complement, and despite the many fora for coordination and shared learning, each donor has its own analysis of a given emergency, its own policies and strategies, and its own organizational and political imperatives. The multiplicity of actors, the overlapping and underlapping mandates, the history of weak field-level collaboration, and the competition for funds by front-line agencies all undercut the UN's coordinating mandate and potential.

The move to greater earmarking and direct donor intervention in humanitarian financing results from three converging influences. The first was the end of the Cold War and the ongoing mainstreaming of aid into the international security agenda. The second is greater international engagement in internal wars such as Kosovo and Afghanistan, where donors wanted more visibility and recognition for their humanitarian assistance. Tight earmarking was one way to achieve this. And the third influence is changes in public sector management, with a greater emphasis on results. In the latter scenario, UN agencies fall victim to their own unwillingness to reform. Furthermore, the idea that unrestricted multilateral aid promotes a more equitable allocation of funds than bilateral methods is dismissed out of hand: "There is insufficient evidence," one study concludes, "to support this in practice."[1]

This book has attempted to demonstrate that individualistic donor behavior is considerably less effective than a coordinated multilateral approach among all donors—at least in principle. The truth is that unearmarked multilateral humanitarian funding has almost completely disappeared from the world, and so what might be loses out to what is. The mess that has followed can be laid squarely at the doorstep of those calling the shots, although because donor governments call the shots, they also pass the buck to the implementers—the United Nations, NGOs, and other front-line delivery organizations. Given the clustering of bilateral donor funding around geopolitical hotspots and the consequent growth in "forgotten emergencies," there is not just insufficient evidence to demonstrate donor individualism is any better than the multilateral ideal—there is no evidence at all. The power grab by donors—in the name of improved policy coherence, greater efficiencies and (the last refuge of the bureaucrat) accountability to the taxpayer—has crippled the United Nations and robbed front-line humanitarian delivery agencies of their principles, their independence, and much of their efficiency.

Too strong? Tell that to the 18,000 Angolan refugees in summer 2003, living on half rations in the miserable refugee camps of Namibia. Tell it to the people of Ituri in the Congo, buffeted between rebel armies for years with little or no humanitarian succor. Tell it to the Haitians who wonder whatever happened to Operation Uphold Democracy, or to the people in Zambia or the Sudan or Somalia who receive enough food from the humanitarian machine to stay alive, but not enough to be healthy or productive. Tell it to the Afghans, whose needs were largely forgotten until September 12, 2001. Tell it to the Sierra Leoneans who, celebrating the end of a ten-year war, watch with dismay as the aid agencies pack their bags, just when they are needed most for recovery and reconstruction—because recovery and reconstruction in Sierra Leone are not part of most donors' "strategic framework." Tell it to the many flyblown children over the decades—in Biafra, Eritrea, Ethiopia, and Cambodia—who have been seen dying of starvation on the television screens of the West.

We will do better next time, everyone says. Afghanistan was to be an example of that. ECHO says it will focus in the future on forgotten emergencies (i.e., that it will stop forgetting). Their meeting donors debate humanitarian definitions and principles but cannot "agree" or "endorse them"—so they settle finally on the word "elaborate." They *elaborate* a plan for good humanitarian donorship." And this plan, recognizing the problems of late, short-term, and unpredictable funding to front-line UN agencies, "strives to ensure predictability" and says it will "explore the possibility of reducing, or enhancing the flexibility of, earmarking, and of introducing longer-term funding arrangements."[2]

In fact this meeting, with the benefit of three major background studies submitted in 2003, explored these issues and others for two full days, but could reach almost no agreement on anything that extended beyond a platitude and a vague undertaking to strive to do better. A recommendation that there should be much more independent evaluation of humanitarian interventions, including the role played by donor governments vis à vis the actual delivery of assistance, was modified as follows: "Emphasizing the importance of peer reviews of humanitarian action, donors will invite the OECD Development Assistance Committee (DAC) to consider ways to significantly strengthen the coverage of humanitarian action in existing and/or complementary peer reviews." An invitation to another intergovernmental body "to consider ways" to strengthen "peer reviews" hardly constituted a clarion call to action; nor did it represent a rush to demonstrate accountability to the virtuous but legendarily tight-fisted taxpayer.[3]

Moving on from this dynamic set of conclusions, a fourth study was commissioned in 2003: "Changes in Humanitarian Financing: Implications for the United Nations." This report was a different cup of tea, because where humanitarianism is concerned, the new study recommended turning the United Nations into a "standard-setting" institution with an enhanced coordination function. Indeed, that might be a useful role for the United Nations to play, if donors allowed it. But where delivery is concerned, it was recommended that the United Nations take a seat much further back in the humanitarian bus—in fact it should more or less get off the operational bus. "The UN would deliver humanitarian services only in situations where alternative delivery mechanisms are unavailable or undesirable."[4]

Before taking a look at this extraordinary recommendation, it is worth examining the reaction of the agencies that would ostensibly be emasculated by it. The Interagency Standing Committee (IASC) Working Group, including representatives of UNHCR, WFP, WHO, UNICEF, UNDP, OCHA, the Red Cross movement, and NGOs, was perhaps stung by charges that the UN system was not adequately assessing needs and evaluating performance. But instead of addressing the recommendation that their hands-on role be severely curtailed, if not cancelled, they agreed that the principal action point would be to "Establish a technical sub group to the current IASC WG [Working Group] on the CAP to develop common approaches for integration, inter-agency and cross-sectoral needs assessment and objective criteria for vulnerability analysis. Such work should furthermore lead to the development of results-oriented monitoring and evaluation systems. The first task would be to define the parameters of vulnerability."[5]

While they are doing this (assuming that anyone knows what it actually means), donors presumably pondered the dissolution of UNICEF's direct delivery capacity, along with those of UNHCR, WHO, and others.

Source: © Jeff Danziger. Los Angeles Times (August 22, 2003).
Reprinted with permission.

The problem with this startling idea is that while it acknowledges the weakness of UN agencies as front-line delivery mechanisms, it does not say *why* they are weak. The reasons involve donor earmarking; unpredictable, late, and inadequate funding; inadequate evaluation; and all the standard problems of large bureaucracies whose senior staff are appointed for political reasons and under donor pressure. And the report says virtually nothing about the alternative. It is assumed that NGOs, much criticized in other studies (not to mention in donor capitals), will now do most everything. Or possibly they will be complemented by greater humanitarian efforts on the part of the private sector and the military. In this model, the UN would assess needs, set priorities, and somehow coordinate the dozen or five dozen or even twenty dozen NGOs that would do all the running around, commissioned by a dozen donors according to their own priorities, policies, and predilections. Backward runs the logic until it boggles the mind.

There are other possibilities, not quite as anarchic, not a million miles removed from the ideals set forth in the Charter of the United Nations, and although politically awkward, not impossible. As a starting point, it is worth recalling that the Charter itself, signed in June 1945 and subsequently approved by all 191 member nations, begins this way:

> We the peoples of the United Nations, determined to save succeeding generations from the scourge of war, which twice in our lifetime has brought untold sorrow to mankind, and to reaffirm faith in fundamental human rights, in the dignity and worth of the human person, in the equal rights of men and women and of nations large and small; and to establish conditions under which justice and respect for the obligations arising from treaties and other sources of international law can be maintained; and to promote social progress and better standards of life in larger freedom; and for these ends, to practice tolerance and live together in peace with one another as good neighbors; and to unite our strength to maintain international peace and security; and to ensure, by the acceptance of principles and the institution of methods, that armed force shall not be used, save in the common interest; and to employ international machinery for the promotion of the economic and social advancement of all peoples, have resolved to combine our efforts to accomplish these aims.

"Have resolved to combine our efforts to accomplish these aims." Where humanitarianism is concerned, the opposite has happened. Governments have gradually but relentlessly pulled away from the multilateral ideal, and at great expense, this book argues, not just to humanitarian principles, but to the people whom humanitarian action is designed to assist and protect. Donors have, in fact, passed the bucks to the UN and other aid agencies but have failed to accept responsibility for their own direct role in the disappointing results. A promising step forward was taken at a 2003 conference on "good humanitarian donorship." Sponsored initially by the Netherlands and Sweden and subsequently chaired by Canada, the initiative seeks better ways to coordinate humanitarian assistance, recognizing that there are serious supply-side problems among the donor agencies. But its first steps— experimental efforts at field coordination and peer reviews—fall far short of the fundamental changes required.

Drawing on the cases described in this book as exemplars of the problem, six bold steps must be taken to reinvigorate a humanitarianism that focuses on those in need and puts and end to ad hocism, egocentricity and the haphazard, take-it-or-leave-it approach that characterizes today's humanitarian planning and activities.

A Conceptual Humanitarian Center

Chapter 1 discussed the vague articulation in humanitarian law of the right to humanitarian assistance, and the plethora of institutions that now debate, fund, and administer such aid. Chapters 2, 3, 4, and 5 demonstrated that where humanitarian policy was concerned in Sierra Leone, East Timor, Afghanistan and elsewhere, principle almost always takes a back seat to the political and commercial concerns of donors, too often focused narrowly on particular issues or distracted by clamorous events elsewhere. From a conceptual standpoint, there can be no such thing in a real-time, media-pumped world as a "forgotten emergency." Nevertheless, they abound. Chapter 6 described the policy backdrop against which humanitarian action takes place (or does not), finding no lack of definitions, policies, concepts, and frameworks. The problem is not their absence but the confusing and contested grab-bag within and among countries and agencies, allowing explanation and justification for any action, or inaction: In this world, any dream will do.

There must be a conceptual center, not so much a physical entity as a catalytic function, within the humanitarian sector where definitions and norms for humanitarian action are vetted, set, and maintained.[6] The United Nations is ideally suited for this role—as a standard bearer, as a visionary leader, as a place where a global humanitarian framework can be created and where assessments of response can be considered against future action.[7] It could serve as the catalyst enabling the outcomes of global humanitarian action to become more than the sum of its parts. In addition to helping ensure the allocation of resources according to actual need, it could also help to coordinate, or at least set a priority agenda for research. As with the rest of the enterprise, there is a political economy of humanitarian research (of which this book is a part), with individuals and academic institutions vying for attention and funding. They are no less prone to following the patchy and erratic money trail than any other player in the game. In the process, important perspectives may well be overlooked, key lessons ignored, and criticism implicitly or explicitly muted.

In 2004, the OECD opened a discussion on ODA eligibility, that is, on the possibility of changing the definition of official development assistance. This can sometimes be more important for appearances than for substance, as the United States discovered when Israel was taken off the list of ODA-eligible countries, and U.S. foreign aid, as defined by the Development Assistance Committee (DAC) of the OECD, suddenly plummeted. It also can work the other way. By allowing the inclusion of expenditures for resettling refugees during their first twelve months in a donor country, the DAC effectively allowed donors to inflate their humanitarian calculations, making them look more generous than might otherwise be the case. This particular smoke-and-mirrors exercise doubled humanitarian spending totals in some countries and represented a quarter of so-called humanitarian aid by OECD member countries taken together.

The 2004 OECD discussion was more ominous because of pressure from several governments to include in ODA items that had always been disallowed: technical assistance to defense ministries and armed forces; technical assistance related to national security; reform and training of military forces; financing of peacekeeping forces drawn from developing countries; assistance with intelligence gathering on terrorism threats.[8] It is not clear where such discussions will lead, but they suggest two possibilities. The first is the growing encroachment of security and security sector issues into ODA thinking in general and into humanitarian action in particular. The second is that including something new under the ODA rubric allows cutbacks on other forms of development assistance without the appearance of having reduced overall aid spending. Security and security sector reform may well be an essential part of evolving interactions between donors and developing countries, but to throw it into the same basket with emergency relief makes sense only as a means of subterfuge. It is like a person losing weight, but hiding it by putting on more and more clothing.

Definitions have consequences, as does the presence (or absence) of policy. Clearer articulation of humanitarian claims on resources would arguably elevate humanitarian considerations among competing priorities in the public square. It would also promote less confusion in public understanding of the essentials. Unless donors embrace an agreed-upon commitment to proportionality in the resource allocation, improving a system that functions by patchwork rather than principle will remain hard to achieve. Without structural changes, there likely will be recurrent

Iraqs which, commandeering $2.5 billion in aid funds in a single year, swamp all other country allocations and the best efforts at proportionality.

The lack of shared definitions lies at the heart of much of the disarray in the current humanitarian financing system. A common definition of humanitarian response simply for reporting and statistical purposes is long overdue. Greater clarity about what is meant by transition and on how delivery agencies can or should be organized to implement transition initiatives will help coordinate funding and reduce the funding gaps that are now so common.

There must be better synergies between the humanitarian mandate and operations within donor agencies and those of their development counterparts. Too often the humanitarian department and its programming desks are functionally and conceptually divorced from what is regarded as more mainstream and serious development thinking. Nothing could be more inappropriate, especially after a decade of watching development investments disappear down the drain of war, and of famines induced by human agency. Organizations that mount both humanitarian and development activities have a special opportunity to explore and capitalize on such links.

Definitions and mandates aside, investments in the transition from relief to development and in postemergency reconstruction efforts are very much ad hoc. Each humanitarian agency winds down according to its own institutional imperatives, making whatever arrangements for follow-up activities it deems best, which in many cases are none at all. The longer-term factors that contributed to the crisis in the first place are often ignored completely. Pressed at the 2002 Economic and Social Council (ECOSOC) review of humanitarian issues for a policy statement regarding phasing down food aid programs in crisis countries, a senior WFP official replied, perhaps flippantly but also tellingly, that programs cease when donors no longer provide food.

If huge investments in humanitarian assistance are to bear fruit, it is essential that longer-term development issues are approached comprehensively *during* the emergency phase. Donors must develop common strategies to address relief and development issues concurrently and to plan for the longer term. Doing so may be beyond the mandate of humanitarian departments in particular donor agencies, but it is not beyond the mandate of the donor agency itself, whether or not it intends to stay on after the emergency ends. Distinctions of mandates within individual donor governments should not be allowed to interfere with transition planning and funding.[9]

The United Nations should consider disaggregating and defining humanitarian policy and should work for a common donor understanding under the following headings:

- **Humanitarian principles:** These reflect international humanitarian, refugee, and human rights law and can form a mutual basis for humanitarian action. Currently there are widely varying definitions and widely divergent priorities when tensions among principles emerge. Efforts should be made to draw in new ideas and concepts that extend beyond the traditional Northern base of humanitarian thought and resources;
- **Sectoral policies:** Some donors may emphasize some sectors over others in their humanitarian activities. Food is a major priority for the United States but no longer for Canada; the government of Norway has exercised a lead role on issues related to internally displaced persons;
- **Operational policies:** Greater clarity and consistency among donors on their preferred delivery channels and the basis for their choices among UN agencies, NGOs, the IFRC, and ICRC could enhance predictability in humanitarian financing;
- **Geographic policies:** Clearly articulated priorities and preferences would help front-line agencies plan their own response to particular emergencies and also minimize the number of emergencies that lack priority for most donors; and
- **Cross-cutting policy themes:** Protection, gender, children, risk reduction, conflict prevention, capacity-building, coordination, and quality control play a greater (or lesser role) in the humanitarian policy of some donors.

A Strengthened Multilateral Core

Humanitarian action is part of a system of official development assistance that is increasingly rights-based: Rights to life, food, shelter, and basic health and education are core tenets of humanitarian law, the UN Charter, the Declaration of the Rights of the Child and a dozen other charters, codes, and sets of standards. These contain very real implications for donor organizations regarding the quantity and the quality of the humanitarian resources they provide. At the center of humanitarian action lies the multilateral ideal and its manifestation in the United Nations—the software and the hardware of combined efforts to achieve common objectives. And yet almost every case study in this book except East Timor reveals a set of UN agencies in competition with each other, with NGOs, with commercial and political interests, and sometimes even the military. Chapter 8 described the consolidated appeal process (CAP) and the demands from donors for priority setting in a funding climate where secondary priorities will never get money, and where in any case the choice is never between, say, food aid (in financial terms *the* top donor priority) and something else. It is between food aid and nothing.

The major humanitarian challenge today, for the United Nations and for member governments, is not to further weaken but to create a strengthened multilateral core that has the capacity, resources, and mandate from its members to meet humanitarian needs more impartially and effectively. There are four parts to this core.

The first is the need to insulate the UN humanitarian mandate from the current and individual political concerns of its member states. The operative word here is insulate—not divorce. Terrorism, for example, is not a new phenomenon but, redefined since 9/11, it has become a dominant consideration in discussions about official development assistance. Discussions of a new common security policy in Brussels involve proposals that would place emergency assistance more clearly within a political rubric. This inclination undoubtedly holds for other donors as well.

This, too, may pass, but in the short run it is important that humanitarian action and budgets not be diverted into a security mindset, especially one that might undermine efforts at conflict prevention. The United Nations and its agencies should be able to even out some of the peaks and valleys that result from lopsided bilateral action; that was and should remain one of the primary purposes of multilateral action. Individual donor governments may forget certain emergencies, but the United Nations cannot, and should not.

Second is the need for a strong, managerial, but nonoperational UN humanitarian agency that can assess needs, set priorities, and allocate funds. Some aspects of such a body exist in OCHA, but it needs a stronger mandate, a broader job description, and complete separation from the operational UN organizations and others that might benefit from its funding decisions. This body must do more than coordinate; it must lead, and it must have the recognized authority to lead.

Third, such a humanitarian focal point must have access to significant amounts of humanitarian funding that is predictable, timely, and not earmarked. A substantial portion of this funding must be derived from assessed rather than voluntary contributions, as described below. Current mechanisms for funding humanitarian work (called voluntary but, in effect, whimsical) must be comparable to assessed contributions for UN peacekeeping operations.

Fourth, a multilateral institutional core must have a powerful accountability mechanism that limits political interference from member states without alienating them. That will require an executive board that includes some members from donor and recipient countries but that also represents civil society, business, the media, and others concerned and knowledgeable about humanitarian action. As described below, such representation would expand the membership of current UN governing boards and advisory committees, but in some instances reduce the numbers of such structures.

An inherent tension exists between the scale of need for humanitarian action and the absence of adequate funding for assistance and protection activities. At a more fundamental level, there is a contradiction between the rights articulated in the UN Charter and in international humanitarian, human rights and refugee law on the one hand and, on the other, the treatment of humanitarian financing, not as an international obligation of states but as a kind of charitable freewill offering. This approach results in financing arrangements that do not reflect obligations and duties but preferences and idiosyncrasies. A strengthened multilateral financing and implementation system represents an investment in a more proportional and less politicized response to human need.

To propose that some contributions to humanitarian activities be assessed rather than voluntary may seem unrealistic in the current circumstances. But reliance upon hundreds, if not thousands of inadequate, earmarked, voluntary contributions throughout any given fiscal year from a score of donors makes as much sense as trying to run a big-city fire brigade on nothing but donations. The result is not a system but a self-serving, hit-or-miss charitable arrangement that aims to satisfy the givers first and foremost—at the expense of those in need.

The current percentage shares of assessments (for example, to UN peacekeeping operations) could serve as the basis for establishing minimum targets for humanitarian financing by all member states. This would have the virtue of avoiding a bruising discussion of the modalities and percentages of assessments while recognizing the need to generate a more equitable and reliable system of burden-sharing. The idea could be crafted in such a way as to maintain current levels of effort by pace-setting nations while encouraging others to step up their contributions. A target of 75 percent of the previous year's spending by each donor country on humanitarian assistance could serve as a starting point for initial assessments. The balance could be devoted bilaterally to areas of particular concern or interest to individual donors. The point is not to halt all direct bilateral humanitarian spending but to create a core of depoliticized multilateral resources.

In a similar vein, much could be done to improve the governance of individual UN agencies. To expect governments, especially donor governments, to give up their role on governing boards would be unrealistic. However, consideration should be given to reducing their size, bringing in knowledgeable but disinterested professionals, and creating mechanisms where boards or executive committees (including non-government professionals) can discuss issues in greater detail and more often than is currently possible.

A More Disciplined NGO Community

Chapter 9 described the climate of mistrust that exists between bilateral donors and front-line agencies. The United Nations suffers from this phenomenon, but it is more pronounced between donors and NGOs, even though donors depend at least as much on NGOs for the delivery of their funding as NGOs depend on donors for their support. Chapter 8 described the humanitarian scramble, with NGOs vying for attention and money, many of them becoming little more than underpaid contractors in the world's humanitarian soup kitchen, where there are obviously too many cooks. And the case studies of Sierra Leone, East Timor, and elsewhere described NGOs tripping over themselves for contracts, with little ability to operate on their own initiative or to strengthen their counterparts in developing countries.

An estimated 10 to 15 percent of all humanitarian assistance is generated in the form of private donations to NGOs, churches, and the Red Cross family—as much as $1.5 billion annually. On top of that, NGOs receive about one-third of all bilateral contributions to the humanitarian effort in the form of grants and contracts. And they program as much as half of what goes through the UN system. NGOs, therefore, program as much as 60 percent of all humanitarian assistance, or roughly $6 billion per year. And although there are hundreds of NGOs, it is safe to say that 75 percent of their humanitarian spending is handled by fewer than fifteen large transnational organizations.[10]

The size, professionalism, and importance of these major NGOs are not recognized, however, in the way monies are allocated, dispensed, and reported. Most donors moved to multiyear program funding for the development work of these organizations two decades ago. But where emergencies are concerned, even the largest and most professional NGOs are kept on short donor leashes and permitted woefully inadequate overheads. They are made to compete for contracts in ways that lead to tardy and inadequate delivery, dysfunctional behavior, and an absence of learning. NGOs should be an integral part of the UN coordinating role and the proposed assessed funding arrangement.

There should be a preselection mechanism, managed by the United Nations, say, guaranteeing a certain level of predictable program funding for a preselected group of fifteen major NGOs, assessed triennially for participation in such an arrangement. They should be eligible for additional program funding in a given country—along with front-line UN agencies—on the basis of needs assessments, competencies, their willingness to be part of a coordinated effort, and on the basis of the additionalities they might bring to an emergency in the form of their own funding or particular experience. To preserve their independence, however, there would be no compulsion for them to act in any particular emergency, or in any particular way. Other NGOs, both international and local, would be contracted on the basis of merit and diversity. It is assumed that some NGOs would keep their distance from relationships with the newly deputized UN forward-funding entity, and they should be free to do so.

For these NGOs and for others operating outside the core program, burden-sharing of administrative costs should be negotiated and shared proportionally by NGOs and institutional donors. In other words, donors and UN agencies should not expect NGOs to cover a disproportionate share of the overheads on program delivery. This only leads to NGOs having to subsidize institutional donors with hard-won private donor income, or to cutting corners on program delivery. The provision of adequate administrative overheads should be viewed as an integral part of quality control rather than a formulaic and unwanted necessity to be minimized at all costs. Whatever the arrangement, funding must be released quickly, or even preauthorized. A good example is ECHO's primary emergency procedure for proven NGOs such as the Red Cross or MSF, which can release funds within seventy-two hours of a natural disaster.

Capacity-building for local civil society in conflict prevention and emergency assistance needs to be taken much more seriously. It should become an automatic feature of donor funding in any emergency that extends beyond three months. Such an arrangement would represent a fundamental shift in orientation, operation, and accountability. However, it would address a chronic shortcoming of the international humanitarian apparatus: that of failing to leave strengthened local capacity behind.[11] The "heavy footprint" that characterizes most emergency responses must not be allowed to recur.

Predictable funding is a key element in all successful planning and implementation, not least in the humanitarian sector. Short donor timeframes lead to unpredictability and therefore poor planning. Management is exacerbated by a compartmentalizing of donor agencies' funds and departments, which reduces the possibility of funding for recovery and reconstruction and for linking relief and development. This schism should not be repeated in the creation of a stronger UN focal point or in the evolution of assessed funding arrangements. In protracted emergencies, donors and the UN must find ways to make longer-term allocations, even if they are notional and conditional. This would help implementing agencies to plan better, to find and retain good staff, to develop greater synergies between relief and development, and to become more professional in other ways.

Trust in the humanitarian enterprise is a two-way street. It is not only about givers trusting receivers; those who pay the piper are also obliged to change. One small step toward both improved management and greater multilateralism would be to establish common reporting formats for UN agencies and NGOs. Donors complain that reports are late, incomplete, and inadequate. Agencies complain that they have to deal with myriad forms, templates, definitions, and queries. If donors are serious about coordination and about reducing the costs of administration, and if UN agencies and NGOs are serious about building better donor confidence, developing a common reporting format could represent a breakthrough that might help establish greater two-way trust.

Greater Accountability

The mistrust that pervades the humanitarian system, described at length in Chapter 9, must end. At various points in this book, donors have been criticized for their choice of implementation strategies, partners, and structures, based not on the merits of available options but on an amalgam of extraneous factors, including political pressures, habits and assumptions, personal connections, and the need for political visibility and immediate effects. However, decision-making based on the merits—for example, of bilateral or multilateral, civilian or military, Northern or Southern implementing partners—is difficult, if not impossible. Comparative data does not exist to support such decisions.[12]

The long-identified gaps in data and knowledge should be the subject of new action-oriented policy research. Why should rigorous analysis and cost-effective criteria not be applied to the program impacts of civic action programs conducted by the military, so that these may be contrasted with the costs of assistance and protection efforts by humanitarian agencies? Why not examine the correlation, whether positive or negative, between donor conditionalities and effective programs? Why not seek to calculate the impacts on beneficiary populations that result from undersubscribed UN appeals? Clearly enough experience is available to assess whether an architecture that connects humanitarian work more closely with conflict prevention and resolution, peace-making and peace-building, democratization and good governance produces more effective assistance and protection activities than does an architecture that separates humanitarian and other activities. However, that, too, would require additional research and reflection.

A recurrent theme in the book is that the issue of accountability has been taken, in general terms, to the point of dysfunctionality. The consumers of the product, who should be the beneficiaries, have no say in the quality, quantity, delivery, or process. The real consumers, in fact, are taxpayers, donors, and politicians. This is like General Motors ignoring its customers and allowing its board members to design automobiles. The demand for accountability ostensibly aims to satisfy taxpayers that money channeled through UN agencies, NGOs, and others is being spent well. It would not be difficult routinely to include the recipients of humanitarian assistance in evaluations. Certainly such an approach is long overdue.

In its standard application, evaluation contains a large element of control—and threat. Because of low donor tolerance for failure and because effective humanitarian action involves a high element of risk and innovation, accountability processes as currently applied can actually drive real lessons underground, especially the important lessons that might be derived from failure. The upshot is an evaluation approach that is limited in scope, imagination, and potential for learning. Useful lessons can be learned from evaluating difficult and risk-prone enterprises, if punishment is not a likely outcome. This is not to suggest that willful or repeated mistakes should be ignored but that mistakes are much less likely to be repeated if they are identified and addressed.

A more holistic approach to evaluation puts learning at center stage. If this is done well, donors' accountability requirements will also be satisfied, but as a byproduct rather than as the only product. Evaluations should transcend one organization, one emergency, and one donor. And the focus should be broadened from the delivery end of the chain to encompass the entire system, from design and supply to result. In other words, there should be much greater emphasis on multidonor evaluations that take a variety of approaches—geographical, sectoral, comparative, assessing the role of donor organizations, comparing delivery mechanisms, and examining results. Joint evaluations should be widely posted on the Web sites of donors, agencies, and evaluators.[13]

More Funding

Each major case study in this book has described the inadequacy of humanitarian funding levels. The only exception was East Timor, which—when the time came—was well endowed for historical, political, and commercial reasons, with humanitarian objectives arguably in somewhat distant second place. From a global vantage point, the humanitarian effort is underfunded by at least half, if not more. It is fashionable among donors and academics studying the issue to argue that, in the absence of good assessments, we don't really know what the actual needs are. Or that by reducing costs and inefficiencies, we could get a bigger bang for the buck—"do more with less." UN agencies, after all, are very expensive.

Maybe they are, but consider the $87 billion package approved by the U.S. Congress for defense and reconstruction purposes in Iraq alone, against the $10 billion provided by all DAC and non-DAC governments and all NGOs in a year for all of the refugees and all of the victims of all the wars, all the floods, all the cyclones and hurricanes and droughts in the entire world. Consider the $10 billion spent on humanitarian assistance and postconflict peace activities against the $749 billion on global military expenditures. Consider the fact that in 2003 a very bad film called *Charlie's Angels: Full Throttle* cost $130 million to produce and a further $40 million to distribute, about five times what the United Nations, all government donor agencies, and all NGOs combined spent on humanitarian assistance in Sierra Leone in any twelve-month period during the 1990s, when more than half of the country's population was on the run from rampaging rebels, living destitute and hungry in filthy squatter camps.

Former U.S. Secretary of State Madeleine Albright puts the cost of running the United Nations—the entire United Nations—into perspective:

> The annual budget for core UN functions—based in New York City, Geneva, Nairobi, Vienna and five regional commissions—is about $1.25 billion, or roughly what the Pentagon spends every 32 hours. The UN Secretariat has reduced its staff by just under 25 percent over the past 20 years and has had a zero-growth budget since 1996. The entire UN system, composed of the Secretariat and 29 other organizations, employs a little more than 50,000 people, or just 2,000 more than work for the city of Stockholm. Total annual expenditure by all UN funds, program and specialized agencies equal about one fourth the municipal budget of New York.[14]

The question is not so much whether more money is needed for humanitarian work, but where it will come from and how to get there from here. Increases can no longer be taken from the development side of the ODA house. This is not just robbing Peter to pay Paul; it makes no sense to reduce spending on efforts that are designed to prevent human and natural disasters. Given how little most OECD member countries devote to ODA as a whole, however, it does not seem to be asking too much for an increase in global aid spending, and to suggest that at least a portion of the increase be devoted to the humanitarian effort.

A New Approach to Public Understanding

It might well be asked how all this very fundamental change is to happen. Is it even remotely conceivable that governments might loosen the political purse strings on humanitarian action in a world beset by rampant unilateralism, the quest for commercial advantage, and concerns about terror? Perhaps. *Perhaps:* If governments could be made to see that the long-term cost of bad development and weak, politicized humanitarian action will be higher than what might be "lost" to reform in the short run; if humanitarian agencies could make common cause around their ailing enterprise and create so much noise about the problem that they could not be ignored; if instead of more conferences for powerless bureaucrats, they engaged decision makers at much higher levels and beneficiary populations on the front lines; if they stopped worrying about the next contract and started saying more forthrightly in public what they mumble among themselves in private; if researchers received more hard-hitting terms of reference and their recommendations did not shy away from speaking truth to power.

The humanitarian response is a part of human nature. Taxpayers and those who contribute individually to assuage humanitarian need do so from basic human instincts that are common to all societies. Most are not concerned about political calculation or commercial advantage, and they would be surprised, even shocked, to discover the role these play in their government's management of humanitarian budgets. If there is to be any hope of a more adequate, timely, and proportional humanitarian response, all players must work to better inform parliamentarians, taxpayers, individual donors, and the media and public about the nature of humanitarian action and about the causes of complex emergencies. Governments must have *permission* from their citizenry to provide the amounts of money needed—and to provide it in creative and effective ways—for more comprehensive approaches to emergencies.

While some of the dysfunctional foreign and domestic political pressures on humanitarian action are unavoidable, many could be mitigated by more proactive initiatives from the humanitarian community, including government agencies, UN organizations, and NGOs. Many spend as much time promoting themselves as the issues. Joint briefings and study missions for journalists could be encouraged, as well as for key parliamentarians and members of financial oversight bodies. Better contextualization of evaluations and broader dissemination of findings might help build a better climate of understanding among potential critics. Joint studies that demonstrate the human cost of politicized choices could also be supported. If one percent of the $10 billion global humanitarian and postconflict budget (roughly U.S.$100 million) was devoted to creative and responsible worldwide public education, the investment would likely pay for itself in cash and kind many times over.

It is a steamy April day at a derelict fish processing plant on the edge of a mangrove swamp west of Freetown. The buildings have been commandeered for Liberian refugees, and several thousand now live here in a collection of leaky UNHCR tents, outbuildings, and a massive hangar that once served as a trawler maintenance shed. An international NGO operating under the auspices of UNHCR manages the camp. Food is supplied by WFP, and UNICEF provides some health services. Small children, half naked, are playing a game with a stick and a broken bicycle wheel. Although it is midday, many people are dozing on makeshift beds and mats. There is not much to do all day long.

The refugees have organized a management committee and one of the leaders introduces himself. "I was a primary school teacher in Liberia," he says. He speaks excellent English, which reduces the distance between him and the visitor. Language barriers often make it difficult for refugees to communicate directly with outsiders, and the use of an interpreter introduces yet another filter and, on occasion, agenda. People become the objects of conversation, unaware of what other people are deciding for them.

"My family and I have been here for six years," he says. He describes conditions in the camp: bad. "I want to show you something." He sends a young man out, and he soon returns with a bottle of cooking oil and a plastic pail filled with bulgur wheat. "This is what we live on," the teacher says. "A bucket of wheat and a liter of oil for each of us every month. No fish, no meat, no vegetables. We have to sell some of this to traders from Freetown if we want anything else. They cheat us, of course, but then who in Freetown wants bulgur wheat?" He explains that some of the men are able to get past the camp guards and go to Freetown themselves, where they work as day laborers. "My children have become teenagers in this place," he says. "They no longer have any respect for me. I have nothing to give them; nothing to teach them."

Time passes. From somewhere a bottle of Fanta is produced for the visitor, who eyes the white Pajero and driver waiting under a tree to take him back to Freetown. "We just want to go home," the schoolteacher says. "We just want to go home."

Appendix 1:
Donor Response to Six Crises:
A Comparison

Angola CAP 2002

Mid-2002: 4 million IDPs, "life-saving aid to 2m"
Overall response rate: 68.21%
• WFP, UNICEF over 95% funded;
• OCHA, 68.6%;
• UNHCR, 38.9%;
• IOM, UNDP, UNFPA all less than 15% of request;
• NGO funding recorded as zero.

Out of $202 million funded inside the CAP:
• 71.6% was for food;
• 10% was for coordination and support services;
• 8.3% was for health;
• 2.5% was for agriculture;
• 2.36% was "multisector" (UNHCR or IOM);
• 1.89% was for education;
• 1.7% protection/human rights/rule of law;
• 0.9% was for water and sanitation;
• 0.5% was for security.

$43.3 million (18% of all donor funding) was channelled outside the CAP framework. Percentage and channel for funding outside the CAP:
• Germany   80%   NGOs and ICRC
• Denmark   78%   NGOs and ICRC
• Switzerland   68%   NGOs and ICRC
• Netherlands   38%   NGOs and ICRC
• Ireland   38%   NGOs
• Sweden   37%   NGOs and ICRC
• EC   17%   NGOs
• Canada   16%   NGOs and ICRC
• Norway   16%   NGOs and ICRC
• United States   5%   NGOs and ICRC
• France, U.K., Italy, and Japan   0

Funding for food aid under the CAP:
• United States   71.5%
• EC   19.2%
• France   4.7%
• Netherlands   2.5%
• United Kingdom   2.1%
• Ireland   1.5%
• Germany   1.0%
• Italy, Sweden, Denmark, Norway, Canada   Less than 1%

Sudan CAP 2002

Mid-2002: Food for 2.9 million
• Overall response rate: 61.12%
• WFP, UNHCR, OCHA over 80% funded;
• UNICEF, 36.9%;
• WHO, UNFPA less than 10%;
• UNDP, less than 5%;
• UNCHS, IOM zero;
• NGO funding recorded as zero.

Out of $167 million funded inside the CAP:
• 5.4% was for food;
• 2.48% was for coordination and support services;
• 4.65% was for health;
• 3.26% was for agriculture;
• 7.3% was "multisector";
• 1.42% was for education;
• 1.76% protection/human rights/rule of law;
• 2.17% was for water and sanitation;
• 0.9% was for security.

$94.2 million (36% of all donor funding) was channelled outside the CAP framework. Percentage and channel for funding outside the CAP:
• United Kingdom 85%   NGOs, ICRC, UN Security
• EC   85%   NGOs and WFP
• Ireland   72%   NGOs
• Denmark   65%   NGOs and UNICEF
• Sweden   64%   NGOs and ICRC
• Germany   44%   NGOs
• Canada   43%   NGOs
• Netherlands   38%   NGOs
• United States   30%   NGOs, WFP
• Belgium   20%   Caritas
• Japan   4%   NGOs

Funding for food aid under the CAP:
• United States   87.3%
• Japan   6.5%
• Netherlands   2.8%
• Italy   1.5%
• Belgium, Denmark, Germany, Italy   Less than 1%
• EC, Canada   0

DRC CAP 2002

Mid-2002: 2.4 million IDPs, 16 million food insecure
Overall response rate: 46.87%
• WFP, 117% funded; OHCHR, 100%;
• UNHCR, 76%;
• OCHA, 41.4%;
• UNICEF, 27%;
• FAO, 23%;
• WHO, 2%;
• IOM, UNDP, ILO, UNIFEM, UNFPA, UNESCO, 0%;
• NGO funding recorded as zero.

Out of $94.8 million funded inside the CAP:
• 49.2% was for food;
• 5.6% was for coordination and support services;
• 5.4% was for health;
• 5.3% was for agriculture;
• 28.9% was "multisector" (UNHCR or IOM);
• 0.4% was for education;
• 3.5% protection/human rights/rule of law;
• 0% was for water and sanitation;
• 0.9% was for security.

$38.3 million (28.8% of all donor funding) was channelled outside the CAP framework. Percentage and channel for funding outside the CAP:
• Germany   70% NGOs and ICRC
• United Kingdom   65% NGOs
• Switzerland   59% ICRC, NGOs, OCHA
• Sweden   49% Merlin, ICRC
• United States   33% NGOs, OFDA, OTI
• Denmark   31% ICRC
• Canada   31% MSF, Red Cross
• Netherlands   27% NGOs
• Ireland   38% NGOs
• Sweden   37% NGOs and ICRC
• EC, Japan, Italy   0

Funding for food aid under the CAP:
• United States   81.5%
• EC   8.5%
• Netherlands   4.4%
• Sweden, Belgium, Canada, Germany, Switzerland   Less than 1.5% each

Tajikistan CAP 2002

Mid-2002: 734,000 food insecure
Overall response rate: 95.3%
• WFP, 116%;
• UNICEF, 83%;
• OCHA, 73%;
• WHO, 46%;
• IOM, 56% (UNHCR absent);
• UNIFEM, UNFPA, 0;
• NGO funding recorded as zero.

Out of $72.8 million funded inside the CAP:
• 93.9% was for food;
• 3.5% was for water and sanitation;
• less than 1% each was devoted to agriculture, coordination and support services, health, economic recovery, and infrastructure.

Part of the reason for WFP "overfunding" was a carryover of $36 million.

$17.2 million (32% of all donor funding) was channelled outside the CAP framework (this does not include the food carryover). Percentage and channel for funding outside the CAP:
• Sweden   99% IFRC
• Norway   54% IFRC
• Switzerland   50% NGOs
• EC   48% NGOs
• Canada   44% IFRC
• Germany   44% Red Cross, GTZ
• United Kingdom   10% NGOs
• Ireland   7%   NGOs
• United States, Japan, Italy   0
Note: With the exception of the U.S., EC, Germany, U.K., and Japan, all contributions were less than $1 million.

Funding for food aid under the CAP (not including carryover):
• United States   59.43%
• EC   25.3%
• Germany   8.0%
• United Kingdom   4.4%
• Ireland, Canada   Less than 1%

Sierra Leone CAP 2002

Mid-2002: 350,000 food insecure; 50,000 refugees
Overall response rate: 44.3%
- OCHA, 110%;
- OHCHR, 114%;
- FAO, 78.8%;
- UNHCR, 68.3%;
- WFP, 51.7%;
- UNICEF, 49.6%;
- IOM, 8.7%;
- ILO, UNAMSIL, UNFPA, UNV, 0
- No NGO requests in the appeal.

Out of $31.5 million funded inside the CAP:
- 2.6% was for food (but food represented 22% of total donor response; USAID used NGO delivery channels);
- 9.7% was for coordination and support services;
- 7.6% was for health;
- 6.2% was for agriculture;
- 58.8% was "multisector" (UNHCR)
- 4.7% was for education;
- 8.3% protection/human rights/rule of law;
- 2.8% was for water and sanitation.

$52.4 million (62.5% of all donor funding) was channelled outside the CAP framework. Percentage and channel for funding outside the CAP:

• Canada	96%	NGOs and IFRC
• United States	86%	NGOs
• EC	74%	NGOs
• United Kingdom	60%	NGOs and IFRC
• Switzerland	54%	NGOs
• Netherlands	43%	NGOs and IFRC
• Sweden	41%	NGOs and IFRC
• Ireland	36%	NGOs
• Norway	6%	IFRC
• Japan, Italy	0	

Funding for food aid under the CAP:
- Less than $1 million was provided to WFP through the CAP; $18 million in food aid was provided by the United States through CARE, CRS, and World Vision.

Afghanistan CAP 2002

Mid-2002: 860,000 returnees; food caseload 1.6 million
Overall response rate: 66.3%
- UNHCR, 96.6%;
- FAO, 89.7%;
- WFP, 85.2%;
- UNICEF, 75.3%;
- UNFPA, 96.6%
- UNEP, 33.3%;
- WHO, 17.8%;
- ILO, 0
- Many NGOs in the CAP; response rate mixed; many (e.g., CARE, Concern = zero)

Out of $1.18 billion funded inside the CAP:
- 42.2% was for food;
- 4.9% was for coordination and support services;
- 6.4% was for health;
- 5.2% was for agriculture;
- 25.6% was "multisector" (HCR, IOM, NGOs)
- 5.6% was for education;
- 1.0% protection/human rights/rule of law;
- 2.17% was for water and sanitation;
- 1.0% was for security;
- 2.8% for economic recovery and infrastructure.

$424 million (28% of all donor funding) was channelled outside the CAP framework. Percentage and channel for funding outside the CAP:

• Finland	38%	IFRC, ICRC, NGOs
• United States	34%	IFRC, ICRC, NGOs, OFDA, UN, bilateral
• United Kingdom	34%	NGOs, IFRC
• Canada	34%	NGOs, IFRC, ICRC
• EC	32%	NGOs, ICRC
• Germany	30%	NGOs, IFRC, ICRC
• Denmark	28%	NGOs
• Norway	27%	IFRC, UN agencies, NGOs
• Sweden	22%	ICRC, NGOs, IFRC
• Australia	20%	NGOs, ICRC, UN agencies
• Italy	16%	ICRC, NGOs
• Japan	10%	IFRC, ICRC, UN agencies

Funding for food aid under the CAP:

United States	45.0%	Italy	3.1%
EC	7.5%	Australia	1.5%
Japan	9.5%	Carryover	16.5%
United Kingdom	2.8%	Smaller donors	
Netherlands	2.0%		

Observations

- Within the CAPs, WFP is usually significantly better funded than any other UN agency. In the case of Sierra Leone, low funding for food inside the CAP was offset by funding from USAID to WV, CARE, and CRS for food. With the exceptions of Sierra Leone and Afghanistan, food represented more than 70% of funding to the CAP.
- OCHA is usually well funded in relation to other UN agencies.
- UNICEF was very well funded in Afghanistan, Tajikistan, and Angola, less well in Sierra Leone, DRC, and Sudan.
- UNHCR was well funded in Afghanistan, Sudan, Sierra Leone, and DRC, but received only 39% of its request in Angola.
- Most other UN organizations received 15% or less of what they requested. Many received nothing.
- NGOs are recorded as having received nothing of what they requested through the CAP in most countries except Afghanistan.
- Taking CAP and non-CAP contributions together, food received most of funding: 50% in the DRC, 71.65% of the total in Angola and 75.4% in Sudan; 94% in Tajikistan.
- Relative to food—health, education, protection, agriculture, water, and sanitation received little attention in all cases.
- In four countries, roughly one-third of donor spending was outside the CAP—mainly to NGOs, the ICRC, and IFRC. In Angola, the proportion was significantly lower (18%) and in Sierra Leone it was significantly higher (62.5%).
- There does not appear to be any pattern by donor country for funding outside the CAP.
- The United States is by far the most significant funder of food aid under the CAP (45% in Afghanistan, 81.5% in DRC, 59.4% in Tajikistan). In most cases, the EC is the next largest, with percentages ranging from 7.5% to 25%. Japan was a significant contributor of food aid in Afghanistan (9.5%) and Sudan (6.5%). Although there were several food donors in each country, none provided more than 5% and most were under 3%. Canada, once a significant provider of food aid, provided less than 1% in a few cases, and nothing in others.

Errors and Omissions

- USAID says that some of its contributions are not recorded in the Angola statistics (e.g., a contribution of $2 million to Oxfam GB). It is possible that this is a financial year recording problem.
- In OCHA statistics, NGOs are recorded as having received nothing inside the CAP funding framework in most countries, although NGOs are reported as having received large sums *outside* the CAP framework. CARE, for example, requested $1.14 million via the CAP in the Sudan, and was reported as having received none of this. But

donors provided CARE with over $6 million *outside* the CAP (and perhaps more, as ECHO funding for NGOs is not disaggregated). The total CAP request for UN agencies and NGOs was $3.8 million. Against this, $873,000 was recorded as having been met. Outside the CAP, however, NGOs received at least $85 million from donors.

Conclusions

- Whether or not UN agencies are setting priorities in the CAP, donors are clearly funding what they deem to be their priorities. With the exceptions of WFP, UNHCR, UNICEF, and OCHA, most UN agencies receive little or nothing of what is requested through the CAP.
- Food is a higher priority for donors (at least for the United States) than it is for UN agencies. Although food represents about half of what was requested in most CAPs, it usually received about 75% of donor resources (with the exception of Sierra Leone).
- Other sectors (agriculture, water and sanitation, health and education) therefore received less priority attention from donors than is reflected in CAP requests.
- Donors channelled much more of their funding through UN agencies in Angola than in the other countries, and much less in Sierra Leone. This may represent the availability of other options (i.e., more NGOs with a better track record). It could also represent lower donor confidence in Sudan-based UN agencies.
- NGOs simply do not figure in the CAP statistics. While they represent a small part of the appeal, they are recorded in most countries as having received nothing. In fact NGOs received at least as much as was requested on their behalf outside the CAP. In Sudan they received nine times what was requested for them in the CAP. (It is not known whether the NGOs included in the CAP were funded, however, and if they were, if they were funded for the projects identified in the CAP.) NGOs appear not to be taken seriously in the CAP process and do not appear to take it seriously themselves.
- The response to these six CAPs suggests that they do not reflect donor priorities very well. Another way of saying this is that UN priorities are not being met very well, except where food and OCHA coordination are concerned.
- Further, the CAP is not a full reflection of need as perceived by donors, as significant funding is going to delivery agents not included in it.

Notes

Introduction

1. David Rieff, "Humanitarian Intervention: A Forum," *The Nation*, July 14, 2003, 15–16.
2. William G. O'Neill, *A Humanitarian Practitioner's Guide to International Human Rights Law* (Providence, R.I.: Watson Institute, 1999), 62.

Chapter 1

1. Purists might refer to Article 23 of the Fourth Geneva Convention and Articles 70 and 18 of Protocols I and II respectively. These make a case for the unimpeded passage of relief goods in conflict situations, and specify that where people are in need, efforts "shall" be made to assist, but in fact the clauses are hortatory and reinforce the voluntary nature of the overall enterprise.
2. The figures are taken from Development Initiatives' *Global Humanitarian Assistance 2003* and are larger than the $6 billion provided by DAC governments to "humanitarian assistance" activities.
3. Public Papers of the Presidents, Dwight D. Eisenhower, 1960, 1035–1040.
4. Development Initiatives, *Global Humanitarian Assistance 2003*, 3.
5. There is considerable debate, however, as to whether domestic resettlement costs should be counted as part of a given government's international humanitarian assistance totals. In the wake of the terrorism attacks on September 11, 2001, U.S. government admissions and resettlement of refugees have fallen off significantly.
6. Organization for Economic Co-operation and Development/Development Assistance Committee Web site: www.oecd.org.
7. Amadou Toumani and Blaise Compaoré, "Subsidizing the rich: Africa needs a level playing field for trade." *New York Times*, July 12, 2003.
8. William G. O'Neill, *A Humanitarian Practitioner's Guide to International Human Rights Law* (Providence, RI: Watson Institute, 1999), 6.
9. Marc Lindenberg and Coralie Bryant, *Going Global: Transforming Relief and Development NGOs* (Bloomfield, Conn.: Kumarian, 2001), 13.

10. For an examination of their influence, see Don Hubert, *The Landmine Ban: A Case Study in Humanitarian Advocacy* (Providence, RI: Watson Institute, 2000).

11. Margaret E. Keck and Kathryn Sikkink, *Activists Beyond Borders* (Ithaca and London: Cornell University Press, 1998), 3.

12. Keck and Sikkink, *Activists Beyond Borders*, 52–53.

13. Lindenberg and Bryant, *Going Global*, 36.

14. For a more detailed description, see Larry Minear and Peter Walker, "The Strategy for the Red Cross & Red Crescent Movement: A Review of the Evolving Partnership," (Medford, Mass.: Feinstein International Famine Center, 2003).

15. Elizabeth G. Ferris, "The Role of Non-Governmental Organizations in the International Refugee Regime," in Niklaus Steiner, Mark Gibney, and Gil Loescher, eds., *Problems of Protection: The UNHCR, Refugees, and Human Rights* (London and New York: Routledge, 2003), 117.

16. For an elaboration of this conclusion, see Larry Minear and Philippe Guillot, *Soldiers to the Rescue: Humanitarian Lessons from Rwanda* (Paris: OECD, 1996).

17. Dan Baum, "Nation Builders for Hire," *New York Times Magazine*, June 22, 2003, 34.

18. Frederick Schieck, quoted in Mark Matthews, "U.S. defends private sector's Iraq contracts," in *Baltimore Sun*, August 10, 2003.

19. Jonathan Foreman, "The Real Scandal of Iraqi Relief," *New York Post*, May 11, 2003.

20. Humanitarian Policy Group, "According to Need? Needs assessment and decision-making in the humanitarian sector" (London: Overseas Development Institute, 2003).

21. Development Initiatives, *Global Humanitarian Assistance 2003*, 37.

22. Sarah Collinson, "Introduction," in Collinson, 17. Columbite-tantalite—coltan—is a metallic ore found in the eastern Congo. When refined, it becomes metallic tantalum, a heat-resistant powder that can hold a high electrical charge, making it a vital element in creating capacitors used in cell phones and other electronics.

23. Max P. Glaser, "Negotiated humanitarian access in the voids of sovereignty," initial draft, unpublished paper, 17.

24. Stephen Jackson with Siobhan Calthrop, *Making Sense of Turbulent Contexts: Analysis Tools for Humanitarian Actors* (World Vision International, July 2002 [updated January 2003]).

Chapter 2

1. David Keen, "Blair's Good Guys in Sierra Leone," *The Guardian*, November 7, 2001.

2. UNDP, "Development Cooperation: Sierra Leone," 1994 Report, Freetown, August 1995.

3. Mukesh Kapila, "Sierra Leone Humanitarian Aid Assessment Mission, 24–29 April 1995," ODA, London.

4. John Hirsch, *Sierra Leone: Diamonds and the Struggle for Democracy* (Boulder, Colo.: Lynne Rienner, 2001), 40.

5. Michael Young, "Practising principles of humanitarian assistance in conflict: the experience of ActionAid-Sierra Leone," ODI HPN Report, http://www.odihpn.org/report.asp?ReportID=2344.

6. Marc Sommers, *The Dynamics of Coordination*, Occasional Paper #40 (Providence, R.I.: Watson Institute, 2001), 32. Sommers' study offers a detailed review of developments on the humanitarian front.

7. Toby Porter, "The Interaction Between Political and Humanitarian Action in Sierra Leone, 1995 to 2002," Centre for Humanitarian Dialogue, Geneva, March 2003.

8. Unnamed official, cited in Sommers, *The Dynamics of Coordination*, 33.

9. Toby Porter, "The Interaction Between Political and Humanitarian Action in Sierra Leone," 6.

10. Alex de Waal, "Humanitarianism Unbound?" African Rights, London, November 1994.

11. *Minutes of Evidence*, Select Committee on International Development, U.K. Parliament, 8 December 1998, para. 621.

12. Letter from ActionAid to the Chairman of the Select Committee on International Development, U.K. Parliament, *Minutes of Evidence*, 18 December 1998.

13. David Keen, "Blair's Good Guys in Sierra Leone," *The Guardian*, November 7, 2001.

14. Lizza Ryan, "Where Angels Fear to Tread," *The New Republic*, July 24, 2000.

15. Ryan, "Where Angels Fear to Tread."

16. Ryan, "Where Angels Fear to Tread."

17. Steve Coll, "The Other War," *Washington Post Magazine*, January 9, 2000.

18. Confidential interview, quoted in Toby Porter, "The Interaction Between Political and Humanitarian Action in Sierra Leone," 33.

19. Médecins sans Frontières, "Populations affected by War in the Mano River Region of West Africa: Issues of Protection," Freetown, May 2002.

20. See for example Sommers, *The Dynamics of Coordination*, and Porter, "The Interaction Between Political and Humanitarian Action in Sierra Leone."

21. "Note . . . by UNHCR and Save the Children-UK on Sexual Violence and Exploitation: The Experience of Refugee Children in Guinea, Liberia and Sierra Leone," Freetown, February 2002.

22. *The Guardian*, February 28, 2002.

23. Reuters Foundation AlertNet, http://www.alertnet.org/thefacts/relief resources/417778.

24. Ian Christopolos, "Evaluation Report: The Humanitarian Accountability Project First Trial in Sierra Leone," Humanitarian Accountability Project Geneva (July 16, 2002): 6.

25. WFP, "Protracted Relief and Recovery Operation—West Africa Coastal 10064.1" (Draft), September 18, 2002.

26. UN Office of Internal Oversight Services, "Investigation into Sexual Exploitation of Refugees by Aid Workers in West Africa," New York, October 11, 2002.

27. Statistics are drawn from UNHCR's *Global Report 2000*, and from data provided by UNHCR in Geneva.

28. In fact, of the funds actually spent during this period, $1 million had been drawn from UNHCR's Operational Reserve against the hope that it could be reimbursed, if and when donor funds were received. Figures are accurate to August 27, 2002.

Chapter 3

1. Timothy Mo, *The Redundancy of Courage* (London: Vintage, 1992), 110.

2. Xanana Gusmão, *To Resist is to Win: The Autobiography of Xanana Gusmão with Selected Letters and Speeches*, Sarah Niner (ed.) (Victoria, Australia: Aurora Books, 2000), 133.

3. "White House Memorandum of Conversation" at Camp David, July 5, 1975, declassified June 20, 2001, Gerald Ford Library, University of Texas, www.ford.utexas.edu/library/document/memcons/750705a.htm.

4. U.S. Department of State, Telegram from U.S. Embassy Washington to "Secstate," December 6, 1975, declassified photocopy from Gerald R. Ford Library.

5. Secret cable from Australian Ambassador Woolcott to Canberra, leaked in 1976; Rodney Tiffen, *Diplomatic Deceits: Government, Media and East Timor* (Sydney: UNSW Press, 2001), 12.

6. Secret cable from Australian Ambassador Woolcott to Canberra, Rodney Tiffen, *Diplomatic Deceits*, 75.

7. Matthew Jardine, *East Timor: Genocide in Paradise* (Chicago: Odonian Press, 1999), 50.

8. Sharon Scharfe, *Complicity: Human Rights and Canadian Foreign Policy* (Montreal: Black Rose Books, 1996), 29.

9. Article in *The Guardian* (London), July 5, 1994, reproduced in Jardine.

10. Sharon Scharfe, *Complicity: Human Rights and Canadian Foreign Policy*, 114.

11. Eilís Ward and Peter Carey, "East Timor Issue in the Context of EU-Indonesian Relations, 1975–1998," *Indonesia and the Malay World* 9 (March 2001): 51–74.

12. Jamsheed Marker, *East Timor: A Memoir of the Negotiations for Independence* (Jefferson, N.C.: Macfarland & Company, 2003), 129.

13. Secret cable from Australian Ambassador Woolacott to Canberra, Rodney Tiffen, *Diplomatic Deceits*, 96.

14. In fact, Australian forces had been preparing for action in East Timor for several weeks.

15. World Bank, *East Timor: Policy Challenges for a New Nation* (May 2002): 5.

16. Australian Strategic Policy Institute, *New Neighbour, New Challenge, Australia and the Security of East Timor*, Canberra, 2002.

17. "Brace for Fight Over Oil Australia Told," *Sydney Morning Herald*, May 21, 2002.

18. Asia Pacific Defence Forum, http://forum.apan-info.net/Summer_02/44_48/48.html.

19. King's College London, *A Review of Peace Operations: A Case for Change, East Timor Study*, 10 March 2003, para vii.

20. King's College London, *A Review of Peace Operations*, para 26.

Chapter 4

1. James Morris, *Pax Britannica: The Climax of an Empire* (New York: Penguin, 1979), 277.

2. This interaction is the subject of a number of recent studies including Michael Bhatia and Jonathan Goodhand, with Haneef Atmar, Adam Pain, and Mohammed Suleman, "Profits and poverty: Aid livelihoods and conflict in Afghanistan," HPG Report 13 in *Power, livelihoods and conflict: Case studies in political economy analysis for humanitarian action* (London: HPG, 2003); Fiona Terry, *Condemned to Repeat? The Paradox of Humanitarian Action* (Ithaca, N.Y. and London: Cornell University Press, 2002), chapter 2; Nicholas Stockton,

Strategic Coordination in Afghanistan, Afghanistan Research and Evaluation Unit, Issues Paper Series, August 2002; Johnson and Leslie, "Afghans have their Memories," *Third World Quarterly* 23 (2002): 861–874; Mark Duffield, Patricia Gossmann, and Nicholas Leader, Strategic Framework Review (Kabul: AREU, 2001); ALNAP, Global Study: The Case of Afghanistan (London: ALNAP, 2003) [prepared by Francois Grünewald and colleagues at URD]; Paula R. Newberg, "Politics at the Heart: The Architecture of Humanitarian Assistance to Afghanistan" (Washington, D.C.: Carnegie Endowment, 2001); Greenberg Research, Inc., *Country Report: Afghanistan* (Geneva: ICRC, 1999) [ICRC worldwide consultation on the rules of war]; Antonio Donini, Norah Niland, and Karin Wermester, eds., *Nation-Building Unraveled? Aid, Peace and Justice in Afghanistan* (Bloomfield, Conn.: Kumarian, 2003).

3. ICRC, "Country Report: Afghanistan," in the *People in War* Series: ICRC worldwide consultation on the rules of war (Geneva: ICRC, 1999), 1.

4. Nicholas Leader and Mohammed Haneef Atmar, "Political Projects: Reform, Aid, and the State in Afghanistan," in Donini, Niland, and Wermester, 185.

5. "Humanitarianism and Communism," *The Washington Star*, May 10, 1985, quoted in Larry Minear, *Helping People in an Age of Conflict: Toward a New Professionalism in U.S. Voluntary Humanitarian Assistance* (New York and Washington: InterAction, 1988), 36.

6. Fiona Terry, *Condemned to Repeat?*, 71.

7. Kenneth Katzman, "Afghanistan: Current Issues and U.S. Policy Concerns," (Washington, D.C.: Congressional Research Service, May 20, 2002), 2.

8. Helga Baitenmann, "NGOs and the Afghan War: The politicization of humanitarian aid," *Third World Quarterly* 12: 1, 1990.

9. T. Barry, et al., "The New Right Humanitarians," (Albuquerque, N.M.: The Inter-Hemispheric Education Resources Center, 1986), quoted in Baitenmann.

10. For a more extended discussion, see Norah Niland, "Justice Postponed: The Marginalization of Human Rights in Afghanistan," in Donini, Niland, and Wermester, 61–82.

11. For an elaboration of this conclusion, see Minear, *Helping People in an Age of Conflict*.

12. The changes from Cold War to post–Cold War aid activities are reviewed by Donini, *The Policies of Mercy: UN Coordination in Afghanistan, Mozambique, and Rwanda*, Occasional Paper 22 (Providence, R.I.: Watson Institute, 1996).

13. Minear, "Report to the Headquarters Colloquium on the InterAgency Strategic Framework Mission to Afghanistan," October 1997, 2. [available at hwproject.tufts.edu under "Publications."]

14. For an analysis of the responses of different relief organizations to the Taliban's human rights violations, see Julie A. Mertus, *War's Offensive on Women: The Humanitarian Challenge in Bosnia, Kosovo, and Afghanistan* (Bloomfield, Conn.: Kumarian, 2000), 60–69.

15. International aid levels grew from $250 million per year under the Taliban to $2 billion committed at the Tokyo conference in early 2002.

16. MSF, "Humanitarianism Threatened: The Policy and Praxis of Aid in Afghanistan," Germany Colloquium (November 27, 2001), 1.

17. Fiona Terry, *Condemned to Repeat?*, 81.

18. Norah Niland, "Justice Postponed," in Donini, Niland, and Wermester, 79.

19. Ian Smillie and Larry Minear, "The Quality of Money: Donor Behavior in Humanitarian Financing," (Medford, Mass.: Tufts University, 2003), 9. www.reliefweb.int/cap/hfs.html.

20. Antonio Donini, "Principles, Politics, and Pragmatism in the International Response to the Afghan Crisis," in Donini, Niland, and Wermester, 118.

21. Kate Clark, "The Struggle for Hearts and Minds: The Military, Aid, and the Media," in Donini, Niland, and Wermester, 83.

22. Voluntary Organizations in Cooperation in Emergencies [VOICE], "Afghanistan: The Road to Recovery and the Role of NGOs." [Seminar organized by Euronaid and VOICE, Brussels, February 14, 2002], 2.

23. Graham T. Allison, "Bombing Afghanistan with Food: War's Second Front," *Boston Globe*, October 14, 2001.

24. Colin Powell, Conference at U.S. Department of State, October 26, 2001.

25. UN Security Council Resolution 1401, March 26, 2002.

26. ACBAR Press Release, "ACBAR voices deep alarm at second fatal attack on NGO community in eleven days," Kabul, February 26, 2004.

27. David Rohde and Ismail Khan, "Pakistan Adopting a Tough Old Tactic to Flush out Qaeda," *New York Times*, January 31, 2004.

28. Antonio Donini, "Principles, Politics and Pragmatism," in Donini, Niland, and Wermester, 121.

29. "Like the Saudis, American [intelligence] officers involved in the secret war in Afghanistan regarded Bin Laden as an asset at the time, because of his success as a fundraiser." Quotation from Jane Corbin, *The Base: Al-Qaeda and the Changing Face of Global Terror* (London, Sydney, New York, Tokyo, Singapore, and Toronto: Pocket Books, 2003), 24.

30. NGO Policy Dialogue X, "Humanitarian Action and the Afghanistan Crisis," (November 15, 2001), 1.

31. Nicholas Stockton, *Strategic Coordination in Afghanistan*, 7–8.

32. Development Co-operation Directorate, Development Assistance Committee, "Aid Responses to Afghanistan: Lessons from Previous Evaluations," DCD/DIR (2001) 31, DAC Senior Level Meeting (December 12–13, 2001), 1.

33. Development Co-operation Directorate, Development Assistance Committee, "Aid Responses to Afghanistan," 7.

34. Minear, "Report to the Headquarters Colloquium," 6, 9.

35. UN Secretary-General Kofi Annan, "Afghanistan needs $1.3 billion to cover immediate needs, $10 billion over the next five years, Secretary-General tells [Tokyo pledging] conference," SG/SM 8108, January 21, 2002.

36. NGO Policy Dialogue XI, "Afghanistan Revisited," 8.

37. NGO Policy Dialogue XI, "Afghanistan Revisited," 2.

38. Ed Schenkenberg, "NGO Coordination and Some Other Relevant Issues in the Context of Afghanistan from an NGO Perspective," (April 9, 2002), www.interaction.org. The report quotes an NGO official in Afghanistan as saying "When it comes to learning the lessons from experiences in previous humanitarian crises, . . . these lessons and the policy implications they bring with them are certainly not discussed by the NGOs together."

39. Stockton, *Strategic Coordination in Afghanistan*, 31.

40. Stockton, *Strategic Coordination in Afghanistan*, 35.

41. Stockton, *Strategic Coordination in Afghanistan*, 40.

42. Duffield, Gossmann, and Leader, Strategic Framework Review, 28.

43. VOICE, 14.

44. Security Council Resolution 1401, March 28, 2002, para. 4.

45. Duffield, Gossmann, and Leader, Strategic Framework Review, 4.

46. Duffield, Gossmann, and Leader, Strategic Framework Review, 24.

47. Carlotta Gall, "Threats and Responses: Help for Kabul. O'Neill, in Afghanistan, promises to push $2.3 billion aid bill," *New York Times* (November 19, 2002).

48. Johnson and Leslie, 861, 872.

Chapter 5

1. Michael Ignatieff, *Empire Lite: Nation Building in Bosnia, Kosovo and Afghanistan* (London, Penguin: 2003), 25.

2. In 2004, violence by government-sponsored militias against Muslims in Western Sudan was being described as the worst humanitarian crises at the time anywhere in the world.

3. "UN appeals for $465 million for emergency relief and recovery aid for Sudan in 2004," ReliefWeb, November 19, 2003 [dateline Brussels/Khartoum/Nairobi], 1.

4. The incident is recounted in Larry Minear, et al., *Humanitarianism under Siege: A Critical Review of Operation Lifeline Sudan* (Trenton, NJ: Red Sea Press, 1990), 131.

5. Presaging the narrow focus on relief, the UN appeal issued in October 1988 at the time of massive famine- and war-related deaths made no mention of the SPLA or human rights abuses by the government. See African Rights, *Food and Power in Sudan: A Critique of Humanitarianism* (London: African Rights, 1997), 114.

6. For a detailed listing of such events, see Masood Hyder, "Nurturing Humanitarian Space in Sudan: A Practitioner's Viewpoint (privately printed, July 2002).

7. African Rights, *Food and Power in Sudan*, 364.

8. Barbara Hendrie, ed., with Ataul Karim, Mark Duffield, Susanne Jaspars, Aldo Benini, Joanna Macrae, Mark Bradbury, Douglas Johnson, and George Larbi, *Operation Lifeline Sudan: A Review* (July 1996).

9. African Rights, *Food and Power in Sudan*, 125.

10. African Rights, *Food and Power in Sudan*, 354.

11. Adrian Wood, Raymond Apthorpe, and John Borton, *Evaluating International Action: Reflections from Practitioners*, 211 (London and New York: Zed Books and ALNAP, 2001) [emphasis added].

12. African Rights, *Food and Power in Sudan*, 360.

13. Minear, *Humanitarianism under Siege*, 33.

14. This section is based in part on studies by the Humanitarianism & War Project: Ian Smillie, *Relief and Development: The Struggle for Synergy* (Thomas J. Watson Jr. Institute for International Studies, Brown University, 1998); and Kathy Mangones, "Alternative Food Aid Strategies and Local Capacity Building in Haiti," in Ian Smillie, (ed.), *Patronage or Partnership: Local Capacity Building in Humanitarian Crises*, (Bloomfield, Conn.: Kumarian Press, 2001).

15. Bob Shacochis, *The Immaculate Invasion* (New York: Penguin, 1999), 63.

16. Serge Picard, *Aide Alimentaire; le Cas d'Haiti* (Port-au-Prince, Forums Libre du Jeudi 21 sur l'Aide et Securité Alimentaires en Haiti, 1996), cited in Mangones, "Alternative Food Aid Strategies."

17. Mangones, "Alternative Food Aid Strategies," 69.

18. Shacochis, *The Immaculate Invasion*, 255.

19. L.M.G. Carlier, "Review of the Impact and Effectiveness of Donor-Financed Emergency Poverty Alleviation Projects in Haiti," in *Haiti: The Challenges of Poverty Reduction*, Vol. II (Washington, D.C: World Bank, March 1998).

20. Carlier, "Review of the Impact," 9.

21. Ian Smillie, *The Land of Lost Content* (Toronto: Deneau, 1985), 81–87.

22. Mary Anderson and Peter Woodrow, *Rising From the Ashes: Development Strategies in Times of Disaster* (Boulder, Colo.: Westview, 1989).

23. Robert Maguire, Edwige Balutansky, Jacques Fomerand, Larry Minear, W.G. O'Neill, Thomas Weiss, Sarah Zaidi, *Haiti Held Hostage: International*

Responses to the Quest for Nationhood 1986 to 1996, Occasional Paper #23 (Thomas J. Watson Institute for International Studies and the United Nations University: Brown University, 1996).

24. USAID information sheet on OTI, undated.

25. Sally Patterson, *A Report on a Survey of the Former FAd'H in Haiti* (Washington, D.C.: Winner, Wagner and Francis, September 1996).

26. Jonathan Dworkin, Jonathan Moore, Adam Siegel, *Haiti Demobilization and Reintegration Program: An Evaluation Prepared for USAID* (Alexandria, Va.: CNA Corporation, March 1997).

27. Mark Duffield, *Social Reconstruction in Croatia and Bosnia: An Exploratory Report for SIDA* (Stockholm: Swedish International Development and Co-operation Agency (SIDA), 1996).

28. Ian Smillie and Goran Todorović, "Reconstructing Bosnia," in Ian Smille, ed. *Patronage or Partnership* (Bloomfield, Conn.: Kumarian Press, 2001), 33.

29. Evaluation of a Bosnian NGO by Oxfam GB; quoted in Smillie and Todorović.

30. Smillie and Todorović, "Reconstructing Bosnia," 62.

31. Smillie and Todorović, "Reconstructing Bosnia," 25.

32. Ignatieff, *Empire Lite*, 42.

33. Thomas R. DeGregori, "The Uncivil Society" (Washington, D.C.: Cato Institute, October 7, 2002), www.cato.org.

34. Private communication.

35. World Food Programme, "Summary Report of the Real-Time Evaluation of WFP's Response to the Southern Africa Crisis 2002–2003" (September 10, 2003), 7.

36. WFP, "Summary Report," 6.

37. "A Stitch in Time?" Independent Evaluation of the DEC Southern Africa Crisis Appeal, Valid International, Oxford, January 2004.

Chapter 6

1. William Sloane Coffin, *Credo* (Louisville and London: Westminster, John Knox Press, 2004), 80.

2. Politics at the level of the regions experiencing crises, not to say of the crisis countries themselves, also come into play, although they are not treated here in detail. For a detailed review of the impacts of regional and local political factors on the contours of humanitarian action, see S. Neil Macfarlane, *Politics and Humanitarian Action* (Providence, R.I.: Watson Institute, 2000).

3. Macfarlane, *Politics*, 79.

4. Macfarlane, *Politics*, 62.

5. See Larry Minear, *The Humanitarian Enterprise* (Bloomfield, Conn.: Kumarian Press, 2002), 102–3.

6. The comment is from then-AID Administrator Peter McPherson, quoting President Ronald Reagan. See Larry Minear, *Helping People in an Age of Conflict: Toward a New Professionalism in U.S. Voluntary Humanitarian Assistance* (New York and Washington, D.C.: InterAction, 1998), 30.

7. Macfarlane, *Politics*, 71.

8. Development Initiatives, *Global Humanitarian Assistance Flows 2003*, 32. For the trends in donor government thinking about recalibrating country aid allocations in the service of antiterrorism concerns, see Development Assistance Committee, "A Development Co-operation Lens on Terrorism Prevention: Key Entry Points for Action" (Paris: OECD, 2003).

9. Oxfam, *Beyond the headlines: An agenda for action to protect civilians in neglected conflicts* (Oxford, UK: Oxfam International, 2003), 2.

10. Jerome Amir Singh, "Is donor aid allocation to Iraq fair?" *Lancet* 362 (November 15, 2003).

11. Quoted in Minear, *The Humanitarian Enterprise*, 81.

12. In early 2004, UN Under-Secretary-General for Humanitarian Affairs Jan Egeland visited Chechnya and neighboring republics in what may signal the beginning of newly energized humanitarian diplomacy.

13. Kevin Maguire, "How British charity was silenced on Iraq," *The Guardian*, November 28, 2003; Save the Children (U.S.) *Annual Report 2002*, Westport, Conn.

14. Associated Press, "UN Report Wars of Al-Qaeda WMD Risk," November 17 [dateline UN, New York].

15. Gorm Rye Olsen, Nils Carstenssen, and Kristian Heyen, "Humanitarian Crises: What Determines the Level of Emergency Assistance: Media Coverage, Donor Interests, and the Aid Business," *Disasters* 27, 2: 118.

16. *Global Humanitarian Assistance 2003*, 4–5.

17. Olsen, et al., 109.

18. Ian Smillie and Larry Minear, "The Quality of Money: Donor Behavior in Humanitarian Financing," (Medford, Mass.: Humanitarianism and War Project, April 2003), 5. www.reliefweb.int/cap/hfs.html.

19. Documents prepared for and resulting from an International Meeting on Good Humanitarian Donorship, Stockholm, June 16–17, 2003.

20. Singh, "Is donor aid allocation to Iraq fair?"

21. David Rieff, "Did Truly Independent Relief Agencies Die in Kosovo?" *Humanitarian Affairs Review*, Autumn 1999.

22. Oxfam, "The UN's 50th Anniversary: An Opportunity to Reduce Conflicts," Oxford, January 1995.

23. Quoted in Minear, *The Humanitarian Enterprise*, 102.

24. Ted van Baarda, letter to Larry Minear, June 22, 2001.

25. Larry Thompson, "Iraq: Lessons from going it alone," *Refugees International*, November 17, 2003, 1. Also on www.reliefweb.int.

26. "UN Refugee Agency suspends activities in Afghan province after murder of staffer, November 17 (dateline UN, New York).

27. Press release, ANSO security officer comments on escalating frequency of attacks, November 2003.

28. ALNAP Global Study, *Consultation with and participation by beneficiaries and affected populations in the process of planning, managing, monitoring and evaluating humanitarian action: Afghanistan* (London: ALNAP/URD, 2003), 47.

29. Larry Minear, Ted van Baarda, and Marc Sommers, *NATO and Humanitarian Action in the Kosovo Crisis*, Occasional Paper #36 (Providence, R.I.: Watson Institute, 2000), 50.

30. Hugo Slim, "International Humanitarianism's Engagement with Civil War in the 1990s: A Glance at Evolving Practice and Theory," A Briefing Paper for ActionAid (December 1997), Oxford, U.K.

31. "U.S. Sees Evidence of Overcharging in Iraq Contract," *New York Times*, December 12, 2003.

32. See Minear, van Baarda, and Sommers, *NATO and Humanitarian Action in the Kosovo Crisis*. The figures were not forthcoming even though the researcher requesting them had security clearance.

33. The 2004 prisoner abuse scandal in Iraq underscores this question.

34. UN Office for the Coordination of Humanitarian Affairs, "The Use of Military and Civil Defense Assets to Support United Nations Humanitarian Activities in Complex Emergencies," March 2003.

35. UN Office for the Coordination of Humanitarian Affairs, "General Guidance for Interaction between UN Personnel and Military Actors in the Context of Iraq," March 21, 2003.

36. Swedish Armed Forces, *Joint Military Doctrine: Peace Support Operations,* Stockholm, 1997, 5–3.

37. Conference at U.S. State Department, October 26, 2001.

38. "Example Field Guidelines" in "CARE International's Relationship with the Military," Draft Discussion Paper, Barney Mayhew, February 5, 2000.

39. Larry Minear and Philippe Guillot, *Soldiers to the Rescue: Humanitarian Lesson from Rwanda* (Paris: OECD, 1996), 142.

40. British Agencies Afghanistan Group, "Monthly Review October 2003," November 8, 2003.

41. Mark Duffield, *Global Governance and the New Wars* (London: Zed Books, 2001), 11.

42. Antonio Donini has introduced the concept of "copyright" and "non-copyright" humanitarianism and suggests that mandate creep on the part of donors and aid agencies may be as responsible for problems as political intrusions.

43. "Attack suspected in copter collision," *International Herald Tribune,* November 17, 2003 [dateline Mosul, Iraq], 1.

Chapter 7

1. Robert W. Cox, "Critical Political Economy," in Hettne, Bjorn (ed.) *International Political Economy: Understanding Global Disorder* (London, Zed Books: 1995), 41.

2. Some donors were able to provide funding to East Timor before 1999, usually within the context of larger programs for Indonesia as a whole.

3. Chalmers Johnson, "The War Business: Squeezing profit from the wreckage in Iraq," *Harper's Magazine,* November 2003, 54.

4. Robert Schlesinger, "In Iraq, a door shuts on France, Germany, and Russia," *Boston Globe,* December 10, 2003, A22.

5. Development Initiatives, 2003, *Global Humanitarian Assistance 2003,* 20–21.

6. BBC World Service, November 11, 2001.

7. Naomi Klein, "Bush to NGOs: Watch your mouths," *Globe and Mail,* June 20, 2003.

8. Jim Lobe, "U.S. Conservatives Take Aim at NGOs," June 12, 2003, OneWorld.net.

9. "Remarks by Andrew S. Natsios, Administrator, USAID," InterAction Forum, May 21, 2003.

10. Jim Lobe, U.S. Conservatives Take Aim at NGOs."

11. For further detail about conflict diamonds, see Ian Smillie, "Trouble at the Hard Rock Café: Diamonds and corporate social responsibility" (with Ralph Hazleton) in Rupesh Shah, David Murphy, and Malcolm McIntosh (eds.) *Something to Believe In* (Sheffield, U.K.: Greenleaf Publishing, 2003). On the dynamics of the landmine ban, see Don Hubert, *The Landmine Ban: A Case Study in Humanitarian Advocacy,* Occasional Paper 42 (Providence, R.I.: Watson Institute, 2000).

12. S. Neil Macfarlane, *Politics and Humanitarian Action,* Occasional Paper 41 (Providence, R.I.: Watson Institute, 2000), 5.

13. http://www.time.com/time/international/1995/951023/cover4.html.

14. "Tonya Harding Got More Coverage," *Ottawa Citizen,* March 14, 2004.

15. Michael Maren, *The Road to Hell: The Ravaging Effects of Foreign Aid and International Charity* (New York: The Free Press, 1997), 205–6.

16. Comparisons of media coverage are taken from Gorm Rye Olsen, Nils Carstensen, and Kristian Høyen, "Humanitarian Crises: What Determines the Level of Emergency Assistance? Media Coverage, Donor Interests, and the Aid Business," *Disasters* 27, 2.

17. Rodney Tiffen, *Diplomatic Deceits: Government, Media and East Timor* (Sydney: UNSW Press, 2001).

18. Ibos were subject to terrible massacres in Northern Nigeria before the declaration of Biafran independence in 1967. But they were not the only ethnic group in Biafra. And as Biafran territory was taken over by Nigerian troops, there were no massacres. Likewise, when Biafra finally collapsed, there were no massacres. What looked like a tribal war at its outset was actually a war of secession that failed; it was not a genocidal war. For more on this subject, see, for example, John J. Stremlau, The *International Politics of the Nigerian Civil War 1967–77* (Princeton, N.J.: Princeton University Press, 1977).

Chapter 8

1. Mukesh Kapila, "Time for a humanitarian compact," *International Herald Tribune*, January 8, 2003.

2. We have not included informal transfers such as *zakat* and *wakf* in this generalization and have limited the discussion to "Western" nations, not to ignore the contributions of countries such as Saudi Arabia (derived from oil revenues rather than taxpayers) but to focus the discussion on the major donor and delivery mechanisms.

3. Development Initiatives, *Global Humanitarian Assistance 2003*, 46.

4. During 2003, ECHO signed new cooperation agreements with UN agencies, a trend toward greater recognition of their larger mandate and role.

5. In recent years, UNHCR has followed UNICEF's lead in establishing national citizens committees to cultivate individual funding sources and in tapping celebrities to serve as goodwill ambassadors. UNV does the same.

6. The term "cherry-picking" refers to donors' practice of funding the most attractive projects (for example, in the area of microcredit), leaving equally essential priorities (e.g., infrastructure) underresourced.

7. This discussion builds on an earlier OCHA study on the consolidated appeal process: Toby Porter, "An External Review of the CAP," (OCHA, April 2002).

8. The CAP-equivalent in Afghanistan in 2002 was called the Immediate and Transitional Assistance Program for the Afghan People (ITAP).

9. Cited in Abby Stoddard, "Humanitarian NGOs: Challenges and Trends," *Humanitarian Action and the Global War on Terror*, Joanna Macrae and Adele Harmer (eds.), HPG Report 14 (London: Overseas Development Institute, 2003), 28.

10. Cited in Abby Stoddard, "Humanitarian NGOs: Challenges and Trends," 28.

11. Alex de Waal, *Humanitarianism Unbound*, Discussion Paper No. 5 (November 1994), 17.

12. Alex de Waal, *Famine Crimes: Politics & the Disaster Relief Industry in Africa*, African Rights & the International Africa Institute in association with James Currey (London, Oxford & Bloomington, Ind.: Indiana University Press, 1997), 138–9.

13. Antonio Donini, Larry Minear, and Peter Walker, "The Future of Humanitarian Action: Implications of Iraq and Other Recent Crises," Alan Shawn Feinstein International Famine Center, Tufts University, Medford Mass., January 2004.

14. Development Initiatives, *Global Humanitarian Assistance 2003*, 56.

15. Larry Minear, Ted van Baarda, and Marc Sommers, *NATO and Humanitarian Action: The Kosovo Crisis*, Occasional Paper #36 (Providence, R.I.: Watson Institute, 2000), 37.

16. Tom Kines to Ian Smillie, personal conversation.

17. World Food Programme, "Comparison Study of WFP and NGOs," Executive Board Document, Rome, February 2003.

18. Alexander Cooley and James Ron, "The NGO Scramble: Organizational Insecurity and the Political Economy of Transnational Action," *International Security* 27, 1 (Summer, 2002): 16.

19. The WFP Comparison Study of WFP and NGOs found that while WFP has economies of scale not enjoyed by NGOs, it also has a global mandate, which adds significantly to its costs. No real cost comparison was therefore possible.

20. Fiona Terry puts it another way: that MSF was one of the few NGOs willing to call a "genocidaire" a "genocidaire." The problem of feeding children and adults in a camp managed by genocidaires, however, is not solved by name-calling.

21. For a detailed discussion of relationships between international humanitarian actors and local civil society in emergency situations, see Ian Smillie (ed.) *Patronage or Partnership: Local Capacity Building in Humanitarian Crises* (Bloomfield, Conn.: Kumarian Press, 2001).

22. For a discussion of capacity building in Afghanistan, see Larry Minear, *The Humanitarian Enterprise*, 195–8.

23. Thomas Turay, "Sierra Leone: Peacebuilding in Purgatory," in *Patronage or Partnership: Local Capacity Building in Humanitarian Crises*, Ian Smillie (ed.), 166.

24. *Toronto Telegram*, January 21, 1970.

Chapter 9

1. Michael Maran, *The Road to Hell: The Ravaging Effects of Foreign Aid and International Charity* (New York: Free Press, 1997), 97.

2. Mukesh Kapila, "Putting the Human Back in Humanitarian," International Meeting on Good Humanitarian Donorship, Stockholm, June 2003.

3. The issue of how needs are conceived as well as how they are assessed is explored in *According to need? Needs assessment and decision making in the humanitarian sector*, James Darcy and Charles Antoine Hofmann, HPG Report 15 (London: Overseas Development Institute, September 2003).

4. "Coping strategies" and the interaction between people in need and outsiders have been widely explored in recent years. See, for example, Mary B. Anderson and Peter J. Woodrow, *Rising from the Ashes: Development Strategies in Times of Disaster* (Boulder, Colo.: Lynne Rienner, 1989).

5. HPG Report 15, 69.

6. Mukesh Kapila, "Time for a Humanitarian Compact," *International Herald Tribune*, January 8, 2003.

7. For a discussion of the methodological and practical issues involved, see Stephen C. Lubkemann, Larry Minear, and Thomas G. Weiss, *Humanitarian*

Action: Social Science Connections, Occasional Paper 37 (Providence, R.I.: Watson Institute, 2000).

8. E. Hereward Phillips, *Fund Raising Techniques and Case Histories* (London: Business Books, 1969); quoted in Jørgen Lissner, *The Politics of Altruism* (Geneva: Lutheran World Federation, 1977), 131.

9. Quoted in Jonathan Benthall, *Disasters, Relief and the Media* (London: I.B. Taurus, 1993), 133.

10. Genevieve Butler, "NGOs urge end to two-tier aid financing," AlertNet, Brussels, November 20, 2003.

11. The fact that the possibility had been discussed with NGOs in early December and that AusAID had asked for a "capacity statement" rather than a full-fledged proposal did not make the timeframe more manageable. The capacity statement would be instrumental in making funding decisions for an emergency that had been going on for months. While AusAID views this as a non-issue, Australian NGOs see it very differently, illustrating more than the timing issue under discussion.

12. In fact OCHA financial tracking showed that at the time of the reconstruction pledging conference in New York, less than $3 million had been raised for emergency assistance. Some of the requested food aid, however, had been included in a regional appeal.

13. For a more extended discussion, see Ian Smillie, *Relief and Development: The Struggle for Synergy*, Occasional Paper 22 (Providence, R.I.: Watson Institute, 2000).

14. Mark Duffield, *Global Governance and the New Wars* (London: Zed Books, 2001), 75.

15. Joanna Macrae, et al., *Uncertain Power: The Changing Role of Official Donors in Humanitarian Action*, HPG Report 12 (London: ODI, December 2002), 9.

16. Macrae, et al., 9.

17. Macrae, et al., 10.

18. *The Annual Review of 2002* by the Active Learning Network for Accountability and Performance in Humanitarian Action (ALNAP) surveyed forty-six evaluation reports and nine syntheses conducted during 2000–2001. ALNAP, Humanitarian Action: Improving performance through improved learning (London: Overseas Development Institute, 2002), 90. Its Annual Review serves as a barometer for the number and thrusts of evaluations.

19. A cross-cutting British evaluation of the drought *was* conducted in 2004 (see Chapter 5), but it focused more on delivery problems than results.

20. An evaluation of the Sphere impact was scheduled for completion in 2004.

21. Sphere Project: www.sphereproject.org; ALNAP: www.alnap.org; HPG/ODI: www.odi.org.uk/hpg; Red Cross/Red Crescent Code of Conduct: www.ifrc.org/publicat/conduct; Humanitarian Accountability Project: www.hapgeneva.org; Humanitarianism & War Project: www.hwproject.tufts.edu; Do No Harm/Local Capacities for Peace Project: www.cdainc.com/lcp/lcp-publications; People in Aid: www.peopleinaid.org.uk.

Chapter 10

1. ODI, "The Changing Role of Official Donors in Humanitarian Action: A Review of Trends and Issues," HPG Briefing No. 5, December 2002.

2. "Implementation Plan for Good Humanitarian Donorship, Elaborated in Stockholm," June 17, 2003.

3. Sweden did, however, send a person to the DAC to help develop the idea further.

4. Mark Dalton, Karin von Hippel, Randolph Kent, and Ralf Maurer, "Changes in Humanitarian Financing: Implications for the United Nations" (October 11, 2003), 39.

5. Dalton et al., "Changes in Humanitarian Financing," 59.

6. As noted earlier, two key definitions needing attention involve the appropriateness of including the costs of domestic refugee resettlement within donor tallies of humanitarian contributions (six DAC countries do, the others do not) and the current DAC use of "multilateral" to apply only to those contributions provided to UN agencies without conditions. In the first instance, it is more logical to exclude domestic resettlement costs from international humanitarian assistance; in the second, all resources going to the agencies of the UN system should be included, not only those without earmarks. (For an elaboration of these issues, see Development Initiatives, *Global Humanitarian Assistance 2003*, 1–9).

7. These terms and the idea of giving the UN primarily a standard-setting function are elaborated at length in Dalton et al. Our difficulty with this study is not this idea, but the study's larger concept of a nonoperational UN where humanitarian action is concerned.

8. OECD, Development Cooperation Directorate, "ODA Eligibility Issues for Discussion," DCD/DAC/CPDC, January 2004, 1.

9. For a more extended discussion, see Ian Smillie, *Relief and Development: The Struggle for Synergy* (Providence, R.I.: Watson Institute, 2000), http://www.hwproject.tufts.edu.

10. For a review of the major families of NGOs, see Marc Lindenberg and Coralie Bryant, *Going Global: Transforming Relief and Development NGOs* (Bloomfield, Conn.: Kumarian, 2001).

11. Strengthening the capacity of local civil society is an enormous subject, which can only be touched on here. For more on the subject, see *Ian Smillie, Patronage or Partnership: Local Capacity Building in Humanitarian Crises* (Bloomfield, Conn.: Kumarian Press, 2001).

12. Chapter 6 mentioned to the impossibility of making cost comparisons between humanitarian actors and the troops from donor countries who contributed to the Rwanda relief effort in 1994. See Minear and Guillot, *Soldiers to the Rescue*, 37 ff., 152 ff.

13. In recent years, UNHCR has taken the unusual but welcome step of posting its evaluations on its Web site.

14. Madeleine K. Albright, "Think Again: The United Nations," *Foreign Policy*, August 13, 2003, www.foreignpolicy.com.

Selected Bibliography

Anderson, Mary B., and Peter J. Woodrow. *Rising From the Ashes: Development Strategies in Times of Disaster.* Boulder, Colo.: Lynne Rienner, 1989.

Benthall, Jonathan. *Disasters, Relief and the Media.* London: I. B. Taurus, 1993.

Dalton, Mark, Karin von Hippel, Randolph Kent, and Ralf Maurer. "Changes in Humanitarian Financing: Implications for the United Nations." October 11, 2003.

Darcy, James, and Charles Antoine Hofmann. *According to Need? Needs Assessment and Decision Making in the Humanitarian Sector.* HPG Report 15. London: Overseas Development Institute, September 2003.

de Waal, Alex. "Humanitarianism Unbound?" London: African Rights, November 1994.

———. *Famine Crimes: Politics and the Disaster Relief Industry in Africa.* African Rights & the International Africa Institute, in association with James Currey. London, Oxford and Bloomington Ind.: Indiana University Press, 1997.

Donini, Antonio, Norah Niland, and Karin Wermester, eds. *Nation-building Unraveled? Aid, Peace and Justice in Afghanistan.* Bloomfield, Conn.: Kumarian, 2003.

Donini, Antonio, Larry Minear, and Peter Walker. "The Future of Humanitarian Action: Implications of Iraq and Other Recent Crises." Alan Shawn Feinstein International Famine Center. Medford, Mass.: Tufts University, January 2004.

Duffield, Mark. *Global Governance and the New Wars.* London: Zed Books, 2001.

Global Humanitarian Assistance 2003. Development Initiatives, 2003.

Gusmão, Xanana. *To Resist is to Win: The Autobiography of Xanana Gusmão with Selected Letters and Speeches,* ed. Sarah Niner, Victoria, Australia: Aurora Books, 2000.

Power, livelihoods and conflict: Case Studies in Political Economy Analysis for Humanitarian Action. HPG Report 13. London: HPG, 2003.

Hubert, Don. *The Landmine Ban: A Case Study in Humanitarian Advocacy.* Providence, R.I.: Watson Institute, 2000.

Humanitarian Policy Group. "According to Need? Needs Assessment and Decision-making in the Humanitarian Sector." London: Overseas Development Institute, 2003.

Ignatieff, Michael. *Empire Lite: Nation Building in Bosnia, Kosovo and Afghanistan*. Penguin: London, 2003.

Jardine, Matthew. *East Timor: Genocide in Paradise*. Chicago: Odonian Press, 1999.

Keck, Margaret E., and Kathryn Sikkink. *Activists Beyond Borders*. Ithaca and London: Cornell University Press, 1998.

King's College London. *A Review of Peace Operations: A Case for Change; East Timor Study*, March 10, 2003.

Lindenberg, Marc, and Coralie Bryant. *Going Global: Transforming Relief and Development NGOs*. Bloomfield, Conn.: Kumarian, 2001.

Macfarlane, S. Neil. *Politics and Humanitarian Action*. Occasional Paper 41. Providence, R.I.: Watson Institute, 2000.

Macrae, Joanna, and Adele Harmer, eds. *Humanitarian Action and the Global War on Terror*. HPG Report 14. London: Overseas Development Institute, 2003.

Macrae, Joanna, et al. *Uncertain Power: The Changing Role of Official Donors in Humanitarian Action*. HPG Report 12. London: ODI, 2002.

Maren, Michael. *The Road to Hell: The Ravaging Effects of Foreign Aid and International Charity*. New York: The Free Press, 1997.

Marker, Jamsheed. *East Timor: A Memoir of the Negotiations for Independence*. Jefferson, N.C.: Macfarland & Company, 2003.

Minear, Larry. *The Humanitarian Enterprise*. Bloomfield, Conn.: Kumarian Press, 2002.

Minear, Larry, Ted van Baarda and Marc Sommers. *NATO and Humanitarian Action in the Kosovo Crisis*. Occasional Paper #36. Providence, R.I.: Watson Institute, 2000.

ODI. "The Changing Role of Official Donors in Humanitarian Action: A Review of Trends and Issues." HPG Briefing No. 5. London: ODI, December 2002.

Porter, Toby. "The Interaction Between Political and Humanitarian Action in Sierra Leone, 1995 to 2002." Geneva: Centre for Humanitarian Dialogue, March 2003.

———. "An External Review of the CAP." OCHA, April 2002.

Rupesh Shah, David Murphy, and Malcolm McIntosh, eds. *Something to Believe In*. Sheffield, U.K.: Greenleaf Publishing, 2003.

Scharfe, Sharon. *Complicity: Human Rights and Canadian Foreign Policy*. Montreal: Black Rose Books, 1996.

Sommers, Marc. *The Dynamics of Coordination*. Occasional Paper #40. Providence, R.I.: Watson Institute, 2001.

Smillie, Ian, and Larry Minear. "The Quality of Money: Donor Behavior in Humanitarian Financing." Medford, Mass.: Tufts University, 2003. www.reliefweb.int/cap/hfs.html

Smillie, Ian. *Relief and Development: The Struggle for Synergy*. Thomas J. Watson Jr. Institute for International Studies, Brown University, 1998.

Ian Smillie, ed. *Patronage or Partnership: Local Capacity Building in Humanitarian Crises*. Bloomfield, Conn.: Kumarian Press, 2001.

Tiffen, Rodney. *Diplomatic Deceits: Government, Media and East Timor*. Sydney: UNSW Press, 2001.

World Bank. *East Timor: Policy Challenges for a New Nation*, May 2002.

Index

About the Authors

Ian Smillie is an Ottawa-based development consultant and writer. He has lived and worked in Sierra Leone, Nigeria, and Bangladesh. He was a founder of the Canadian development organization, Inter Pares, and was Executive Director of CUSO. Recent books include *Patronage or Partnership: Local Capacity Building in Humanitarian Crises* (Kumarian Press, 2001) and *Managing for Change: Leadership, Strategy and Management in Asian NGOs* (Earthscan, 2001). In 2000 and 2001, Ian Smillie served on a UN Security Council expert panel investigating the links between illicit weapons and the diamond trade in Sierra Leone. Today he serves as Research Coordinator on Partnership Africa Canada's "Diamonds and Human Security Project" and is a participant in the intergovernmental "Kimberley Process" which is developing a global certification system for rough diamonds.

Larry Minear directs Tufts University's Humanitarianism and War Project. He has worked on humanitarian and development issues since 1972. A posting in the southern Sudan was followed by advocacy work in Washington, D.C. on behalf of Church World Service and Lutheran World Relief. Over the years he has served as a consultant to governments, UN agencies, NGOs, and the Red Cross movement. Since cofounding the Humanitarianism and War Project in 1991, he has conducted and coordinated research on many humanitarian crises and written extensively for specialized and general audiences. His most recent book, *The Humanitarian Enterprise: Dilemmas and Discoveries* (Kumarian 2002) reviews the findings and recommendations of this research group.

The present volume builds on the work of the HUMANITARIAN-ISM AND WAR PROJECT, an independent policy research initiative underwritten since its inception by some fifty UN agencies, donor governments, nongovernmental organizations, and foundations. It has conducted thousands of interviews on complex emergencies around the world, producing an array of case studies, training materials, books, articles, and opinion pieces. It is located at the Feinstein International Famine Center in Tufts University's Gerald J. and Dorothy R. Friedman School of Nutrition Science and Policy. A detailed list of its contributors and publications is available at the web site below.

THE HUMANITARIANISM AND WAR PROJECT
Feinstein International Famine Center
Tufts University
11 Curtis Avenue
Somerville, MA 02144
(617) 627-5949
e-mail: h&w@tufts.edu
web site: hwproject.tufts.edu

Also from Kumarian Press...

International Development and NGOs

Aiding Violence: The Development Enterprise in Rwanda
Peter Uvin

Ethics and Global Politics: The Active Learning Sourcebook
Edited by April L. Morgan, Lucinda Joy Peach, and Colette Mazzucelli

Going Global: Transforming Relief and Development NGOs
Marc Lindenberg and Coralie Bryant

The Humanitarian Enterprise: Dilemmas and Discoveries
Larry Minear

New Roles and Relevance: Development NGOs and the Challenge of Change
Edited by David Lewis and Tina Wallace

Nongovernments: NGOs and the Political Development of the Third World
Julie Fisher

Southern Exposure
International Development and the Global South in the Twenty-First Century
Barbara P. Thomas-Slayter

Worlds Apart: Civil Society and the Battle for Ethical Globalization
Michael V. Bhatia

Humanitarianism

Human Rights and Development
Peter Uvin

Nation-Building Unraveled? Aid, Peace and Justice in Afghanistan
Edited by Antonio Donini, Norah Niland and Karin Wermester

Patronage or Partnership: Local Capacity Building in Humanitarian Crises
Edited by Ian Smillie for the Humanitarianism and War Project

War's Offensive on Women
The Humanitarian Challenge in Bosnia, Kosovo and Afghanistan
Julie A. Mertus for the Humanitarianism and War Project

War and Intervention: Issues for Contemporary Peace Operations
Michael V. Bhatia

Visit Kumarian Press at **www.kpbooks.com** or
call **toll-free 800.289.2664** for a complete catalog.